# THE STORY OF ISLAM

## from Muhammad to Suleiman the Magnificent

Suzanne Strauss Art

PEMBLEWICK PRESS
Lincoln, Massachusetts

This book is dedicated to the spirit of peace and mutual understanding in the global community.


Printed in the United States of America
ISBN 0-9718507-1-2



**Other books by the same author:**

EARLY TIMES: THE STORY OF ANCIENT EGYPT
EARLY TIMES: THE STORY OF ANCIENT GREECE
EARLY TIMES: THE STORY OF ANCIENT ROME
EARLY TIMES: THE STORY OF THE MIDDLE AGES
WEST MEETS EAST: THE TRAVELS OF ALEXANDER THE GREAT
*QUINTET: FIVE LIVELY PLAYS FOR KIDS
*THE STORY OF THE RENAISSANCE
*ANCIENT TIMES: THE STORY OF THE FIRST AMERICANS, BOOK I
*NATIVE AMERICA ON THE EVE OF DISCOVERY: THE STORY OF THE FIRST AMERICANS, BOOK II
*THE STORY OF ANCIENT CHINA (China series Book I)
*CHINA'S LATER DYNASTIES (China series Book II)

*available through Pemblewickpress.com
others through Wayside Publishing

email Pemblewick@aol.com

# TABLE OF CONTENTS

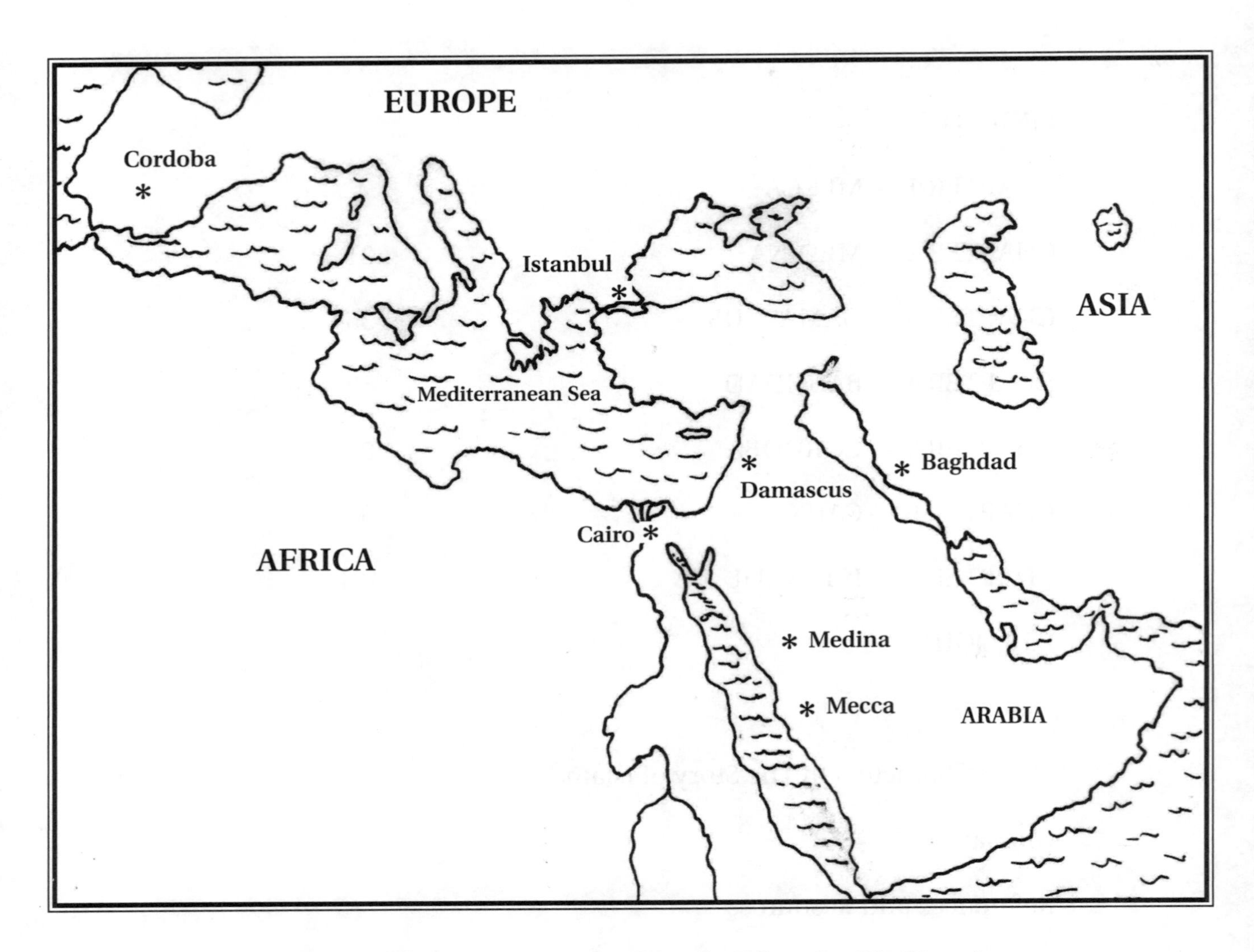


Seven Cities: Beacons of Early Islamic Civilization

# PROLOGUE

Today there are over 1.2 billion Muslims in the world. That's roughly one out of every five people. Islam is practiced on all continents except Antarctica. It is the religion of the majority in 56 countries and the fastest growing religion in North America.

Until September 11, 2001, most Americans had little awareness of the Islamic community. On that day, 19 Muslim extremists hijacked four passenger jets. They flew two into the World Trade Center in New York City and one into the Pentagon in Washington, DC, killing more than 3,000 people. The fourth plane crashed in Pennsylvania. The tragic events on that day dramatically brought the activities of the radical members of the Islamic community into sharp focus, and ever since reports of violence and terrorism instigated by extreme fundamentalist Muslim groups have filled the media on a daily basis. But although Americans are now very aware of Islam, their image of this very complex culture is generally limited to what they see and read about in the news. Few realize that Islam was founded upon principles of equality, compassion, and peace, and that most Muslims abhor violence and terrorism. This lack of knowledge leads to misunderstandings that foster unwarranted suspicions and intolerance. In our age of globalization, it is more important than ever to learn about the beliefs and values of the other peoples with whom we share the planet, not only to appreciate their culture but also, more urgently, to promote world peace.

This book tells the story of early Islam, tracing its evolution from its origins in 7th century Arabia, through its transformation into a vast empire and up to its entry into modern times in the 16th century. Each chapter focuses upon one of the great Muslim cities that flourished as centers of Islamic culture during this period — Mecca, Medina, Damascus, Baghdad, Cordoba, Cairo, and Istanbul. Muslim cities were the most sophisticated in the medieval world. In an age when Paris and London were mired in mud and superstition, these cities had paved streets with streetlights, running water, garbage collection, hospitals, bathhouses, well-tended parks and gardens, schools and colleges, bookstores, public libraries, and research institutes. As the thread of the story progresses from city to city, you will encounter major figures of Islamic history, from Muhammad, the camel driver whose visions form the substance of Islam's sacred book, the *Quran,* to the caliphs and sultans who ruled empires extending over three continents, to scholars, poets, artists, architects, and philosophers who created one of the richest civilizations of the world.

As the story unfolds, you will learn about the basic tenets of Islam and how this faith relates to two other great religions of the world, Judaism and Christianity. You will discover the meaning of the word "jihad," the differences between Shi'ite and Sunni Muslims, the rituals of the annual pilgrimage to Mecca, the reasons for wearing a veil, the role of morality and ethics in Islamic law, and many other aspects of the Muslim way of life. And you will see how the traditions of earlier times continue to influence the lives of present-day Muslims. As you gain a clearer understanding of what Islam is all about, you should be able to cast aside the myths associated it with it and to appreciate how similar its core values and ideals are to those of the Western world.

# THE STORY OF ISLAM

# Chapter 1 — MECCA

Mecca is the holiest city of Islam. Five times a day, Muslims throughout the world offer prayers while facing toward Mecca's ancient shrine, the *Kaaba* (KAH ba). Every year, over two million Muslim pilgrims arrive in the city to participate in rituals that date back over a millennium. This was the birthplace of the Prophet Muhammad, and it is here that the story of Islam begins.

## Early Cultures in Arabia

Mecca is in Arabia, the largest peninsula in the world, covering over a million square miles. That's about twice the size of the state of Alaska. Arabia is bordered by the Red Sea to the west, the Indian Ocean to the south, and the Persian Gulf to the east. The landscape is mostly salt flats, gravel plains, and sand dunes. Temperatures in summer average above 100 degrees F., and the scant annual rainfall (a mere four inches) comes in sudden torrential bursts that quickly dry up. In winter, nighttime temperatures dip way below freezing. The most desolate part of the peninsula is known as the "Empty Quarter," since few people venture there. Its sand ridges are hundreds of miles long and the dunes are as high as mountains. Scattered throughout the vast Arabian desert are oases — waterholes surrounded by groves of date palms that offer welcome relief from the harsh elements.

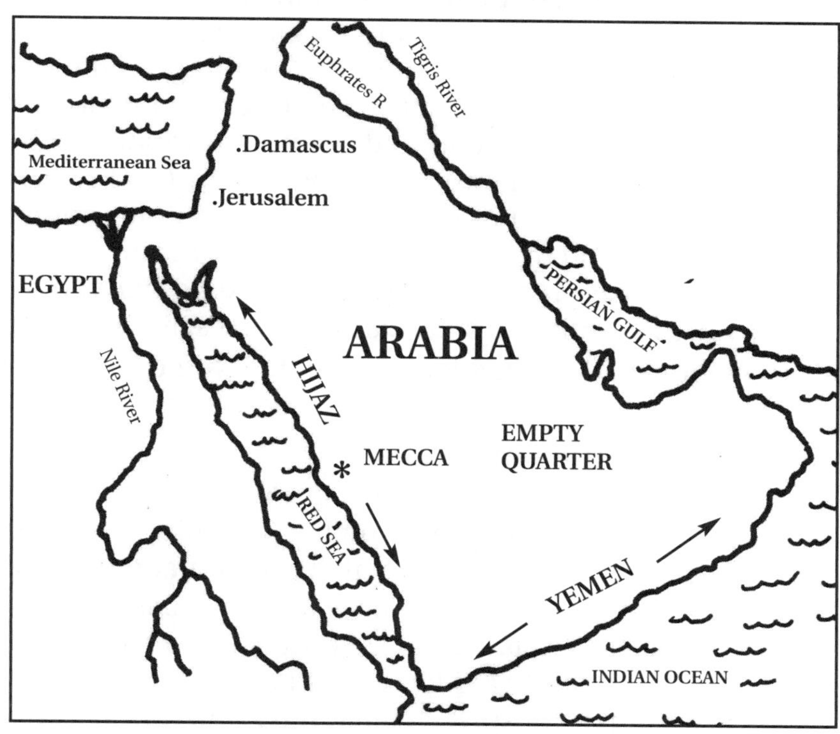


The only green part of Arabia is the strip of land along the southern coast (modern Yemen). Summer monsoons from the Indian Ocean, trapped by a range of mountains, provide up to 30 inches of annual rainfall. As early as the second millennium BCE, groups of tribesmen settled here. They cut terraces into the hillsides to create farmland, then built dams and reservoirs to catch runoff rainwater and channeled it to the terraces through a network of irrigation canals. These innovations enabled them to grow plentiful supplies of barley and wheat. While agriculture made the region prosperous, trade made it rich. Frankincense and myrrh, fragrant gum resins obtained from the trunks of local balsam trees, were in demand as incense for religious ceremonies. They were loaded onto camels and taken north to be traded in Egypt, Palestine, and Syria. Gems, silk, and spices arriving on merchant ships from the Indian Ocean were also transported in the caravans.

In contrast to the settled lands of the south, the vast Arabian desert was the home of nomadic people called Bedouins. They traveled from oasis to oasis with their herds of camels, sheep, and goats, owning only as much as they could carry. The Bedouins spoke Arabic, a Semitic tongue, and lived in tribes, which were divided into family clans. Tribal leaders, called *shaykhs* (pronounced "shakes"), were chosen for their courage and wisdom. For important decisions, the *shaykhs* consulted tribal councils made up of the heads of the clans.

A Bedouin counted upon the support of his kinsmen for his very survival in the desert. In return, he was fiercely loyal to his tribe, prepared to fight to the death to protect its common interests. When someone was murdered, the members of his clan carried out a vendetta against the kinsmen of his murderer. A less violent desert tradition was the raiding party: one tribe would invade the territory of another to steal camels, horses, livestock, or weapons. During these raids bloodshed was avoided, since this would lead to a vendetta.

## Early Times in Mecca

Over the years, small groups of Bedouins settled in the oases, where they harvested dates, grew small quantities of wheat, and grazed their animals. Caravans often stopped at these settlements to rest their camels and obtain water and supplies. Mecca was a small oasis in a mountainous region in western Arabia known as the Hijaz. It was situated in a rocky ravine about 45 miles inland from the Red Sea. Mecca was known for the cool, refreshing water that flowed from a natural spring called the ZamZam. Because it lay near a major corridor through the Hijaz linking southern Arabia with the trading centers of the north, Mecca became an important caravan stop.

Towards the end of the 5th century CE the Quraysh (Kor AYSH), one of the largest Bedouin tribes, settled in Mecca. They established close ties with local camel breeders and began marketing the animals to caravan leaders. They also offered their services as escorts to protect against desert raiders. By the 6th century, many Quraysh had become successful merchants.

In those early times, each of the Bedouin tribes worshiped its own nature gods, which were believed to dwell in certain trees, rocks, springs, and wells. These gods controlled the weather, the sun, moon, and stars, and even the destinies of the people. Reigning above the tribal deities was the all-powerful *Allah* (a name derived from the Arabic *al-ilah*, which simply means "the god"). Although revered as the creator of the heavens and the earth, *Allah* was considered a remote deity who took little interest in the daily lives of human beings. He had three daughters — *Allat, al-Uzza,* and *Manat.* They served as mediators between him and his worshippers.

Long-distance overland trade was made possible by the single-humped camel, a hardy creature that could travel across the desert sands carrying over 300 pounds without food or water for up to a week. In addition to being a beast of burden, the camel provided milk (and occasionally meat) and served as a desert warhorse. Its hair was woven into ropes, its skin was tanned into leather, and its dried dung was burned as fuel on cold nights. The camel was also a unit of exchange, the wealth of a man often measured by the number of camels he owned.

Shrines housing stone idols of the tribal gods were set up in various locations across the Arabian peninsula. A central shrine stood in Mecca. This was the *Kaaba,* a windowless, roofless cube-shaped building made of stone and mudbrick. (*Kaaba* means "cube" in Arabic.) The corners of the shrine pointed in each of the four cardinal directions. Embedded in the eastern corner was a black meteorite. This was considered a sacred stone, linking the site to the heavens. In the 6th century the *Kaaba* housed 360 stone idols in its inner chamber and just outside the entrance. The area surrounding the shrine was considered sacred, and visitors there were forbidden to carry arms, to spill blood, or even to speak a cross word. The Quraysh, as the ruling tribe of Mecca, were the proud caretakers of the *Kaaba.*

In the 2nd century CE, Greek geographer Ptolemy wrote in his journals about Mecca. He called it Macoraba, which means "temple" in several Semitic languages.

Every year, Bedouins throughout Arabia traveled great distances to worship and offer sacrifices to their idols at the *Kaaba*. Such a pilgrimage is known in Arabic as a *hajj* (HAHJ). The pilgrims circled the shrine seven times, pausing once to kiss the black stone. (The circle was an ancient symbol of the infinite powers of the gods.) After completing these ritual circles (known as circumambulations, or *tawaf* in Arabic), the pilgrims visited the hollow of Muzdalifa, the abode of the Thunder God, just outside Mecca. Then they hurled pebbles at the three sacred pillars of the goddess Mina. They made an all-night vigil on the plain beside Mount Arafat. The next day, after shaving their heads (to symbolize the cleansing of their inner selves), they performed an animal sacrifice. As you will see, these rituals would later become part of Muslim tradition.

The Bedouins had no concept of an afterlife. Their main concern was survival in the difficult environment in which they lived.

A truce was observed just before and during the *hajj*. This was a welcome respite from tribal rivalries and warfare. The resourceful Quraysh took advantage of the peaceful interlude and sponsored a large fair, which brought them considerable profits. One of the highlights of the fair was a competition among poets. The power of the spoken word has long been important in Arabia. Every tribe had its own poet, who was believed to be inspired by *jinns* (nature spirits). He entertained his kinsmen by reciting colorful tales about tribal feuds and vendettas. Some poets even explained the meanings of dreams and predicted the future. (Like the Greek oracles, they wisely made their predictions so vague that they could be interpreted in several ways.)

## The Neighboring Superpowers

In the early 6th century two powerful empires dominated the regions to the north of Arabia — the Byzantine and the Sasanian. The Byzantine Empire was the successor to the mighty Roman Empire. It stretched around the eastern Mediterranean from the Balkan peninsula (Greece) to Egypt. The Byzantine capital, Constantinople, sat strategically on the waterway linking the Black Sea and the Mediterranean, giving it control of this important trading corridor. (Vessels sailing past Constantinople were obliged to pay a tax.) The Byzantines were Orthodox Christians and they spoke Greek.

The Sasanian Empire had succeeded the ancient Persian Empire. Its territory extended from the Byzantine border to the Oxus River (modern Pakistan) in the east. Its capital, Ctesiphon, overlooked the Tigris River. The official reli-

Around the 6th century CE, certain Bedouin poets began reciting long odes known as *qasidas* about tribal life. They contained intricate meter rhythms, interior rhymes, and colorful imagery. The poems marked the beginning of Arabic literature.

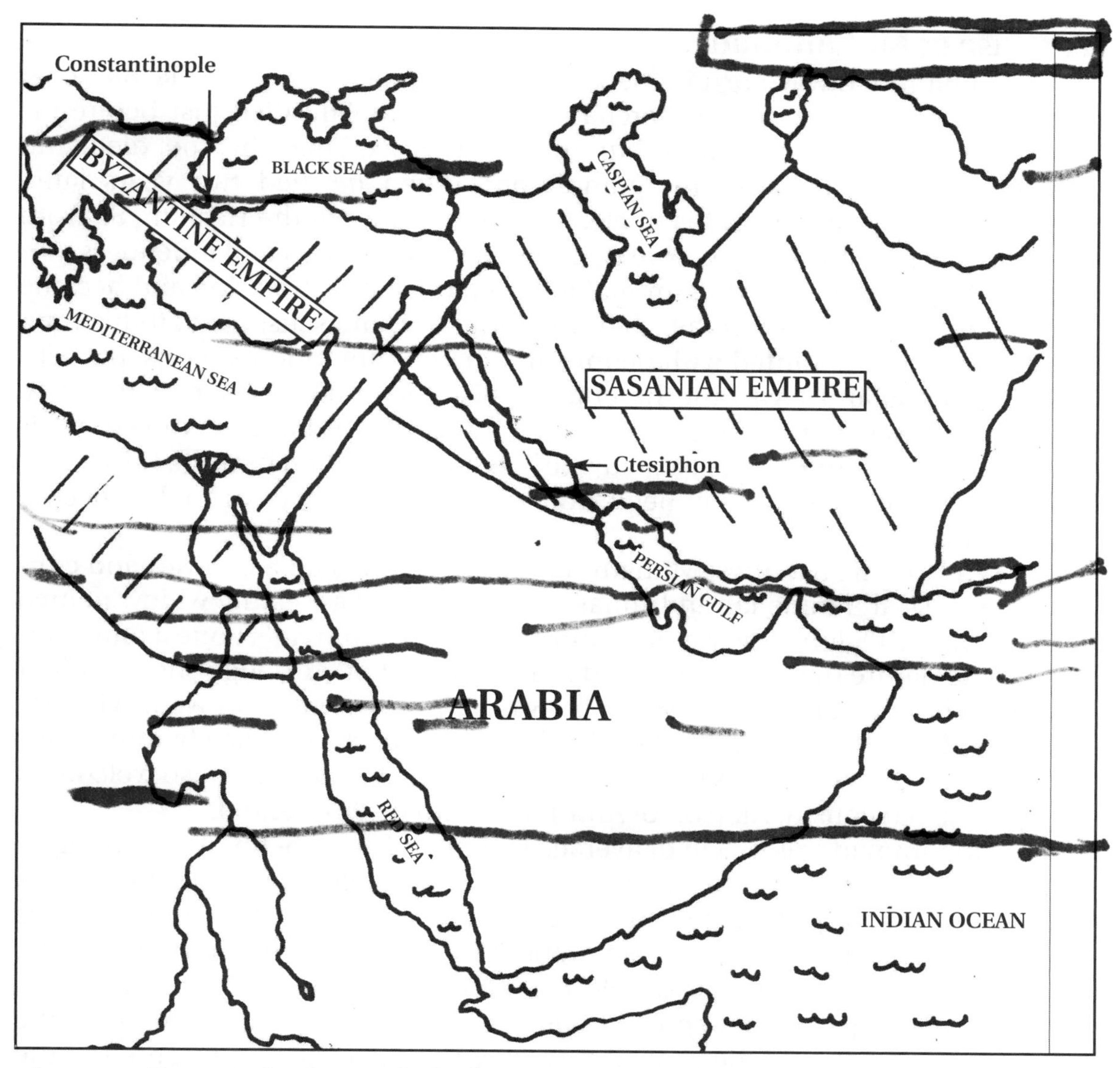


gion was Zoroastrianism (a belief in a supreme god of goodness, Ahura Mazd, who constantly battled the spirit of evil, Ahriman). The language of the Sasanians was Pahlavi, an early form of Persian.

The Byzantine and Sasanian rulers were bitter enemies, who engaged in long wars over territory and resources. They took little interest in Arabia, which they considered a vast wasteland. Their constant warfare, however, had a positive effect upon the Arabian economy. By blocking trade routes between the Persian Gulf and the Mediterranean, they impelled all the ships from the Indian Ocean to unload their goods at ports in southern Arabia and along the Red Sea, bringing a great deal of business to the local merchants.

## The Rise of Muhammad

Muhammad was born in Mecca in 570. He belonged to the Hashim clan of the Quraysh. His father, a merchant named Abdullah, died just before his birth. His mother, Amina, raised him until he was six. Then she, too, died, and the boy went to live with his grandfather. When *he* died two years later, Muhammad moved in with his uncle, Abu Talib, leader of the Hashim. So from an early age, he experienced more than his share of sadness and loneliness.

When he grew up, Muhammad followed the family tradition and became a merchant. He often led caravans from Mecca to Damascus, Syria. In his travels, he became acquainted with people of other cultures and religions, particularly Christians and Jews, and he enjoyed discussing their beliefs with them. Muhammad was admired for his personal integrity and became known in his community as *al-Amin* ("the trusted one"). Being an orphan himself, he sympathized with those who were in need, and he generously gave part of his income to the poor.

While in his twenties, Muhammad was hired to lead a caravan and conduct business at a trade fair in Damascus on behalf of a wealthy widow named Khadija (Kah DEE juh). She was so impressed by Muhammad's honest and compassionate nature that she later asked him to marry her. Although she was older than he (she was allegedly 40 while he was 25), they were soon wed. With her wealth and his business skills, they lived quite comfortably. They had two sons and four daughters. (The sons died at an early age.) Muhammad also welcomed his six-year-old cousin, Ali (son of Abu Talib), into his household.

Muhammad was a man of average height and compact build, with a light complexion, brown eyes, thick, curly black hair that fell to his shoulders, and a full beard. Because of his open-mindedness, he was often called upon to solve disputes. When the *Kaaba* was being rebuilt by a group of Meccans after a fire, the question arose as to who should place the sacred black stone in the wall. Muhammad suggested they spread a sheet of cloth on the ground and place the stone in the middle. He then asked a member of each tribe represented in the group to help carry the cloth to the wall, where he put the stone in position. In this way, tribal rivalry was replaced with the spirit of community effort.

## The Revelations

It was customary in those times for devout men to go on a spiritual retreat during Ramadan, a month in the Arabic calendar. In 610, at the age of 40, Muhammad was on such a retreat. He spent most of his time in a cave on Mount Hira, which overlooks Mecca, meditating upon the meaning of life. One evening, he suddenly felt himself bathed in a glowing light. A vision appeared of the archangel Gabriel, holding a scroll and commanding him to read the words written on it. But Muhammad was illiterate. Trembling and uncertain, he cried out, "I can't read!" So Gabriel read the words aloud and had Muhammad repeat them, committing them to memory as he did so.

These are the words Muhammad heard:

> **Read!*
> *In the name of the Lord (Allah) who created man*
> *From a clot of blood.*
> *Read!*
> *Your Lord is most generous.*
> *He taught by the pen what was not*
> *Known before.*
>
> *Quran* 96:1-5

What did this mean? Gabriel seemed to be representing the Arabic creator god, *Allah*. But far from being remote and unapproachable, He (*Allah*) was described as generous and helpful to mankind. And the reference to teaching "by the pen" suggested that a new scripture would be revealed.

After his vision, Muhammad ran home, frightened and confused. He told Khadija what had happened, and she comforted him. More revelations came to Muhammad, and he began to share them with his family and closest friends. After talking with Khadija's Christian cousin, he came to believe that he was receiving the same messages as those sent by God to the prophets of the Jews and Christians — a long list that included Adam, Abraham, Moses, and Jesus. He was simply the newest prophet, chosen to spread the word among his fellow Arabs. He was the Messenger of God, and his task was not to preach a new religion but to reaffirm one that was very old.

> In Islam the word "prophet" does not mean one who prophesies the future. It is translated as "messenger of God."

The early revelations focused upon the power and unity of God, who had created the universe and organized it a way that kept all things in proper relationship to one another. The revelations decried paganism (the worship of idols) as a deadly sin. More ominously, they warned that the end of the world was near. On the Day of Judgment God would reward or punish people based upon how they had lived their lives. Those who chose to worship Him and obey His Will would spend eternity in Paradise, a blissful place where rivers flow through cool, fragrant gardens. (For a people dwelling in the desert sands, what could be more appealing?) But nonbelievers would suffer unending anguish and despair in a hell where the heat was 70 times that of the earth, fountains flowed with hot,

* The first word can also be translated as "recite."

stinking water, and the trees bore rotten fruit. There was still time to avoid this terrible fate. God was calling upon the people to turn from the petty rivalries of their daily lives, to acknowledge the greatness of the universe and the Spirit behind it, and to become more generous towards one another. Those who did so would be forgiven for their former errors and could look forward to entering Paradise.

Khadija was the first to accept the words of the revelations. Ali, who was then 13, was the second to do so. Other early converts to the faith included Muhammad's best friend, Abu Bakr, and close acquaintances Umar ibn al-Khattab and Uthman ibn Affan. Those in his "inner circle" of followers would come to be known as the Companions. They prayed together in the mornings and evenings by prostrating themselves (kneeling and touching the ground with their foreheads) to express their submission to God. The word "Islam" means submission to the Divine will, and one who submits is called a Muslim.

As Muhammad received new revelations, he recited the words while others who were literate wrote them down. Since there was no paper in Arabia at the time, the words were copied on bits of leather, pottery fragments, palm fibers, and even bones (the shoulder blades of camels). In time, the writings would be gathered in a collection known as the *Quran* (kur AHN), the holy book of Islam. (*Quran* literally means "recitation" or "reading" in Arabic.)

## Spreading the Word

After three years, Muhammad was told by Gabriel to declare himself openly to his kinsmen. So he hosted a dinner for 40 of the most prominent men in his clan. After the meal, he rose to his feet and described his visions. Many in the audience greeted the news with disbelief — even derision — while others felt drawn to his words. A few believed that, like the poets, Muhammad had been inspired by the *jinns*.

He then set about preaching his new beliefs to the general public. Much of what he said tied in closely with the tribal values of the Bedouins. For example, he stressed the equality of all believers and the need for mutual support, both important values in a desert community. He spoke in favor of moderation in one's lifestyle, arguing against the extremes of wealth and poverty that had become common in commercial centers like Mecca. He even proposed that the rich give a tenth of their income to the poor.

Many early converts were members of the smaller clans, who felt bullied by the wealthy and powerful elite. Others belonged to the lowest social levels — the orphans, jobless workers, and slaves. But Muhammad's teachings were not welcomed by the leaders of the Quraysh. They shunned his concept of a single god, preferring the nature deities of their ancestors. They worried that changes in the pagan culture would threaten the yearly pilgrimages to the *Kaaba* and the fair associated with it. And the concept of sharing one's wealth was viewed with disdain by the prosperous merchants, who enjoyed spending their profits. They took great offense at Muhammad's suggestion that those who hoarded their goods would be condemned on the Day of Judgment.

As Muhammad won more followers, the Quraysh began to openly express their disapproval. They accused Muhammad of making up the revelations, of letting his imagination run away with him, even of being crazy. He was jeered in the streets and garbage was thrown at his front door. New converts were more forcefully bullied and harassed. To avoid trouble, groups of Muslims often gathered outside the city to perform their prayer rituals. One day, a fight broke out and a Companion wounded one of his assailants with the jawbone of a camel. This marked the first shedding of blood between Muslims and non-Muslims.

As conditions grew worse, Muhammad sent groups of followers across the Red Sea to take refuge with the Christian ruler of Abyssinia (modern Ethiopia). Soon afterwards, the Quraysh imposed a boycott on the Hashim clan. All members, whether or not they were Muslims, were confined to their quarter of the city and forbidden to engage in trade. This led to a great shortage of food and water. When the sanctions were finally lifted, several people had died.

## The Night Journey

One morning in 619, Muhammad announced to his followers that he had just taken a spiritual journey. While visiting his cousin, who lived near the *Kaaba*, he had gotten up in the middle of the night and gone to the shrine to recite the words of the *Quran*. Afterwards, he had fallen asleep in the *hijr*, the enclosed area near the *Kaaba*. (Bedouins often slept in the *hijr* in hopes of having dreams of divine content.)

Muhammad dreamed that he was woken by Gabriel and lifted on to a horse-like creature (the *Buruq)*, which carried him through the night, every stride taking them to the furthest extent of his eyesight. They alighted on the site of the Temple Mount in Jerusalem, and from there Muhammad and Gabriel climbed a ladder to the seven levels of Heaven. At each level they encountered one of the great prophets. At the seventh level Muhammad passed through a gate guarded by thousands of angels into Paradise. There he spoke with God, who explained to him, among other things, the importance of regular prayer. (God told him that Muslims must pray 50 times a day, but Moses later said that 50 prayers were too many. So he went back and the number was reduced to five. This has remained the number of daily prayers required of a devout Muslim ever

Today, Muhammad's ascension to heaven is celebrated every year with speeches, celebrations, and readings of the legend on 27 Rajab, the 7th month in the Muslim calendar.

Descriptions of this event later inspired Dante's account of his imaginative journey through hell, purgatory and heaven in his famous epic, *The Divine Comedy.*

since.) After this celestial visit, Muhammad and Gabriel returned to Jerusalem and then to Mecca.

When Muhammad described his journey, many of his followers were uncertain how to react, but they were then reassured by the words of Abu Bakr: "If Muhammad himself said it, then it's true." Jerusalem was already the holy city of Jews and Christians. After the Night Journey (called the *Miraj*), it had great religious meaning for Muslims as well, and they would face in its direction each time they prayed.

## The Migration

Muhammad was able to continue his preaching as long as he received protection from his uncle, Abu Talib. No one could kill him without bringing on a vendetta by the Hashim clan. But when Abu Talib died in 619, his successor withdrew the clan's protection. As hostility against him and his followers increased, Muhammad began to think about leaving Mecca. (Around this time, he was also saddened by the death of his beloved wife, Khadija.)

During the annual *hajj* in 620, Muhammad visited with a group of pagan pilgrims camping in the valley of Mina. They came from the city of Yathrib, a lush farming oasis 280 miles to the north. When he spoke with them about his visions, they listened attentively, being drawn as much to his persuasive per-

As in Judaism and Christianity, Islam acknowledges the realms of heaven, earth, and hell, accords a superior status to the angels, recognizes the existence of Satan, and confirms the punishments that await nonbelievers in the hereafter.

According to Muslim belief, God created humans out of clay to be His representatives on earth. Man alone was given free will, and it was his choice to submit to God's will and to live a moral life or to turn away. Angels are immortal beings that God created out of light. They have intellect but no free will, their function being to serve as a link between God and man. Muslims believe that two angels are assigned to every person to keep a record of all of his deeds and actions. Upon his death the records are given to God, who decides whether he goes to Paradise or Hell. Satan represents the dark side. When God created Adam, the first man, He had commanded all the angels to bow before him. One angel, Satan, refused to accept man's unique status and was expelled from Paradise. He became the leader of other fallen angels. He spends much of his time tempting humans to perform immoral or unkind acts. Between the angels and humans are the *jinns*, invisible, intelligent spirits that were created from fire and often assume visible form. They tempt human beings in their moral struggles on earth, but, as we've seen, they've also inspired poets.

sonality as the message he delivered. Yathrib was made up of various tribal groups, three of them Jewish, so the men were familiar with the concept of monotheism. Their community was presently torn by tribal rivalry and conflicts between the merchants and farmers. Muhammad seemed like the ideal candidate to help resolve these conflicts and the pilgrims asked him to consider helping them out. They agreed to carry his religious message home, and the following year, they returned with about 60 kinsmen. After meeting with Muhammad, all converted to Islam. When they went back to Yathrib, Muhammad sent along some of his close followers to instruct the new converts and to recite the *Quran*.

By 622 conditions in Mecca were becoming so intolerable for the Muslims, who now numbered about 70, that Muhammad urged them to emigrate to Yathrib. They left in small groups over several days so as not to attract attention. (Muhammad assumed that the Quraysh would oppose the further spread of Islam.) A report then surfaced of an impending assassination plot. A gang of young men, one from each of the Meccan clans, was to stab the Muslim leader, each with his own sword, so that no single family could be blamed. In this way, the Quraysh could avoid a vendetta, since the Hashim could hardly fight everyone. But when the conspirators gathered outside Muhammad's house, he had already left for Yathrib with Abu Bakr. Ali stayed in the house, wearing his cousin's clothes. When he came outside the next morning, the gang realized that they had been tricked. The Quraysh offered a reward of a hundred camels for the capture of Muhammad, dead or alive. According to legend, a search party actually passed by the cave he was hiding in. Since an enormous spider's web covered the entrance, the pursuers rode on. Muhammad and Abu Bakr eventually arrived at the outskirts of Yathrib, where they were joined by Ali. They entered the city together and were warmly greeted.

The move from Mecca is known as the *Hegira* (or *hijra*, meaning "migration"). It marks a major turning point in the career of Muhammad and the history of Islam. No longer a persecuted minority of believers, Muslims would now form a strong, autonomous community, called the *umma*. The local people who had converted to Islam offered housing and protection to the immigrants. They were known as the *Ansar* ("helpers"). They formally abandoned their old clan and tribal ties to live in together in an egalitarian society with the newly arrived Muslims. Faith replaced kinship as the social and political bond. An attack upon any other Muslim was strictly forbidden.

Yathrib was renamed Medina (Me DEE na, from *Madinat al-Nabi*, "The City of the Prophet"). A charter was written to define the relationships between the Muslims and the other residents of the city. Known as the Constitution of Medina, it was Islam's earliest political document.* (It survives to this day.) The Jewish residents had the same legal rights as Muslims and were free to practice

* A government based upon religion is known as a theocracy.

their religion without interference. They came to be known as *dhimmis* ("protected people") and were required to a pay a poll tax as a price for this protection. All inhabitants were expected to contribute to the cost of defending the city and were forbidden to make treaties with Mecca and its allies.

## The First Mosque

When Muhammad first entered Medina, he had to choose a place to live. So he gave free rein to his camel, Qaswa. As she plodded along, local people begged him to stay in their houses, but he continued on until Qaswa stopped and fell to her knees beside a small shop belonging to two orphan brothers. Muhammad paid them generously for their property, and construction soon began on a simple structure of mud bricks. Once his house was completed, Muhammad had his family brought from Mecca. (He had taken a new wife after Khadija died, and he was also betrothed to Aisha (ah EE sha), the young daughter of Abu Bakr.)

Muhammad's house had a spacious rectangular courtyard enclosed by a wall. Usually such a courtyard was used to fence in camels at night. In this case, however, it became a place for Muslims to gather for meetings as well as formal prayers. The trunks of two palm trees stood like pillars along the northern wall to show worshippers the direction of Jerusalem, towards which they faced during prayer. The wall indicating the direction of prayer is called the *qibla.* Other tree trunks supported a roof of palm branches over a section of the courtyard as protection from the hot desert sun. This simple enclosure served as the first mosque. (The word "mosque" is derived from the Arabic *masjid* meaning "place of prostration." )

At first, people turned up to pray at different times during the day. To regulate these visits, Muhammad appointed an Abysinian former slave named Bilal to announce the official times for prayer. Every morning, just before dawn, he would climb to the rooftop of the tallest house near the mosque. When he saw the sun begin to rise, he chanted the first call to prayer (the *adhan*). The same call has been given ever since from the minarets of mosques five times a day:

> **God is the most Great! I testify*
> *That there is no god but God*
> *I testify that Muhammad is the*
> *Messenger of God. Come to prayer!*
> *Come to salvation! God is the most*
> *Great! There is no god but God!*

* "God is the most Great" is translated in Arabic as *Allahu Akbar*. These words are among the most familiar to members of every Muslim community throughout the world today.

Muhammad continued to receive revelations in Medina. Some would come to him while he was praying, others while he was in the midst of ordinary activities. At such times, he would feel faint and break into a sweat before experiencing visions and sounds that were often difficult to decipher. Afterwards, he would try to determine what the message had been so that he could share it. These revelations were of a more political or social nature than the earlier ones in Mecca. For example, when questions arose in the community, such as how to distribute the property of someone who had died or how to deal with theft, a revelation often provided the answers. Muhammad discussed his visions as well as his social and moral views with the Companions. In later years, collections of writings referring to these conversations would become important sources of Islamic culture.

## Severing Ties

Muhammad had hoped to establish close relations with the Jews of Medina, since their faith and scriptures were so closely tied to those of Islam. Both Muslims and Jews worshiped the same God, who had communicated with them through revered prophets. And just as the words revealed to Muhammad were written down to form the *Quran*, the Jews had a written scripture, the *Torah*. Muhammad regarded the Jews as spiritual kinsmen, just as he did the Christians (with their prophet, Jesus, and their written scriptures, the *Gospels*).

In those early times, Arabs had many wives. Muhammad himself would marry nine times after the death of Khadija, often for purely political reasons. Among these wives, one was Christian and another was Jewish. (Only one of the nine bore him a child — a boy who died in infancy.) As Muhammad's household grew, apartments were built around the courtyard for each of his wives. Since they lived in the center of much activity, Muhammad felt a need to seclude them. They were not allowed to visit the courtyard when strangers were there, and within their apartments a curtain was raised to shield them from the sight of any male visitors. The curtain was called a *hijab*. Later, this word came to mean "veil" or "head scarf."

Although the *Quran* prescribed this degree of segregation for Muhammad's wives, it did not require the veiling of all women or even their exclusion in a separate part of the house. These customs were derived from the Byzantine and Sasanian cultures and were adopted by Muslims several generations after Muhammad's death. Muslim women *were* instructed to "lower their gaze and guard their modesty…to cover themselves and not display their beauty except to their close male relatives." This is interpreted by liberal Muslims today as meaning that women should avoid extremes of dress, like short skirts and plunging necklines. More conservative groups advocate wearing head scarves, veils, *chadors* (black, loose-fitting cloaks that cover body, head and hair), or even *burqas* (full-length garments with mesh covering the face).

The words of one revelation advised Muslims to "Dispute not with the *People of the Book* save in the fairer manner, except for those of them that do wrong."

Both groups were referred to as the "People of the Book." The *Quran*, in Muhammad's view, simply completed and therefore superseded the scriptures of the two earlier religions.

Judaism and Islam also shared a common ancestor, Abraham. He was a biblical patriarch born sometime in the 3rd millennium BCE in ancient Mesopotamia (modern Iraq). As a child, Abraham did not accept his people's worship of stone idols. When he grew older, the archangel Gabriel appeared to him, telling him that he had been chosen to spread the message that there was only one God. Because his own people did not listen to him, he and his wife, Sarah, left their home for a new land — Palestine — where he continued to preach. Since Abraham had no son with Sarah, he took as a second wife an Egyptian slave named Hagar. She bore him a son, Ishmael (*Ismail* in Arabic). A while later, Sarah gave birth to a son, Isaac. Fearing that Ishmael, as first-born, would overshadow Isaac, Sarah pressured Abraham to send Hagar and her son away.

According to Muslim doctrine, Abraham took them on a long journey and finally came to a stretch of barren desert near Mecca. Here he left them with only a single waterskin and a sack of dates. When the supplies ran out, Hagar set out in a frantic search for water, but in vain. When she returned to where she had left her baby, he pressed his little heel into the sand, and water began to gush from a spring. This was the Zamzam ("the well of abundant waters"). Years later, Abraham returned, and together with Ishmael he built a temple where people could pray to God — the *Kaaba*. The black stone was contributed by Gabriel. Ishmael grew up, married, and became the progenitor of the Arab people, while Isaac fathered the Jewish race. This being so, Arab Muslims, Jews, and Christians were all the Children of Abraham. For many centuries, the descendants of Ishmael cared for the *Kaaba* and worshiped God. But in time, the old pagan

This verse in the *Quran* indicates the close ties between Islam, Judaism, and Christianity:

*We believe*
*In God, and the revelation*
*Given to us, and to Abraham,*
*Ismail, Isaac, Jacob,*
*And the Tribes, and that given*
*To Moses and Jesus, and that given*
*To [all] Prophets from their Lord:*
*We make no difference*
*Between one and another of them:*
*And we bow to God.*

*Quran* 2: 136

beliefs resurfaced, and the various tribes began to deposit stone statues of their own deities in and around the shrine. The revelations received by Muhammad simply fostered the return to the tradition of Abraham.

Abraham's faith was put to the test after he dreamed that God ordered him to take Ishmael to the *Kaaba* and sacrifice him. When he awoke, he prepared to do as he was told. At the last moment, God spared the boy and replaced him with a ram. (In the biblical tradition, Isaac was the intended victim, spared by divine intervention in Jerusalem.)

Given all these ties between their religions, Muhammad expected the Jewish leaders of Medina to acknowledge him as the Prophet for all believers, and he was surprised and hurt when they did not. Gradually, he came to realize that Islam was a faith related to but different from Judaism. Until this time, Muslims had prayed facing Jerusalem, the ancient shrine of Judaism as well as the site of Muhammad's Night Journey. In January 624, while leading the Friday prayers, Muhammad suddenly instructed the worshippers to turn and face Mecca, focusing their prayers upon the *Kaaba*. This reinforced ties with Abraham while distancing Islam from Judaism. The change in the direction of prayer required the construction of a second portico (roofed area) on the south side of the mosque's courtyard. Against the new *qibla* was placed a wooden seat on a raised platform, where Muhammad sat to address the faithful. This pulpit, which was a major improvement over the short tree stump he originally stood upon, became known as the *minbar*.

Muhammad had adopted a number of Jewish practices, such as fasting during the Day of Atonement and following dietary laws that forbade the consumption of pork and required the draining of all blood from meat before it was cooked and eaten. (Animals were to be humanely slaughtered.) He now changed the time of fasting to Ramadan, the ninth month of the Arabic calendar, extending it from the ten days of the Jewish tradition to thirty. This marked a return to the long-standing Arabic tradition of fasting and prayer during this time of the lunar year. He also changed the day of prayer from Saturday (the Jewish Sabbath) to Friday. However, the dietary rules remained in effect.

## Battles Against Mecca

The Muslims who had fled from Mecca to Medina were traders and merchants. They had little interest in farming, and many wondered how they could feed their families. Muhammad encouraged them to turn to the old Bedouin tradition of raiding. Since Medina lay near the trade route between Mecca and

Today, Islamic laws determine which foods are *halal* (permissible) or *haram* (forbidden). They are similar to Jewish kosher laws. No consumption of pork or blood is allowed. The slaughter of acceptable animals (sheep, for example) must be quick and merciful, and the carcass drained of all blood. In addition, no alcohol or other intoxicants are allowed.

Syria, groups were organized to intercept some of the caravans. When these activities threatened to disrupt the Meccan economy, the Quraysh launched a series of attacks upon the farmlands of Medina. Animosity between Mecca and Medina began to escalate.

In March 624 Muhammad led about 320 Muslims to intercept a caravan heading for Mecca. It was the largest caravan of the year, with over a thousand camels. The Muslims proceeded to the Well of Badr, a watering hole about 80 miles west of Medina, and waited for the camels to arrive. But Abu Sufyan, a high-ranking member of the Quraysh who was leading the caravan, received word from his scouts that strangers had been sighted near the well. So he skirted Badr and sent a rider to Mecca asking for protection. Nine hundred of the best Meccan warriors were immediately dispatched to deal with the Muslims. When they attacked, Muhammad's men more than held their own, despite their smaller numbers, because they were strongly united behind their leader. The Meccans were divided into tribes, each tribe fighting under its own chief, and had no unified command. By midday, the Meccans had fled in disarray. Muhammed ordered all prisoners rounded up to be ransomed, not killed as was usually the case in tribal warfare. The Muslims returned to Medina in triumph, proud to have driven back the very forces that had once persecuted them.

Abu Sufyan was the head of the powerful and wealthy Umayyad clan of the Quraysh. He would play an important role in the history of Islam.

But all was not peaceful in Medina. The leaders of the three main Jewish tribes had resented Muhammad's takeover of the city, and some proposed siding with the Meccans to drive him out. This, of course, went counter to the Constitution of Medina. Ten weeks after the incident at Badr, a member of the Quraysh elite slipped into the city and was entertained by one of these leaders. When Muhammad heard of this, he expelled his entire tribe as a warning to others. Soon afterward, the discovery of an assassination plot led to strong actions against a second tribe. However, those Jews who did not oppose the Muslims continued to live freely in Medina, practicing their religion as they wished.

In March 625 an army of over 3,000 Meccan warriors, led by Abu Sufyan, headed north, where they were joined by other Bedouin tribesmen. They camped on the plain below Mount Uhud just outside

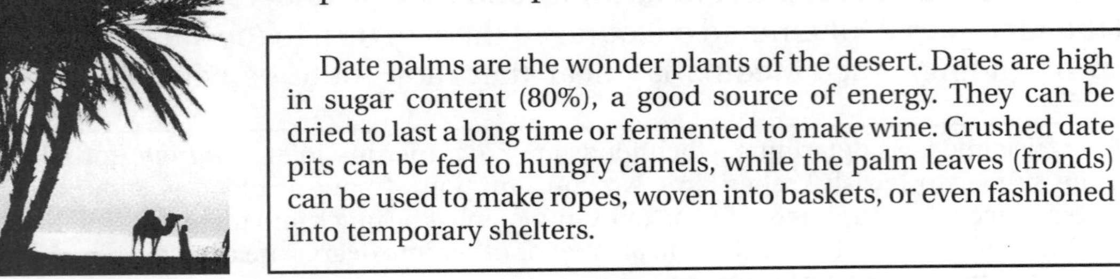

Date palms are the wonder plants of the desert. Dates are high in sugar content (80%), a good source of energy. They can be dried to last a long time or fermented to make wine. Crushed date pits can be fed to hungry camels, while the palm leaves (fronds) can be used to make ropes, woven into baskets, or even fashioned into temporary shelters.

Medina. When Muhammad heard about the approaching army, he summoned a council to discuss whether to wait out a siege or to fight. The decision was made to fight. It was at this time that Muhammad received a revelation informing him that those who died fighting in the defense of the *umma* would be martyrs and therefore automatically admitted to Paradise.

Muhammad led about 1,000 men towards Uhud. When one of his leaders backed out and took his 300 men with him, the odds became even worse — 700 Muslims against 3,000 Meccans. Determined to stand his ground, Muhammad assembled his men in a defensive position, placing 50 archers above a pass to protect his rear. When the Meccans attacked, the Muslim lines held firm — until some of the archers foolishly left their posts and ran onto the field of battle. The Meccan cavalry commander saw what had happened and charged through the pass. Now the Muslims were caught in the middle. The situation looked hopeless when Muhammad was knocked out by a blow to the head, but he soon regained his senses. He and his men then retreated up the mountain, as the victorious Meccans withdrew. The battle had cost the lives of nearly 70 Muslim men. This led to a sudden increase in unattached women, unmarried daughters as well as the recently widowed, who were suddenly in need of support. A new revelation dealt with this issue: it encouraged the men to take as many as four wives, with the stipulation that the husband treat each wife equally.

> Muhammad's men carried a black flag inscribed with white letters that read *Nasr um min Allah*, "with the help of God."

By 627 the Meccans had dramatically expanded their forces with warriors from many parts of Arabia, creating a huge army of over 10,000. In March of that year, Abu Sufyan led this superarmy toward Medina. Muhammad had at most 3,000 men, so there was no question of going out to meet the enemy. Instead, he ordered the people to barricade themselves within the city. Medina was surrounded on three sides by sheer cliffs of volcanic rock, but the fourth side, to the north, was vulnerable. A Persian convert (Salman al-Farsi) suggested digging a deep trench along the edge of the northern wall. Each family dug a part of the trench. The piles of earth were used to build a huge escarpment, which shielded the city's defenders and gave them a superior vantage point from which to hurl rocks and shoot arrows. As expected, the Quraysh attacked from the north, but as they approached the trench they were driven back by the volley of missiles. Those who got to the trench were unable to cross it, as it was too wide for even a horse to jump. After a 40-day siege, the Meccans, frustrated, exhausted and out

> The *Quran* makes men and women partners before God, with identical duties and responsibilities. The women of the first *umma* in Medina took full part in its public life. They prayed beside the men, and some even fought beside them in battle.

of supplies, withdrew.

This episode, known as the Battle of the Trench, increased Muhammad's reputation as a military strategist and won him the support of Bedouins who had earlier sided with Mecca. With this boost in prestige, he was able to form alliances with many tribes, building the foundations of an Arabian confederacy. Even Meccans began to defect and join the *umma* in Medina, much to the anger of the Quraysh leaders.

## Return to Mecca

As the *umma* grew, Muhammad looked for ways to safeguard the lives of its members. This meant ending the conflict with Mecca. But how could he get his avowed enemies, the Quraysh, to listen to him? In March 628 he organized about 1000 of his followers to make a *hajj* to the *Kaaba*. They would bear no arms.

The Quraysh were in a quandary. As guardians of the *Kaaba*, they could not forbid pilgrims from entering the sanctuary, but they cringed at the thought of Muhammad and his people in their very midst. They sent a force of 200 cavalry to intercept the Muslims. Muhammad foiled their plan by taking a different route and then setting up camp at Hudaybiyya, a village bordering the sacred territory. The Meccans sent envoys to his camp, and, remarkably, a treaty was worked out. Both sides agreed to end hostilities and to rein in their allies. Meccan caravans could now pass freely through Muslim territory. Muhammad and his followers were to return to Medina, but the following year they would come back for the *hajj*. At that time, the Quraysh would vacate the city. Just as planned, over 2,000 Muslims arrived in Mecca in 629. And just as promised, the Quraysh left the city so the pilgrims could visit the holy places undisturbed.

## A Peaceful Surrender

But the treaty was short-lived. A tribe allied with the Meccans attacked one with ties to Medina. In response, Muhammad set out in January of 630 at the head of a force of over 10,000 Muslims. They arrived at the outskirts of Mecca at night and made camp on the hills above the city. Each contingent was ordered to light several campfires to make their numbers appear even greater. They certainly made their point. The next day they entered the city without striking a single blow. Abu Sufyan and the other Quraysh leaders surrendered peacefully.

Muhammad later rode his camel around the *Kaaba* seven times, touching the black stone each time and proclaiming that there was no god but God and that he, Muhammad, was His Messenger. His words were taken up by his followers and soon everyone was chanting them. He then turned his attention to the 360 idols in and around the shrine and smashed each one. The interior walls of the *Kaaba* had been decorated with paintings of pagan deities. Muhammad ordered them all obliterated, but he allowed those of Jesus and Mary to remain. He rededicated the shrine to God, restoring it to the pure faith of Abraham. The *Kaaba* was now the sacred center of Islam.

Muhammad issued a general amnesty to the people of Mecca. They were bidden to accept his leadership and to lay aside all pagan beliefs. He did not require anyone to convert (forced conversion is forbidden by the *Quran*), although many Meccans, including leaders like Abu Sufyan, would do so. In his peaceful occupation of Mecca, Muhammad had proven that the message of Islam could be spread without force or violence.

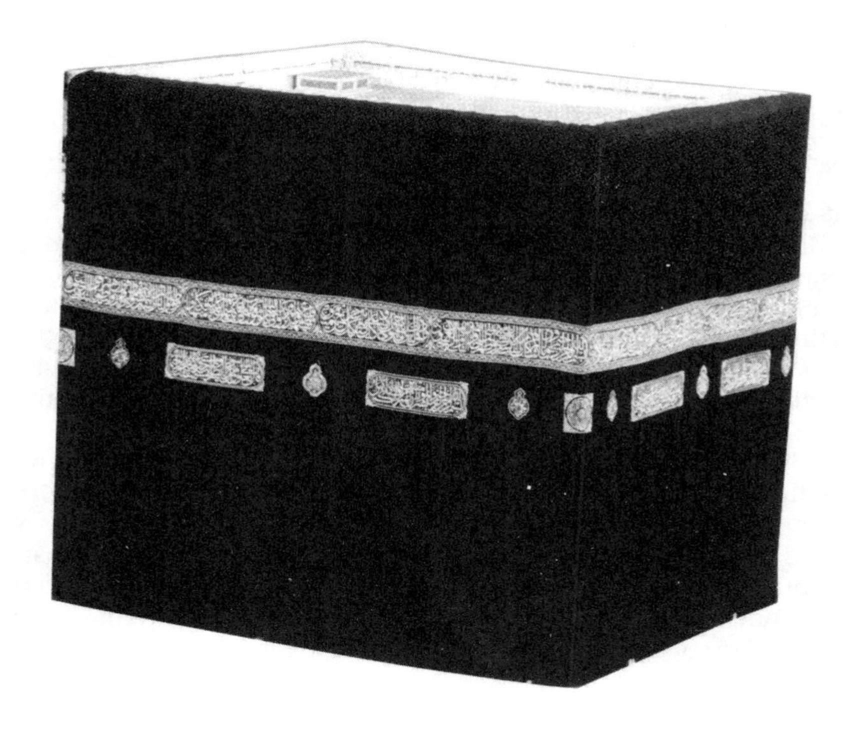

The *Kaaba* has been rebuilt many times. The only original part is the black stone. Today, the shrine rises 50 feet from mortared bases of blue-gray stone. The interior is empty. It has a marble floor, three wooden pillars, and inscriptions on the walls. A ladder leads to the roof. The *Kaaba* is covered with a thick, black cloth, called a *kiswa*, upon which passages from the *Quran* are embroidered in gold. It stands in the center of the Noble Sanctuary (*Haram al-Sharif*) into which only Muslims may enter. The sanctuary includes the Zamzam well, the *Hijr*, and the hills of Safa and Marwa. It is considered the largest mosque in the Islamic world.

## Review Questions:

1. What was the early function of the *Kaaba*?
2. Who were the Quraysh?
3. Describe the Byzantine and Sasanian Empires of the 6th century.
4. What sort of a person was Muhammad?
5. What were the main messages of the revelations that Muhammad received in Mecca?
6. What is the *Quran*?
7. Who were the Companions?
8. Who did Muhammad encounter on his Night Journey?
9. How did the death of Abu Talib affect Muhammad?
10. What was the hegira?
11. Who were the Ansar?
12. What were the main points of the Constitution of Medina?
13. Who were the *dhimmis*?
14. Describe the first mosque.
15. What were the main ties between Islam and Judaism?
16. Why did the Quraysh army first attack the Muslims?
17. What caused Bedouin tribesmen to transfer their allegiance to Muhammad?
18. What were the terms of the Treaty of Hudabiyya?
19. What acts did Muhammad perform in and around the *Kaaba* in 630?
20. What precedent did Muhammad set by his peaceful conquest of Mecca?

## Questions for Discussion

1. How did Muhammad's earliest years influence his views about the "underdog?"
2. What personal characteristics enabled Muhammad to win so many people to his cause?
3. The Day of Judgment was a constant reminder that a person is accountable for his actions. How did this conflict with tribal values?
4. Since a Muslim is someone who submits to the will of God, can one rightfully say that people of many faiths who worship the same God and abide by His will are all Muslims? How might such a statement incite a negative reaction among certain groups?
5. Would you describe Muhammad's battles with Mecca as part of a religious war or a political one, or both? How might his motivations be reinterpreted in later times?
6. In pre-Islamic Arabia, women were regarded as chattel, at the same level as other property. A man could marry as many wives as he wished, and he could easily dispose of one he grew tired of with no obligation to her at all. A woman had no rights of inheritance, and, in fact, was inherited by the firstborn son of the head of the family. In what ways was Muhammad more considerate of and sympathetic to the role of women?

# Chapter 2 — MEDINA

Medina lies 2,000 feet above sea level, wedged between the rugged eastern slopes of the Hijaz mountains and a large lava field. Because of its elevation, the weather is cooler and more pleasant that other desert cities. Today Medina is one of the most sacred shrines of Islam, second only to Mecca among holy places visited on a Muslim pilgrimage.

The first settlers of this oasis were Jewish families, who had been expelled from Palestine by the Romans in the 1st century BCE. The settlement, known as Yathrib, became a thriving farming community — producing fruits, onions, and barley and harvesting dates. In time, many more Jewish settlers arrived, as did Bedouins, who were drawn to the advantages of a settled way of life.

As we've learned, Muhammad and his followers migrated to Yathrib in 622. Renamed Medina, the city became the capital of the growing Islamic realm, and it would remain so until 661.

## Muhammad's Later Years

When Muhammad returned to Medina after his victory in Mecca, he gave a speech, thanking the local people for all the help they had given him and stating his intention to make the city his home for the rest of his life. By now, most inhabitants of Medina had converted to Islam, and mosques had been built in the various neighborhoods. Although Muhammad was acknowledged as the leader of the *umma* as well as the Prophet, he continued to live simply, wearing the rough clothing of an ordinary villager and spending much of his time seated on the ground chatting with his followers. Like a traditional Arab *shaykh*, he acted as the first among equals. He had a regular schedule of meetings with the Companions and the *Ansar* to discuss social and political issues that arose. This tradition of consulting with a representative group had its roots in the pre-Islamic tribal councils, and it would remain an important part of Islam. Muhammad also continued to receive revelations.

With Mecca now firmly in his camp, Muhammad stepped up his campaign to bring other regions into his confederation. Those who resisted were persuaded to do so through force of arms. Within two years he controlled nearly all of the Arabian peninsula. Members of the alliance were forbidden to attack one another, and they were required to furnish troops on demand and to pay taxes to Medina. Although the pagan tribesmen were ordered to smash their idols, they were never pressured to convert to Islam. Muhammad hoped that in time they would be be drawn to the new faith, and, indeed, most of them were.

The cycles of vendettas and tribal warfare were finally ended, and for the first time in history the Arab people were united.

## The Five Pillars

By the end of his life, Muhammad had established the basic religious duties required of all Muslims that came to be known as the Five Pillars of Islam. The first pillar (*shahada*) is to affirm the Islamic faith by reciting the following words: "There is no god but God and Muhammad is His Messenger." Anyone who repeats this statement in all sincerity three times in front of a witness is considered a Muslim. The second pillar (*salat*) is to pray to God while facing Mecca five times a day — at dawn, noon, afternoon, sunset, and evening. Prayers can be performed at home or wherever one finds oneself, although many Muslims go to a mosque for the noon prayer. On Friday all adult males assemble at their local mosque at noon for communal prayers. The worshipper must be in a state of purity before praying (having washed face, hands, arms, and feet) and the prayer area must be spotless. (For this reason, many use a special prayer rug.) Muhammad once compared the purifying power of ritual prayer to a stream of water that washes off a person's sins. (For details of Muslim prayer, see page 50.)

Dates and milk are the traditional first course in the meal after the sun sets during Ramadan. The new moon marks the end of the month of fasting. This is a time of rejoicing and family banquets.

The third pillar (*zakat*) is the alms tax. A Muslim is required to give an amount proportionate to his income to the poor. The fourth pillar (*sawm*) is to fast from sunrise to sunset during the month of Ramadan, the 9th month of the Muslim lunar year. (You can find out more about the Muslim calendar on page 34.) Travelers and people who are ill or very old are excused. Fasting reminds one of the privations of the poor. The fifth pillar (*hajj*) is to make a pilgrimage to Mecca once in a lifetime, if physically and financially able. This is a spiritual as well as a communal experience, since great numbers of Muslims perform the rituals together near the *Kaaba*.

## Updating the Rituals

In February 632 Muhammad, in failing health and sensing that his days were limited, led his final *hajj* to Mecca. Once at the *Kaaba*, he performed the rites that had become a tradition centuries earlier, but he gave them new Islamic meanings, emphasizing events tied to Abraham and Ishmael. As before, the pilgrims walked around the shrine seven times and kissed the sacred black stone. Then they rushed back and forth seven times between the hills of Safa and Marwa, in remembrance of the time when Hagar had frantically searched in the desert for water for her infant son, Ishmael. They stood on the slopes of Mount

Arafat to recall the original covenant God had made with Adam, the very first prophet. They threw pebbles at the pillars at Mina, which now represented the temptations of Satan. They sanctified themselves by shaving their heads, and they slaughtered a sheep to commemorate Abraham's willingness to sacrifice his son to God.

After the rituals, Muhammad preached his Farewell Sermon and shared his final words of revelation. He reminded the pilgrims to deal justly with one another, to treat women kindly, and to abandon all blood feuds. As he spoke, he must have marveled at the vast sea of faces before him. While only 70 followers had migrated with him to Medina 23 years earlier, he now stood before over a hundred thousand believers.

Muhammad died on June 8, 632 at the age of 63. He was buried beneath the mosque he helped build in Medina. Today his grave is marked by the green dome of the greatly enlarged structure. His legacy is inestimable. Prophet, spiritual advisor, model citizen, military strategist, charismatic religious and political leader, he was indeed a figure larger than life. His visions would one day guide the beliefs and conduct of Muslims throughout the world.

## Abu Bakr, the First Caliph

Although Muhammad had depended upon the counsel of the Companions and other community leaders, he had forged no formal government structure. Nor did he leave behind a provision for appointing his successor. His death created an enormous vacuum, and many feared that with him gone, the new Islamic community would whither and die. Abu Bakr, Muhammad's closest friend, had led prayers during his illness. When he announced the Prophet's death to his followers, he addressed this major concern: "If any of you has worshiped Muhammad, let me tell you that Muhammad is dead. But if you worship God, then know that God is living and will never die."

Later that day, the Companions met to discuss the succession. The top contenders were all related to Muhammad through blood or marriage: Abu Bakr, Umar ibn al-Khattab, Uthman ibn Affan, and Ali ibn Abi Talib. Some thought the Prophet would have wanted to be succeeded by his closest male relative, Ali, who was a pious, sensitive, and courageous man. He had married Muhammad's daughter, Fatima, and was now the father of his only grandson. But Ali was young and inexperienced. Instead, the Companions chose Abu Bakr, who was greatly respected for his wisdom as well as his piety. He was given the title of caliph (*khalifa*), which means "successor." His appointment was finalized by the ritual handclasp

Arabic names are often preceded by certain words that denote certain familial relationships: *ibn* (son of), *bint* (daughter of), *abu* (father of), and *umm* (mother of).

(*baya*) used by Arabs to seal a contract. As caliph, his duties were to lead and defend the *umma* and to maintain the heritage of the Prophet. A council could override his authority if he strayed from the tenets of Islam.

Abu Bakr's first task was to reestablish Muslim authority in Arabia. Many of the Bedouin tribes had withdrawn as allies, claiming their allegiance had dissolved with the Prophet's death. (They were no doubt glad to free themselves of the Muslim taxes.) Some resumed raids against members of the confederation and even threatened Medina itself. After seeing to the city's defense, the new caliph set out on a campaign to bring the rebellious tribes back into the fold. Before any fighting took place, he invited the rebels to return peacefully, and many tribes did so. The others were gradually brought back through military means. Within two years, most of Arabia was once again under Muslim control.

Abu Bakr was keenly aware of the warrior tradition of the Bedouins. Since it was unacceptable for Muslims to fight other Muslims, raiding parties in Arabia were out of the question. So to prevent the built-up energies of his soldiers from disrupting the stability of the *umma,* he fixed his gaze northward. In 633 over 8,000 warriors were dispatched to deal with the Sasanian troops who had been backing Bedouin rebels in the north. These skirmishes would eventually lead to a major expansion of Islam.

In 634 Abu Bakr fell gravely ill. He called a special council (*shura*) of the Companions to discuss who should rule next. He suggested Umar ibn al-Khattab, the father of one of the Prophet's wives, and all agreed. A few days later, Abu Bakr died.

## Umar, Commander of the Faithful

Umar was a huge man with a long beard and a totally bald head. He wore coarse clothing, often patched, and ate plain food in order to conform with Muhammad's example of humble living. But he lacked the Prophet's gentleness. Brusque in manner, he often walked about the streets of Medina with a hide whip in his hand, ready to punish anyone who seemed out of step with Muslim rules of behavior.

Umar's talents lay in the military, and he took the title of "Commander of the Faithful." He stepped up raids in the lands beyond the Arabian borders, not simply to keep his warriors engaged, but to expand his empire. The timing couldn't have been better. The Byzantines and the Sasanians had been fighting a long series of wars with one another, and both sides were exhausted. Their soldiers were ill-prepared to deal with the desert-hardened warriors who burst out of Arabia, eager to prove their prowess on the battlefield.

Byzantine rule over Syria and Palestine was particularly shaky at this time. The local people resented their overlords, who spoke an alien language (Greek), were intolerant of all religions except their own orthodox brand of Christianity, and demanded a burdensome rate of taxation. The first major battle between the Muslims and the Byzantines took place at Ajnadayn in southern Palestine in 634. It was a Muslim victory. The following year the Arabs captured Damascus, then moved on and took Antioch and Aleppo. With the fall of these cities, Syria became part of the expanding Muslim empire.

In 636 the Arabs defeated a large Byzantine army at Yarmuk, in northern Palestine. Two years later, they captured Jerusalem in one of the most peaceful takeovers in the long history of that holy city. After its surrender, Umar rode alone through the city gates. The local people were amazed by his simple attire and lack of bodyguards, which contrasted dramatically with the pomp and display of the Byzantine emperors. The caliph was warmly greeted by the local leaders, who were relieved to be released from the oppressive regime of the Byzantines. Jerusalem had been the sacred city of Jews and Christians for centuries. King Solomon had built his temple there in the first millennium BCE, and in the 4th century CE Byzantine emperor Constantine erected the Church of the Holy Sepulcher to mark the site of Christ's tomb. And, of course, Jerusalem was the point of departure for Muhammad's "Night Journey." Now it was in Muslim hands. Apart from a period of occupation by Crusaders in the 12th century, the city would remain so for the next 13 centuries. Umar ordered the site of the Temple of Solomon to be cleansed of the piles of rubble that had accumulated on it and built a small mosque on part of the cleared land. He granted lenient terms to the inhabitants of the Jerusalem. Jews, long banned from living there by the Byzantines, were permitted to return. Christians and Jews could now worship as they wished and live in communities governed by their own laws in return for paying a poll tax.

Further east lay the valleys of the Tigris and Euphrates Rivers. Known as Mesopotamia (a Greek term meaning "the land between the rivers"), this region had been the center of many great ancient civilizations. It was now the westernmost province of the Sasanian empire. In 636 (the same year as Yarmuk) Arab forces clashed with the Sasanians on the plain of Qadisiyya near the Euphrates. Once again, the Arabs were victors. The young Sasanian king, Yazdegerd, withdrew to his capital at Ctesiphon on the east bank of the Tigris. When his enemies

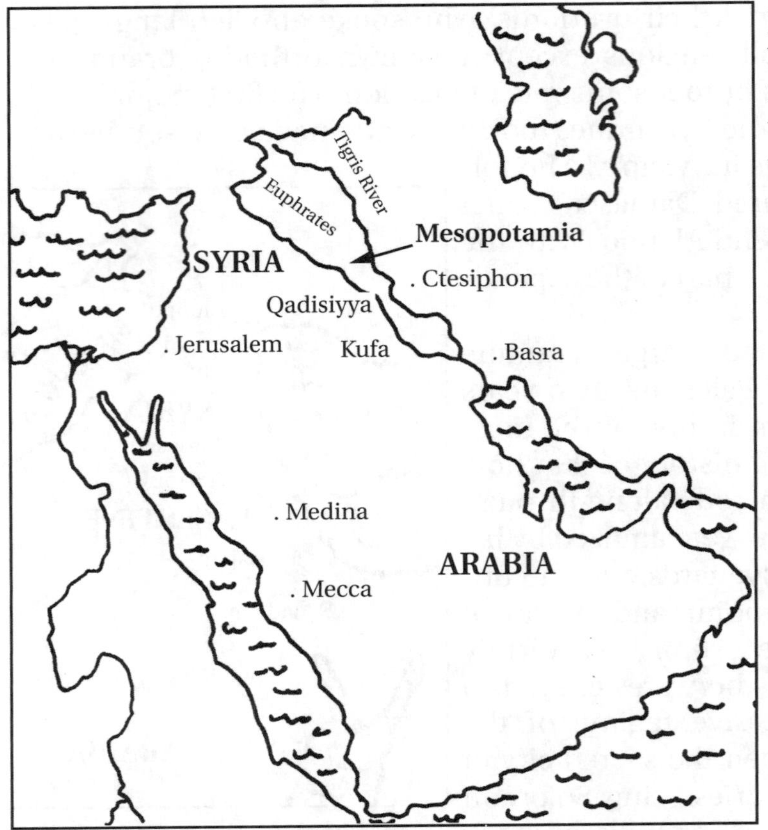


pursued him there, he fled with his family to the eastern mountains and his capital was taken. The Arab warriors were amazed at the city's grandeur — its impressive stone buildings were a far cry from the primitive mud brick houses of Mecca and Medina. Umar's commander established his residence in the royal palace and turned its banquet hall into a mosque. After a number of smaller battles, most of Mesopotamia had fallen to the Muslims.

By 642 Umar controlled all of the former Sasanian Empire and much of the Byzantine. He divided his expanded realm into eight provinces and appointed an emir (governor) to run each one. (The word emir is derived from the Arabic *amir*, meaning "one who gives orders.") He took advantage of the experience of local officials who had worked for the earlier regimes, appointing them to important jobs in his new government. All estates that had belonged to the Sasanian royalty and nobility were confiscated for the caliph, but other lands were left alone so that the local farmers could continue to work on them. The farmers paid a land tax based on the size and productivity of their fields. For the time being, Greek remained the main language in the former Byzantine regions, while Pahlavi was spoken in the Sasanian lands. Daily life in the new provinces continued much as before, although Muslim rule was more flexible and tolerant than that of the powers it replaced. As in Jerusalem, "People of the Book" (Jews and Christians) were free to practice their faith and were protected from foreign aggressors in exchange for paying a poll tax.

Umar kept a tight rein on his Arab warriors. He created a large garrison at Kufu, a settlement on the banks of Euphrates River, so that he could keep them all in one place. The garrison was divided into districts for each tribe, with the residences of the top officers, a mosque, and a marketplace at the center. This became the standard design for new Muslim settlements, civil and military, for the next century or two. The population of Kufa would soon grow to 40,000, as wives and children joined the soldiers. A second large garrison was later established at Basra, a port on the Persian Gulf.

The expansion of the Muslim empire brings up the concept of *jihad* (juh HAHD), a word meaning "struggle." According to the *Quran*, Muslims were called upon to commit themselves to a lifelong struggle, which could be moral, spiritual, or political, to create a fair and just society. There are two levels of *jihad* — greater (the more important) and lesser. Greater *jihad* refers to the personal struggle against the evils encountered in daily living, including one's own vices. Lesser *jihad* is a collective struggle against those who threaten the Islamic way of life. The *Quran* does not sanctify warfare, although it does develop the notion of a just war of self-defense to protect social values. (This refers specifically to Muhammad's conflicts with the Meccans.) But it is important to realize that the spread of Islam throughout the Arabian peninsula and into neighboring regions was politically motivated. Muhammad built a confederation to guarantee a peaceful environment that would enable the *umma* to flourish. Abu Bakr sought a means to channel the fighting spirit of his warriors, while Umar was keen to extend his range of power. The term *jihad* does not apply in these cases.

Umar ruled from a base in Medina for 10 years, until (in 644) a Persian prisoner-of-war stabbed him while he was attending prayers in the central mosque. As he lay dying, Umar appointed a council to choose a new caliph. The most favored candidates were Uthman ibn Affan and Ali ibn Abi Talib. After several days of debate, Uthman was chosen.

## Uthman

Uthman was a member of the Umayyad (OO mah yad) clan, one of the dominant families of Mecca. Under his rule the empire continued to expand. Uthman created the first Muslim navy. His fleets seized the island of Cyprus from the Byzantines, gaining control of the eastern Mediterranean. (They even besieged Constantinople for a short

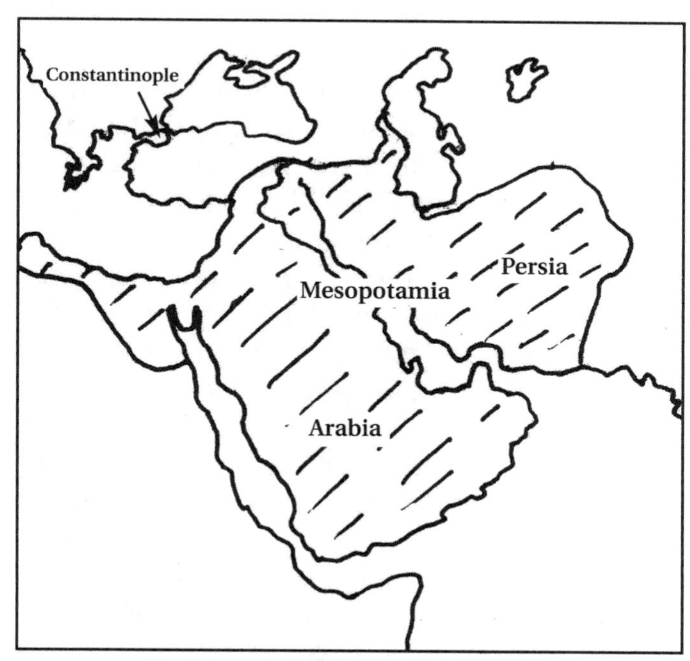


The Muslim Empire Under Uthman

time.) Armies in North Africa extended Muslim borders as far as Tripoli (in present-day Libya). As Islam spread into new regions, special areas were set aside in churches, pagan temples, and ordinary homes to meet the needs of daily prayers until a mosque could be built. The early mosques were very simple mudbrick structures with dirt floors and flat roofs supported by regularly spaced pillars. The direction of prayer (*qibla*) was often indicated by a lance stuck into the ground.

Uthman's most important and long-lasting act was to produce an authorized version of the *Quran*. As we've learned, the revelations were preserved during Muhammad's lifetime on whatever writing materials were available. Since most Arabs were illiterate, a group of devout Muslims known as "the reciters" (*qurra*) chanted the revelations from memory to congregations of worshippers. The reciters were held in great esteem, since they were often the people's only access to the *Quran*. But during the reign of Abu Bakr, 70 of the most prominent members of the group were killed in battle. At that point, the caliph was urged to compile a definitive text of the revelations so that the sacred words would never be lost. This task was completed by Uthman. Copies of the new official version of the *Quran* were sent to the major cities in the Islamic realm. All other versions were destroyed. The *Quran* that has come down to modern times is the very one produced at this time.

Since no one was sure of the exact order in which Muhammad had received his revelations, the *Quran*'s 114 chapters (each representing one revelation) were arranged according to length, from the longest to the shortest. (The exception is the first chapter, the *Fatiha* ("Opening"). The chapters (*suras*) are divided into verses (*ayas*), of which there are 6,000. Each chapter has a name, which refers to an important word or episode it contains, such as "The Star," "The Running Ones," and "The Elephant." The *Quran* is a little shorter than the Christian New Testament.

The longest chapters in the *Quran* are the revelations Muhammad received in Medina. They contain practical guidelines for the organization of the *umma* and include information about moral values, family life, civil disputes, daily prayer, and pilgrimage. The shorter chapters, the revelations received in Mecca, are more dramatic and poetic. They focus upon the Oneness of God, the evil of paganism, and the imminence of Judgment Day. Since the chapters are arranged according to length and have no sequential order, it is common prac-

Memorizing the *Quran* is a goal achieved by many modern Muslims. The art of *Quran* recitation is called *tajwid*. Competitions are held at local, national, and international levels. *Tajwid* often forms part of the ceremony blessing a new house, launching a business, or commemorating a deceased person.

tice to open the *Quran* at random and read a page, as in a collection of poetry.

Scattered throughout the *Quran* are references to accounts and parables that appear in the Jewish *Torah* and the Christian *Gospel*, scriptures with which Muhammad was familiar. However, there are a number of important differences between them. For example, the *Quran* presents Jesus as a prophet, an ordinary man like Muhammad and not the divine Son of God. It does not acknowledge the Christian concept of the Trinity (God represented as Father, Son, and Holy Ghost). Nor does Islam have a doctrine of original sin. In the *Quranic* version of the story of Adam and Eve, both are created at the same time, each for the other's comfort; both eat the forbidden fruit and are driven from the Garden of Eden; and both are later forgiven by God. The message is that man and woman are not inherently sinful, just subject to temptation.

Nearly every chapter begins with the invocation of the *Basmalla*: "In the name of God, the Compassionate, the Merciful." Today, this phrase is also written by Muslims at the head of every letter or document and is repeated before the undertaking of any important activity. Similarly, the mention of Muhammad's name is always followed by the phrase, "God bless him and give him peace."

Unlike the *Torah* and the *Gospels*, which consist of the writings of many individuals collected over a long period of time, the *Quran* is considered the actual word of God, delivered directly by Gabriel to Muhammad. For this reason, when a Muslim reads the *Quran* he senses a close communication with God. Since His message was revealed to Muhammad in his own language, Arabic has become the sacred language of Islam. (Today, all Muslims, regardless of native tongue, read, memorize, and recite the *Quran* in Arabic.) There are, of course, many translations of the *Quran*, but these are intended for a study of the text and are not considered sacred writings. The Arabic verses have a lyrical, musical

The *Fatiha* is repeated five times a day by every Muslim at the beginning of prayers:

*Praise belongs to God, the Lord of all Being,*
*the Merciful, the Compassionate,*
*the Master of the Day of Judgment.*
*You only do we serve; to You alone we pray for help.*
*Guide us in the Straight Path,*
*the path of those whom You have blessed,*
*not of those who earn your anger, nor of those who go astray.*

quality and are intended to be chanted aloud. They are rich with allusions and rhetorical devices, such as alliteration and plays on words (puns), which are not easily translated. The style and language of the *Quran* served as the model for speakers and writers of Arabic for centuries to come. Since the book has never been revised since the time of Uthman, it has preserved the Arabic language of the era of Muhammad. There are no illustrations in the *Quran*, apart from intricate geometric and floral designs. There is nothing in the revelations that forbids images of human beings, but the banning of the worship of idols probably discouraged any sort of figural representation in the sacred book. Over the years, the absence of figures in Islamic religious works (buildings as well as books) became the norm, as you will see.

> Because many sections of the *Quran* assume a certain familiarity with particular events, commentaries were written soon after the death of Muhammad to clarify their content. The interpretation of the revelations would be a major source of discussion and dispute for centuries to come.

Despite his accomplishments, Uthman had many detractors. Ali's supporters felt that he (Ali), and not Uthman, should have succeeded Umar as caliph. Others complained when Uthman placed members of his own family in high positions throughout the empire. (He even gave his relatives financial "gifts" from the government treasury.) They were particularly offended because the Umayyads had been among Muhammad's strongest foes in Mecca. But nearly everyone was shocked when Uthman took the title of "Successor to God." Meanwhile, the Arab soldiers, who now formed a professional army, were tired of being cooped up in the garrison towns. They felt entitled to pieces of the newly conquered lands. In June, 656, a large delegation of Arab warriors from Egypt, Basra, and Kufa brought their grievances to Medina. When Uthman refused to see them, Ali managed to convince them that he would act on their behalf if they would return home. As they left Medina, someone intercepted a message, supposedly signed by Uthman, calling for their punishment. (As it turned out, the message was a fake.) Furious, the soldiers returned and broke into Uthman's house, where they discovered him reading the *Quran*. They drew their swords and killed him, spilling his blood over the holy book that lay open in his lap. It was a terrible omen of things to come.

> Muhammad stressed the importance of using one's intelligence to cultivate a caring and responsible character. Although illiterate himself, he called for the education of all his followers. The first Muslim public school was established in Medina in 653. The need to read the *Quran* in its original language helped spread literacy throughout the Islamic world.

## Ali Becomes Caliph

Most Muslims were deeply grieved by the murder of Uthman. Despite the complaints about his nepotism (family favoritism), the caliph had been admired for his religious devotion. Now he had been murdered by members of his own faith. Did this mark a return to the tribal warfare and vendettas of earlier times? If the *umma* was to survive, who was most capable of leading it? Ali's name was heard in many quarters. He was admired for his piety as well as his close kinship with Muhammad, and his speeches and sermons showed that he was an articulate and perceptive man. Ali was strongly supported in Medina and by those Meccans who resented the power of the Umayyads. And so, amid the confusion following the assassination of Uthman, he was installed as caliph.

Ali's immediate challenge was to deal with Uthman's killers. Although he had not supported Uthman, he could hardly condone his murder. Being of a cautious nature, he took his time, carefully examining all aspects of the crime. His hesitancy to take immediate action was viewed by some as a decision against bringing the killers to justice. Aisha, Muhammad's favorite wife and now his most prominent widow, joined a group of dissidents who were angered by Ali's inaction. They traveled to Basra, where they found some of the killers and executed them. The dissidents, now determined to drive Ali from power, amassed an army of 1000 warriors. In response, Ali traveled to Kufa and made it his base. The following October Ali led an army to meet the rebels, setting up camp in a field near Basra. For the first time, a caliph stood ready to battle an opposing Muslim force. Before any fighting took place, however, Ali and Aisha were able to agree to peace negotiations. Unfortunately, a few men in the front lines began provoking one another with their swords, and then both sides plunged into the battle. Aisha mounted a camel and rode into melee, hoping to get her men to stop fighting, but they assumed she was there to encourage them. After a long bloody battle, Ali's soldiers defeated the rebels. This episode is known as the Battle of the Camel after Aisha's daring ride onto the battlefield. Ali had proven himself as a military leader. Aisha returned to Medina. (She later became an important source of information about the life and teachings of her husband.)

Trouble was now brewing in Syria, where Muawiya (moo ah WEE ya), a Umayyad and the son of Muhammad's former adversary, Abu Sufyan, was governor. He was enraged over the murder of his kinsman, Uthman, and he refused to recognize Ali as caliph. He was in a strong position to argue, since he ruled over a united and orderly province and had a well-trained and highly disciplined army. He was, of course, strongly supported by the Umayyads in Arabia and Syria.

Ali's supporters came to be known as the Shi'ite Muslims (from *shi'at Ali,* "partisans of Ali"). They considered the first three caliphs (Abu Bakr, Umar, and Uthman) interlopers who had stood in the way of the proper line of succession from Muhammad to Ali. Those who joined the Umayyads in opposing Ali were known as the Sunni Muslims (from *ahl al-sunna,* "the people of custom"). They supported the system of an elected caliphate as it had evolved, but with all candidates belonging to the Prophet's tribe, the Quraysh. Their candidate for caliph was, of course, Muawiya.

In May 657 Ali marched an army north and faced Muawiya's troops at Siffin, Syria. After three days of fighting, Ali was on the verge of victory when Muawiya, perhaps sensing imminent defeat, ordered his men to hang pages of the *Quran* on the tips of their spears. This was a signal to settle the question by arbitration. Ali, not wanting to spill any more blood, honored the request. The arbitrators met and decided against Ali, much to the frustration of his followers. A group of these, convinced that Ali had compromised their interests by submitting to arbitration, withdrew from the *umma* to set up their own faction. Known as the Kharijites ("Those Who Withdrew"), they argued that the caliphate should now be open to any observant Muslim of piety and moral excellence. In January 661 a member of this new sect stabbed Ali in front of the mosque in Kufa. He was buried in nearby Najaf.

The Shi'ites, stunned by the loss of their leader, now turned to Ali's son, Hasan. But he was unwilling to dispute the Umayyad claim to leadership, and Muawiya was hailed as the new caliph. He would soon be accepted by the majority of Muslims, although the split between Shi'ite and Sunni would remain and fester. Ali, a man betrayed by his Muslim brothers, was viewed by the Shi'ites as a martyr of the pure faith of Islam. The Sunnis took a more neutral stance. Appalled by the murderous divisions that had torn the *umma* apart, they focused upon preserving the unity of the caliphate.

Ali was the last of the Rightly Guided Caliphs (the *Rashidun*). These four men — Abu Bakr, Umar, Uthman, and Ali — had heard the revelations from the Prophet himself and were guided by his words and his example. Their rule of 30 years was as formative as that of Muhammad. Under their command, Islam had expanded until it stretched from the Atlas Mountains of North Africa to the borders of India. The small community of Medina had evolved into a multi-ethnic empire. A new political structure was needed if Islam was to endure.

What began as a succession dispute between the Shi'ites and the Sunnis would develop and evolve into the major religious schism of Islam. Today Sunnis make up 85% of Muslims worldwide, while various Shi'ite sects form the remaining 15%.

## Review Questions:

1. Describe Muhammad's governing of Medina.
2. What are the Five Pillars of Islam?
3. What traditions did Muhammad establish during his last *hajj*?
4. What did Abu Bakr accomplish during his short period of rule?
5. Why were the Arab armies so successful against the Byzantines?
6. Describe Umar's takeover of Jerusalem.
7. How did Umar administer his growing empire?
8. What prompted the decision to create a standard version of the *Quran*?
9. How is the *Quran* organized?
10. How does the *Quran* differ from the Jewish and Christian scriptures?
11. What are some of the unique characteristics of the *Quran*?
12. What made Uthman unpopular?
13. What caused Ali to lose support within his own party just after he became caliph?
14. Why did Ali fall from power?
15. What were the original descriptions of the Shi'ite and Sunni sects?
16. Who were the Rightly Guided Caliphs?

## Questions for Discussion:

1. How do you explain the fact that Islam was accepted by most people living in Arabia within only 23 years?
2. How is the word "jihad" commonly used in the media today? How does this differ from the actual meaing of the term? How can misuse of the word lead to tensions between Muslims and non-Muslims?
3. In what ways did the Rightly Guided Caliphs follow in the footsteps of Muhammad, and in what ways did they go in new directions? What might Muhammad have thought about their decisions? (Be specific.)
4. What circumstances in Ali's early life might have made him the best candidate to succeed Muhammad? In what ways were Abu Bakr, Umar, and Uthman successful caliphs? How might history have been different if Ali had been chosen over Abu Bakr as the first caliph?

Umar fixed the beginning of the Muslim calendar at the day Muhammad migrated from Mecca to Medina (July 16, 622 CE). The word "Hegira" (*Hijra)* now applied to the new Muslim era and the abbreviation AH (for *Anno Hegirae,* "Year of the Hegira") refers to a Muslim year.

The calendar is lunar, each month beginning with the new crescent of the moon. It is divided into twelve months of 29 or 30 days each. The exception is the last month, the length of which varies to keep the calendar in step with the true phases of the moon. The year has 354 or 355 days, which is ten or eleven days shorter than the solar year.

The Islamic months are:

1. Muharram
2. Safar
3. Rabi' al-Awal
4. Rabi' ath-Thani
5. Jamada' al-Awal
6. Jamada' ath-Thani
7. Rajab
8. Sha'ban
9. Ramadan (the fasting month)
10. Shawwal
11. Dhul Qa'dah
12. Dhul Hijjah (the pilgrimage month)

The dates of the Muslim calendar have no fixed relationship to dates of the Gregorian (Western) calendar, nor do they relate to the seasons of the year. (It is important to remember that in the Arabian desert there were no distinct seasons, and there is little need to divide the year according to an agricultural schedule.) The year 2005 CE corresponds to the Islamic year AH 1426.

There are seven days in a week, just as there are in the Western calendar. The week begins on a Saturday (actually Friday night, the beginning of the sabbath) and ends on a Friday. The names of the days of the week are: al-Sabt (Saturday), al-Ahad (Sunday), al-Ithnain (Monday), ath-Thalatha (Tuesday), al-Arba (Wednesday), al-Khamis (Thursday), al-Jumuah (Friday).

A single day is divided into five periods, marking the five times a Muslim prays. These are: Fajr (Dawn), Zuhur (Midday), Asr (Afternoon), Maghreb (Dusk), and Isha (Night).

# Chapter 3 — DAMASCUS

Damascus is the capital and largest city of Syria. It is situated on a flat terrace nearly 2,000 feet above sea level. Two narrow mountain ranges separate the city from the Mediterranean Sea. The Barada River delivers cool, refreshing water from the mountains to the city's inhabitants before disappearing beneath the sands of the desert to the east.

Damascus is one of the world's oldest continuously inhabited cities. As early as the 8th century BCE it was the capital of the Aramaean kingdom. In 333 BCE it was taken over by Alexander the Great and became a center of Hellenistic civilization. In 64 BCE it fell to the Romans. Damascus became part of the Byzantine Empire in the 4th century CE. As a western terminus of the Silk Road, the network of trade routes linking the Mediterranean world with China, it flourished as a bustling center of commerce.

Under the Umayyads Damascus was expanded and transformed into a majestic center of the rapidly expanding Islamic empire.

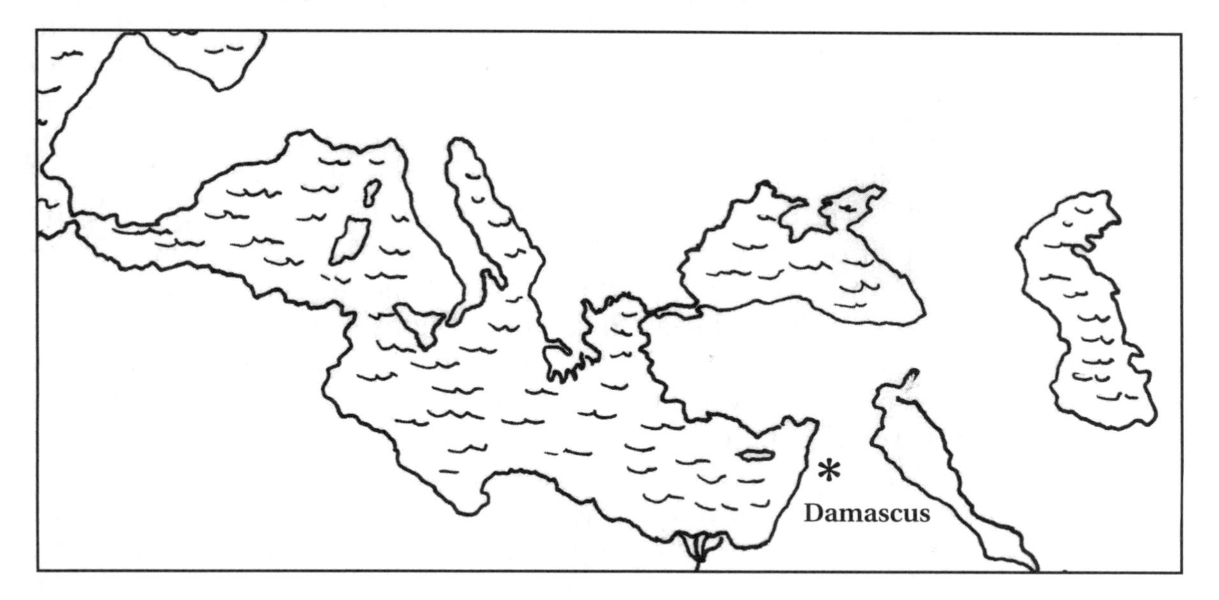


## The Umayyad Caliphate

Since Syria was his power base, the new caliph, Muawiya, made Damascus his capital. The city had many appeals. Its perch above vast expanses of inland desert reminded the Arab warriors of their homeland, yet its close links to the fertile farmland of Mesopotamia kept it well supplied with grain.

Merchants from the east and the west mingled in the city's marketplaces, trading such exotic wares as gemstones, carved ivory, and incense. The food market offered delicious fresh fruits — quinces, melons, and oranges from Persia and bananas from India. (These were a welcome addition to the local diet of bread, onions, dates, and pine nuts.) Damascus was already famous for its fine silk cloth, appropriately known as damask. It was woven in elaborate patterns, often ornamented with gold and silver threads. The city's metalsmiths fashioned strong double-edged swords by heating and hammering together laminated strips of steel and iron. The blades were etched in intricate designs. (In later years, the verb "to damascene" meant "to weave or adorn with elaborate design.") The cloth and swords were particularly popular among those Europeans who could afford them.

The Islamic caliphate had evolved a great deal since the time of Abu Bakr. The changes brought about by the growing empire had altered the sense of a common religious mission that had once held the *umma* together. Politics now seemed to overshadow religion. The Muslim community had been further weakened by the murder of Uthman and the fighting that followed it. Muawiya needed to find ways to strengthen the caliphate and restructure its government to meet the needs of the changing times. His solution was to transform the theocracy created by Muhammad in Medina into something resembling a traditional monarchy, adopting many aspects of the Byzantine bureaucracy. He hired Syrian officials to staff his government, although he appointed his Arab kinsmen to the key posts. Unlike Muhammad and the Rightly Guided Caliphs, who lived unpretentious lives and did not seek to separate themselves from the community they ruled, Muawiya distanced himself from his own people. He lived in an ornate palace and presided over a court similar to those of the Byzantine and Sasanian rulers. He established the office of "doorkeeper" to screen those entering his court, and he received the visitors deemed appropriate with great ceremony. When he *did* appear in public, he had a full escort of bodyguards. His efforts to adopt the regal traditions of the region he now ruled made practical sense, since the people of Syria and Mesopotamia were accustomed to political authority being vested in a powerful and distant monarch. However, many Muslims were uncomfortable with and offended by the caliph's new lofty status.

A regular postal service was set up between Damascus and the provincial capitals. Most official communications were sent by a system of mounted horsemen resembling the pony express of the American West, although urgent messages were sent by carrier pigeon.

Although Medina dropped from the political scene, it remained one of the holiest cities of Islam (the burial place of Muhammad being an important shrine) and it also became an important center of learning.

The Arabs formed an elite military class in Umayyad society. They were exempted from taxes but were forbidden to engage in commercial activities or to own land. Those Muslims who were not Arabs formed a new social class, the *mawali*. Many *mawali* were high-ranking officials who had recently converted to Islam. (No one was forced to convert. However, only Muslims could serve in public office.) Because they could not enter the kinship-based Arab society, they were viewed as second-class citizens. This distinction did not reflect Muhammad's views of social equality, and it would later become a major source of tension. Non-Muslims who were members of "protected" religions (*dhimmis*) now included Zoroastrians as well as Christians and Jews. As in earlier decades, *dhimmis* paid a poll tax in exchange for their protection. They were not allowed to build new churches, temples, or synagogues, although they were free to worship in currently standing structures. They were also told to refrain from "obtrusive" religious practices, such as ringing bells and chanting in public.

*Dhimmi* men could not marry Muslim women. Muslim men could marry out of their faith, however. The wife would convert to Islam, and any children would automatically be Muslims.

The Arab officers commanded well-disciplined troops that included many Syrians. In 667 Muawiya launched a series of annual raids in Khurasan, a region in northeastern Persia, and brought it under his control. In 671 he transferred thousands of soldiers and their families from the crowded garrison cities of Kufa and Basra to bases in the new province. He also sent an army west into North Africa and personally led a campaign into Anatolia (Asia Minor).

Since the time of Abu Bakr, a new caliph had been elected by a council (*shura*) of high-ranking Muslims. Muawiya broke with this tradition when he proclaimed his own son, Yazid, his successor. This enraged many Arabs. The concept of a hereditary dynasty was alien to their tribal values, where leadership was based upon wisdom and courage. Yazid was known to drink wine and to live a wasteful life — two indulgences not allowed in Islam. Most religious scholars and the few surviving Companions openly opposed Muawiya's decision. But when the caliph died suddenly in 680, Yazid wasted no time in claiming the throne, firmly establishing the Umayyad dynasty, Islam's first hereditary regime. The caliphate was looking more and more like the secular empires it had replaced, with the demands of the ruling elite taking precedence over the needs of the *umma*.

Muawiya lived to be 80, presiding over the longest period of peace and prosperity in the short history of Islam. He was buried beside one of the gates in the city wall of Damascus.

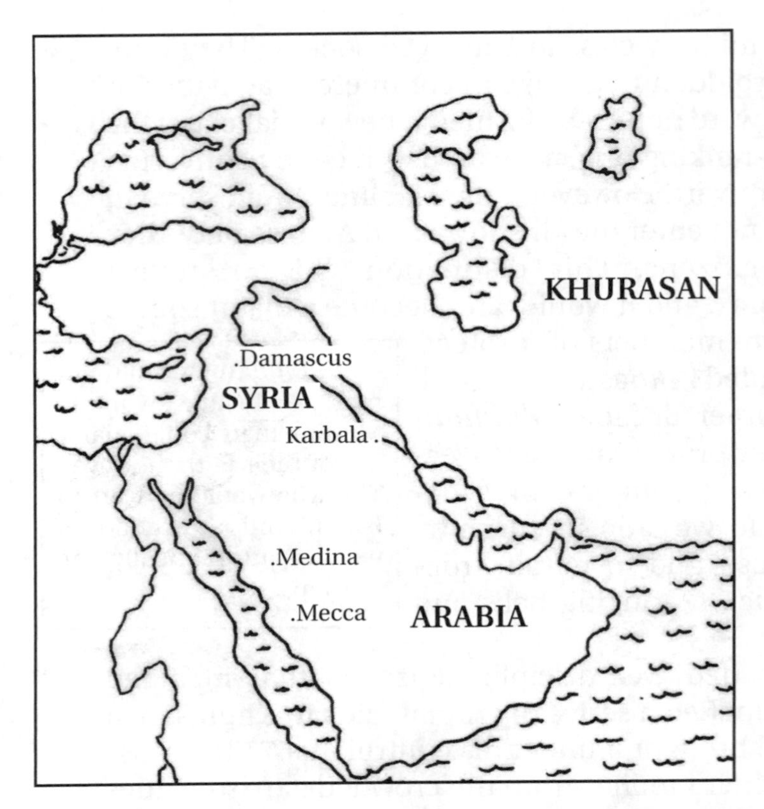


## Tragedy at Karbala

Yazid's rise to power brought the conflict between Sunnis and Shi'ites to the surface again. The Shi'ites refused to accept the new caliph, believing that Ali's younger son, Husayn, was the legitimate leader of the *umma*. (As we learned, Ali's elder son, Hasan, had not pursued a leadership role.) Husayn, who was living in Medina, was persuaded by Shi'ites from Khurasan to lead a rebellion. (Khurasan had become a major Shi'ite stronghold.) Husayn set out with his household, family, and some followers — 200 in all — for Kufa in the fall of 680. He planned to make the garrison his base of action. As they entered the plain of Karbala not far from the city, they encountered an army of 4,000 warriors, sent by Yazid to stop them. Many of Husayn's followers fled in panic, and Yazid's troops easily surrounded the small group that remained. When they refused to surrender, all the men were killed. Husayn was the last to die, allegedly holding his infant son in his arms. His severed head was triumphantly carried to Damascus on the tip of a spear and presented to Yazid.

This event is known as *Ashura*, a term derived from the Arabic word for the number 10. (The event took place on the 10th day of Muharram, the first month in the Muslim calendar.) Like the murder of Ali, the slaying of Husayn symbolized for the Shi'ites the injustice that had denied leadership of the *umma* to Muhammad's descendants. And like Ali, Husayn was viewed as a martyr. The Shi'ites continued to consider Ali and his direct descendants the true leaders of

Husayn's head was later buried with his body at Karbala. This site is one of the most important Shi'ite shrines. The martyrdom of Husayn and his family is remembered by Shi'ites to this day at the mourning rituals of Ashura on the anniversary of his death. In the 13 centuries since Husayn's death, the theology and doctrines of Shi'ites and Sunnis have evolved with the changing times. *Ashura* has come to symbolize for the Shi'ites a longing for freedom and for liberation from unjust rulers.

Islam. They gave these men the title of *Imam* ("spiritual leader") to set them apart from the more worldly and secular Umayyad caliphs. (Among Sunnis, an *imam* was a prayer leader.) All lineal descendants of Ali were known as the *Alids*.

## Protests in Arabia

When Muawiya established his capital at Damascus, Medina and Mecca became suddenly far removed from the seat of power. Of course, the *Kaaba* remained Islam's holiest shrine and the site of annual pilgrimage, while Medina was revered as the cradle of the Islamic community and the burial site of Muhammad. But the leading families in the two cities where Islam had originated now ceased to be important, and this made them resentful. Many devout Muslims residing there were also offended by the luxurious lifestyle of Umayyads, which contrasted so dramatically with the simpler ways of the Prophet. The rift between Arabia and Syria further deepened with the accession to power of Yazid.

Ibn al-Zubayr was the most active member of the second generation of Meccans who protested the rise of the Umayyads. After the murder of Husayn, he declared himself caliph and ordered the Umayyads expelled from Mecca. He hoped that by restoring the center of Islamic culture to the holy cities of the Hijaz, Muslims could return to the pure religion of Abraham and the values of Muhammad.

In 683 Umayyad troops invaded Arabia and sacked Medina. Mecca was only saved from destruction by the death of Yazid. The subsequent death of his infant son and heir led to a chaotic period of civil war in Syria. Once peace was restored, the new caliph, Al-Malik, besieged Mecca and defeated al-Zubayr on the field of battle. Arabia was soon brought back into the fold, and the authority of the Umayyads was no longer challenged there.

## Arabic Becomes the Official Language

With the expansion of the empire and the great influx of non-Arab converts into the *umma*, Muslim society had become multi-ethnic. People living in the newly conquered regions spoke a variety of languages: Coptic (in Egypt), Syriac (in Syria), Pahlavi (in Persia), and a variety of minor tongues and dialects. Muslim scholars worried that this diversity threatened the primacy of the very language that Islam was based upon. This was a major factor prompting Caliph

During the siege of Mecca, the *Kaaba* was nearly destroyed and a fire cracked the Black Stone into three pieces. When the siege was lifted, the stone was repaired with a band of silver and the *Kaaba* was rebuilt on a grander scale.

al-Walid to make Arabic the official language of the empire. This involved all government records and official correspondence. To keep their posts, non-Arab bureaucrats had to learn the language of their rulers. Within a century, Arabic would be fully established as the language of political power as well as religious faith throughout the Muslim world.

In 696 an Arabic coinage replaced the imitations of Byzantine and Persian coins then in use. The new gold coins, known as *dinars*, were covered with writing. On one side, the profession of the Muslim faith, the *shahada* ("There is no god but God and Muhammad is His Messenger") filled the center while a text around the edge contained the invocation, mint, and date. The center of the

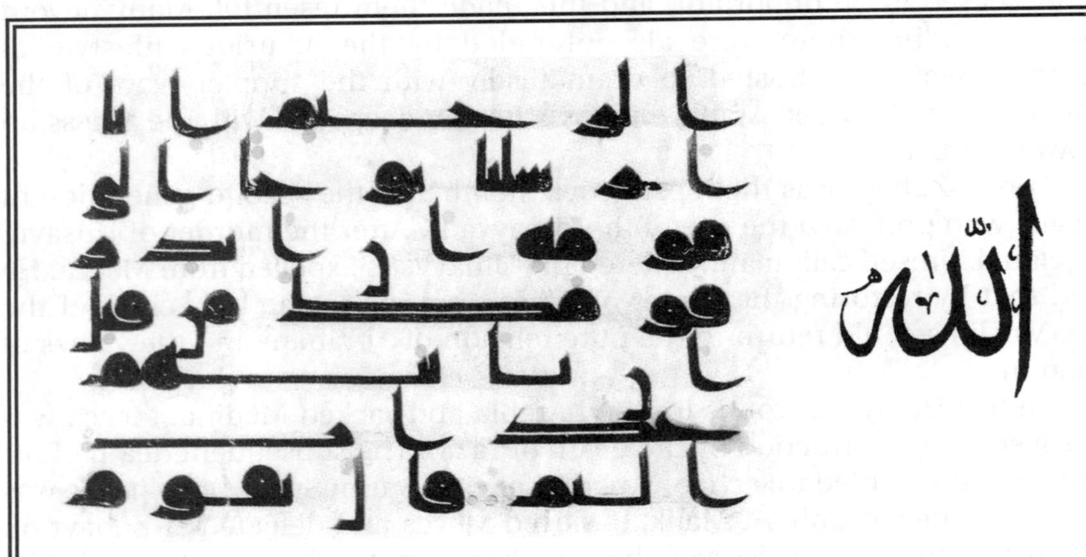

The Arabic alphabet has 28 letters, all representing consonants. Each letter might have up to four forms, depending upon its position in the word. Words are written from right to left, beginning at the top of the page. Originally, there were14 basic letter forms, which represented the 28 consonants. Since there were no vowels represented, the reader had to figure out which vowel sounds to add from the context. In the course of the 7th century, aids to pronunciation were developed. Dots were placed above or below letters to differentiate consonants of similar shape but different pronunciation, while marks above and below the letters indicated the vowel sounds.

The earliest Arabic script was square and angular. Known as Kufic (after Kufa), it was used for the earliest copies of the *Quran* and for architectural decoration. The example above left comes from an early *Quran*. The other major script, Naskhi, developed in Mecca and Medina. This cursive script later evolved into the Maghribi style of writing used today. Above right is an example of the word "God" (*Allah*) written in this style.

reverse side of the coin was inscribed with the *Quranic* verse stating God's Oneness, while around the edge was a long verse about the mission of Muhammad. All of this appeared on a coin smaller than a modern quarter! Similar coins of somewhat lesser value, called *dirhams*, were later minted in silver. (Today, currencies of many Middle Eastern countries include modernized versions of *dinars* and *dirhams*.)

## The Dome of the Rock

When al-Malik first came to power, the civil unrest in Mecca was interfering with the pilgrimages to the *Kaaba*. The caliph decided to redirect Muslim pilgrims to Jerusalem, where the presence of Abraham was felt as strongly as in the Hijaz. Beginning in 685 he oversaw the construction on a large shrine over a sacred rock where, according to Jewish tradition, King Solomon had built his temple to commemorate Abraham's willingness to sacrifice his son, Isaac. This was the same rock from which Muhammad ascended to Heaven on his Night Journey. (There is an indentation in the rock which some claim to be the footprint of the Prophet.) By building a shrine over the rock, al-Malik reinforced the connection between Islam and the legacy of Abraham. The shrine, known as the Dome of the Rock, is the oldest architectural monument in the Islamic world.

The design was entrusted to a Syrian architect with Byzantine training. He created an eight-sided building, with four doors corresponding to the four cardinal points of the compass. The main feature was a large dome, 60 feet in diameter and covered with gold sheathing, which gave the building its name. Domes were commonly used in Byzantine funerary shrines. Centuries earlier, the Romans had discovered that domes and arches were the most effective way of spanning and covering large areas while creating a feeling of openness and space. Not far from the site of the Muslim shrine was the domed church of the Holy Sepulcher, the most sacred shrine of Christianity (it was the burial site of Jesus), which was also built over a rock. Perhaps al-Malik's architect used this as a model. His dome contained 16 windows, which filled the interior of the shrine with light. This had special meaning for the Muslims, since, according to the *Quran*, light is the essence of God. (See page 117.) Beneath the dome, the sacred rock was encircled by an arcade of 16 marble piers and columns, all recycled from nearby Roman ruins. Pilgrims could perform their ritual walks (circumambulations) between this arcade and a larger, octagonal outer arcade.

Artists from Constantinople embellished the interior and exterior walls of the shrine with colorful mosaic tiles. The tiles were a special feature of Byzantine

The gold sheathing of the dome was removed centuries ago. The dome is presently covered with anodized aluminum.

decoration. They often depicted human figures, which were framed by geometric patterns or vegetal designs (stylized fruits, flowers, and trees). Because figures did not appear in Islamic religious art, the artists created elaborate geometric designs for the shrine. Beginning with such simple forms as the circle and the square, they formed patterns and then arranged these in intricate combinations. Among the most popular motifs was the star pattern, derived from triangles and parallelograms inscribed in a circle, like the one shown to the left. Until this time, decoration had been considered secondary to design in architecture, but the artists covered nearly the entire structure of the Dome of the Rock, inside and outside, with brilliant marble and mosaics.

The geometrics were enhanced by beautiful calligraphy, which is an art in itself. Two long bands of inscriptions, written in gold letters against a deep blue background, encircled the inner faces of the shrine's octagonal arcade. They contained pious phrases and verses from the *Quran* about God's omnipotence and Muhammad's prophetic mission. Around the dome itself were verses telling the story of Muhammad's Night Journey. Al-Malik marked the completion of the shrine with this dedicatory inscription: "This dome was built by the servant of God Abd al-Malik ibn Marwan, emir of the faithful, in the year seventy-two." (Hejira 72 in the Muslim calendar is 692 CE.) The Dome of the Rock became a model for later Muslim shrines. While the decoration of the exterior walls of the shrine has been replaced, the inner walls display the most lavish example of mosaics to survive from ancient or medieval times.

The inscriptions on the Dome of the Rock are the first dated example of the written *Quran*. No manuscripts of the holy book have survived form this early date.

## Rediscovering the Ancients

As Islam spread beyond Arabia, Muslim scholars became aware of traditions of learning that dated back to very early times. Many ancient writings had once been preserved in Alexandria, Egypt — a major hub of philosophical, scientific, and medical studies beginning in the first century CE. In 529, however, Byzantine emperor Justinian had ordered the learning centers there closed. (He considered the paganism of the ancient Greek philosophers and scientists a threat to Orthodox Christianity.) He burned the city's famous library. Scholars saved most of the major works and fled east to cities in Syria, Mesopotamia, and Persia. Some of the writings even ended up in Constantinople.

Literacy and knowledge had always been stressed in Islamic culture. Muhammad had counseled his followers to "seek learning as far as China" and noted that "He who travels in search of knowledge travels along God's path to Paradise." Umayyad Prince Khalid, a son of Muawiya, was among the earliest of the ruling elite to express interest in the learning of the ancient past. He recruited scholars from Egypt to translate a number of the texts from Coptic and Greek into Arabic. Such endeavors were the first steps that would lead to an explosion of intellectual activity, which you'll learn about in the next chapter.

## Imperial Splendor

The Umayyads greatly extended the borders of the empire. Muslim soldiers reached the Atlantic coast of Morocco, and in 711 an army crossed the Strait of Gibraltar into Spain. Other forces in the east advanced into India and as far as the border of China. By the middle of the 8th century, the Umayyad empire extended nearly a quarter of the way around the earth. The acquisition of new territories brought in great amounts of revenue (taxes) and tribute, much of it channeled to the caliph and his court. Damascus became one of the great cities of the world. Multi-story buildings of stone and brick rose above the paved

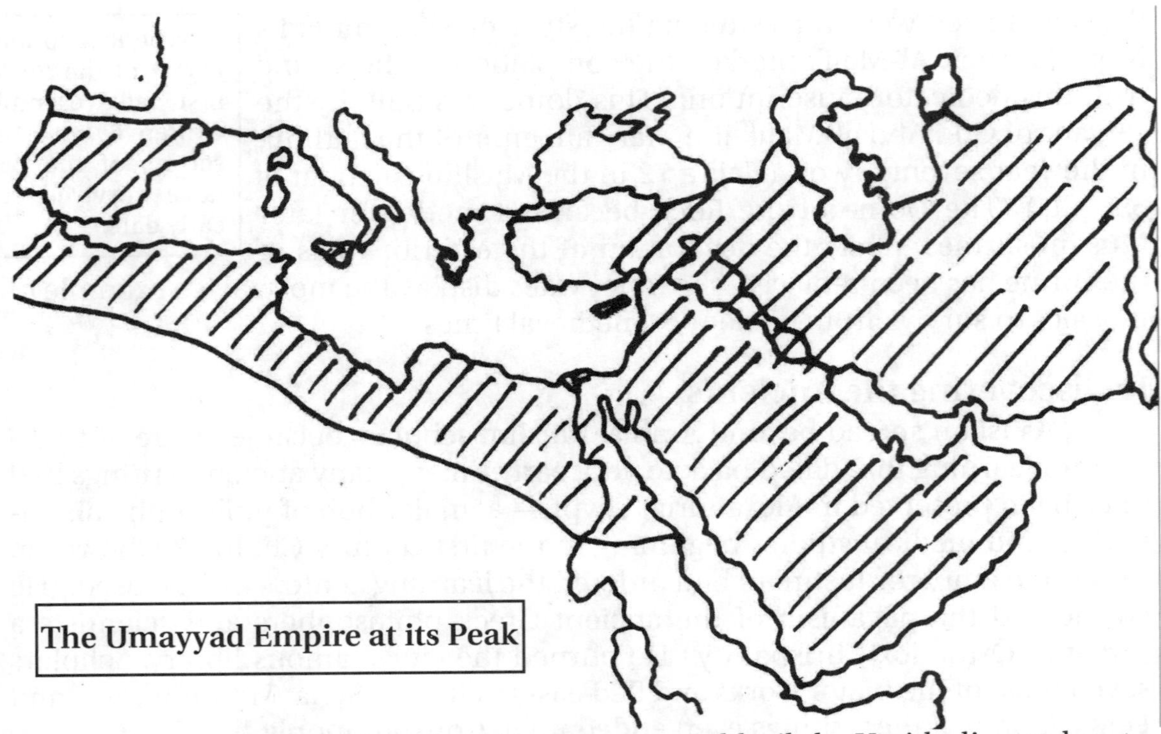

**The Umayyad Empire at its Peak**

streets that were lit at night by oil lamps. A canal built by Yazid diverted water from the Barada River to private homes and supplied the city's many public baths (*hammams*). Parks were filled with flower gardens and bubbling fountains. As the population grew, suburbs sprang up beyond the city walls, interspersed with olive groves and apricot orchards. To the south and west of the city walls were two large open spaces, where the Umayyad princes spent their leisure times watching horse races and tournaments.

The Great Mosque of Damascus was begun by Caliph al-Walid I in 706. It stood upon a prominent site that had been used for worship for nearly two millennia. The Romans had built a massive temple of their god Jupiter upon the foundations of earlier pagan shrines, and in the 4th century CE a Byzantine church dedicated to Saint John the Baptist was built near the temple. (The saint's head was buried there.) When the Muslims first conquered Damascus, they shared this

The giving of alms led to establishment of hospitals and orphanages. The first hospital, possibly for lepers, was built by Al-Walid I in 707 in Damascus. The first Muslim school was opened there in 744.

Before prayer, Muslims perform a ritual washing of the head, face, hands and forearms to elbows and feet. Mosques provided fountains for this in their courtyards. The *hammam* was a bathhouse for the complete washing of the body. As the Muslims expanded into what had been the ancient Roman world, they incorporated the existing waterworks and improved on them to provide water to their cities.

sacred area with the Christians, using the southern arcades of the walled enclosure of the temple as a prayer area. Al-Walid had the church demolished. (The Christians were compensated with other buildings for their religious services.) The temple wall, with its four square corner towers, was preserved, and the mosque was built to fit within the southern part of the enclosure. Thousands of craftsmen from many parts of the empire worked for ten years to create Islam's first imperial mosque.

Unlike Christian churches, with their tall cathedrals and soaring spires, which point towards the heavens, mosques are more "grounded," stressing the community of worshippers itself.

The design of the Great Mosque was a reworking of the elements of a Christian basilica (church). Like a church, it had aisles, but rather than leading to an altar they ran from one side of the prayer hall to the other, parallel to the *qibla*. As a result, the interior of the building was wider and less deep than a Christian church, ideal for Muslims who prayed in long parallel rows facing Mecca. (A small shrine was built within the mosque in honor of Saint John, whom the Muslims consider a prophet. His head was reburied there.) The pitched tile roof of the mosque was supported by marble columns taken from nearby Roman ruins and the church of Saint John. A cupola (a small dome) protruded through the roof, filling the space below it with light. One of the corner towers of the ancient wall was transformed into a minaret from which the *muezzin, or* "crier," called the worshippers to prayer. (This is the earliest known example of a minaret.) Outside the prayer hall was a large courtyard. The panels along its western wall bore a continuous landscape of tall houses and pleasure pavilions nestled beneath shady trees on the banks of a flowing river. (See the picture above.) Most experts believe these were meant to represent Paradise, although some suggest they depict Damascus as it then was.

The Great Mosque became the model for imperial mosques for many centuries. While it was being constructed, the smaller al-Aqsa Mosque was built in front of the Dome of the Rock in Jerusalem. This octagonal structure was the first mosque in Palestine. It was destroyed in an earthquake in the middle of the 8th century and later restored. Since then it has been rebuilt at least five times. Al-Walid also renovated the original mosque in Medina, doubling its dimensions while preserving the design. He added a special recess or niche, known as the *mihrab,* in the middle of the *qibla.* It was adapted from niches already present in synagogues (for the storage of the *Torah*) and churches (to hold religious statues). The *mihrab* served as a symbolic doorway into the spiritual world. In later centuries, it would become the most elaborately decorated feature of a mosque.

In time, every Muslim city had a main mosque as well as smaller mosques in each neighborhood. All mosques would have the same basic design: a covered rectangular prayer hall opening on one side into a courtyard. A *mihrab* marked the center of the *qibla,* which was usually opposite the entrance to the hall. Near the *mihrab* stood a raised platform, the *minbar,* where a member of the congregation led prayers and preached a sermon (the *khutba*) on Friday. The leader was called the *imam,* "one who stands in front." (Women worshiped in a separate area of the mosque, or at home, and did not attend the Friday sermons.) Some mosques had more than one minaret, although the additional towers had a purely decorative purpose. In those early times, the mosque served as a meeting-place, council chamber, courtroom, treasury, and base for military operations as well as prayer center. In between the five daily prayers, scholars often met with students, traders negotiated, meals were served, and the homeless even spent the night. Over the centuries, the mosque would become a more purely sacred place.

As men of the desert, the Umayyads enjoyed the open spaces where they could hunt and ride. Although the caliph had a palace in Damascus, famous for its brilliant green dome, he and his top officers spent a good deal of time in castles bordering the deserts of Syria and Palestine. Some of these buildings were converted Roman or Byzantine forts, while others were entirely new structures. Some were larger and more elaborate than others, but most had a similar plan, with fortified outer walls and central courtyards surrounded by living quarters, a mosque, a reception room, banquet halls, and a bathhouse. One had a vast music hall and a swimming pool. The interior walls were often decorated with mosaics, stone sculptures, and paintings of vines and leaves and even human figures. The bathhouse of Qasr Amra (*qasr* is the Arabic word for castle) had an audience hall decorated with paintings of the three Greek goddesses representing History, Philosophy, and Poetry. (This is another example of the growing interest in the culture of ancient Greece.)

Archaeologists have recently discovered evidence that suggests that these castles were not simply hunting lodges. Many also served as centers of vast farming operations belonging to the caliph or his close associates. These farms had complex systems of irrigation, with dams, reservoirs, canals, wells, aqueducts, and drainage pipes. Thanks to the ingenious Muslim engineers, miles of arid wasteland were converted into fertile fields of rice, sugar cane, and cotton.

## The Weakening Caliphate

The Umayyad dynasty lasted less than a century. The caliphs who followed al-Malik and al-Walid were not especially gifted rulers. A number of poor military decisions led to a depletion of the treasury, and this forced a rise of taxes. In 717, for example, Constantinople was besieged, unsuccessfully, for a year. The cost of supplying the expedition was huge, but even more disastrous was the defeat of the army and the fleet, which deprived the empire of its military muscle. Despite the financial crisis, the caliphs continued their lavish lifestyle, hosting endless banquets where the guests feasted on rare imported delicacies and drank from goblets of gold and silver encrusted with gems. A welcome exception to the worldly caliphs was Umar II, who came to power in 717. A devout Muslim, he tried to bring back the egalitarian spirit of Muhammad. He encouraged the *dhimmis* to convert to Islam, and many did. But this led to a loss of revenue, since as Muslims they no longer had to pay the poll tax. Financial constraints became worse than ever.

Sufism (a type of mysticism) had its roots in the reaction of certain pious Muslims to the worldly ways of the Umayyads. The word "sufi" comes from the Arabic word *suf*, meaning "wool," and it refers to the coarse blue woolen garments worn by mystics to protest the materialism they saw around them. The Sufis longed for a return to the simple ways of the first *umma* and sought a more inward approach to religion. They tried to reproduce within themselves the state

By patronizing artists and writers in their court in Damascus, the Umayyad caliphs encouraged the development of a new secular culture. Toward the end of the Umayyad period, the first literary work in Arabic appeared — *Kalila wa Dimna* of Ibn al-Muqaffa. It was not an original piece, but rather an Arabic translation of the Pahlavi version of a lost Sanskrit original. However, it had definite Arab undertones. The title comes from the names of two jackals, who play leading roles in a long series of amusing anecdotes.

of mind that made it possible for Muhammad to receive the revelations. By concentrating their mental powers while breathing deeply and rhythmically, they believed they could experience the presence of God in the depths of their being. At first, Sufism was a small fringe movement, but, as you will see, it would later have a great influence upon Muslim society.

## The Rise of the Abbasids

Muhammad al-Abbas (of the Abbasid [uh BAH sid] family) was the great-grandson of an uncle of Muhammad. (The elder al-Abbas had fought the Muslims at the Battle of Badr but later joined their cause and accompanied Muhammad on his return to Mecca.) In the early 8th century, Muhammad al-Abbas was a key Shi'ite leader, intent upon denouncing the Umayyads as enemies of the family of the Prophet. He sent "missionaries" into Khurasan to stir up support for a movement against the Umayyads. Many of the *mawali* living in that eastern province, resentful of the privileged Arab elite, were drawn to their cause. Like the Shi'ites, they hoped for a return to the values of equality and justice preached by Muhammad.

When Muhammad al-Abbas died in 743, he was succeeded by his son Ibrahim. He sent one of his most passionate followers, Abu Muslim, to Khurasan to fan the growing unrest. In 747 an open revolt broke out there. Black banners were unfurled and a military attack was launched against the Umayyads. (The black banners expressed mourning for Husayn, victim of the Umayyads, and also provided a visible link to Muhammad, whose standard had been black.)

The last Umayyad caliph, Marwan II, attempted to restore order, but to no avail. In 750 Abu al-Abbas, who had succeeded his brother Ibrahim, defeated Marwan's forces at the Battle of the Great Zab River, a tributary of the Tigris. The caliph was pursued to Egypt and killed. Al-Abbas was then proclaimed the new caliph in Kufa. According to legend, after their triumph the Abbasid leaders invited all male members of the defeated Umayyad clan to a banquet in Jaffa. Before the first course was served, the guests were gruesomely murdered. (All but one, that is. You'll learn about him in Chapter 5.) The banquet then became a victory celebration. A new chapter in Muslim history was about to begin.

## Review Questions:

1. What were the advantages of making Damascus the capital?
2. Describe Muawiya's government.
3. How did the Umayyad caliphs differ from their predecessors?
4. Why did Husayn travel to Kufa?
5. Why is *Ashura* important for the Shi'ites?
6. Who were the Shi'ite Imams and what was their function?
7. What caused the rebellion in Arabia?
8. Why was Arabic made the official language of the empire?
9. Why did domes become central features of Islamic religious buildings?
10. Describe the decoration of the Dome of the Rock.
11. How did the Muslims differ from the Byzantines in their approach to scholarship?
12. In what ways the the Great Mosque of Damascus resemble a Christian church, and how was it different?
13. What is the function of a *mihrab*?
14. What is Sufism?
15. What were some of the causes of the downfall of the Umayyad caliphate?
16. What was Abu al-Abbas?

## Questions for Discussion:

1. The Umayyad caliphs contributed much to the development of imperial Islam. They strengthened the authority of the central government, expanded the borders, and transformed the disparate regions conquered by the Muslim armies into a unified empire. But they also had many negative influences. What were they?
2. Muawiya was known to be generous with his enemies. He once remarked that this cost less than warfare. In what ways did his motivations for peace differ from those of Muhammad?
3. Were the wars and conflicts that arose between Muslims and members of other religions actually religious wars? Or were they political conflicts that might have been improperly associated with religion?
4. In the paintings that do exist of Muhammad, his face (and that of his wife, Khadija) are always covered with veils. Flamelike halos appear above their heads. Why might they been depicted in this manner?
5. The color green is considered a sacred color by Muslims. Why do you think this is so?

Muslim prayer ritual follows specific steps, and the prayers are in Arabic. Prayer is usually uttered to oneself, with eyes kept open looking straight ahead. Prayers can be offered at home or in other private places as well as in a mosque. Before entering a mosque to pray, people remove their shoes and perform an ablution (the washing of face, hands, arms up to the elbow, and feet). Worshippers stand next to each other in straight rows facing the *qibla* to offer congregational prayers. For purposes of modesty, women pray apart from the men, either in a gallery or behind a petition.

To begin prayer, the worshipper stands upright, raises his hands and proclaims four times, "God is most great" (*Allahu Akbar*). Then, folding his hands, he recites the *shahada* "There is no god but God and Muhammad is His messenger") twice and the *Fatiha* (see page 29). Then he bends from the hips, straightens his posture, prostrates (kneels, touching his forehead to the ground between his hands), recites three times, "Glory to the Lord Most High," and sits on his heels. Other verses can also be recited. This is one cycle or *raka*. Each of the five daily prayers consists of a prescribed number of *raka*: at daybreak two; noon four; afternoon four; sunset three; night four. The prayer ends with an invocation of peace as well as blessings on the Prophet and on fellow believers ("May the peace, mercy, and blessings of Allah be upon you"). After the formal prayer, a worshipper can speak privately to God, either in Arabic or in his own native tongue.

Daily prayers, as a constant call to faith, keep Islam at the center of a Muslim's life.

# Chapter 4 — BAGHDAD

Baghdad, the capital of Iraq, sits on both banks of the Tigris River 330 miles north of the Persian Gulf. The city is hot and dry in summer, and the air is often filled with a dusty mist of sand blown in from the western plains. Date palms and poplars provide the only natural shade. Winters are cool and damp. In more peaceful times, Baghdad was a bustling city of museums, universities, galleries, gardens, and cafes. Sadly, it has been greatly damaged by recent wars.

In very ancient times, this was the heart of Mesopotamia, the "land between the rivers" (the Tigris and Euphrates), where the early mastery of irrigation techniques enabled farmers to produce bountiful harvests of grain. This, in turn, led to the rise of the world's first great cities — Ur and later Babylon.

Baghdad was built by the Abbasids as their capital in the 8th century. The city would long be associated with a period of peace and prosperity that lasted from its founding through the 9th century, fostering a golden age of scholarship.

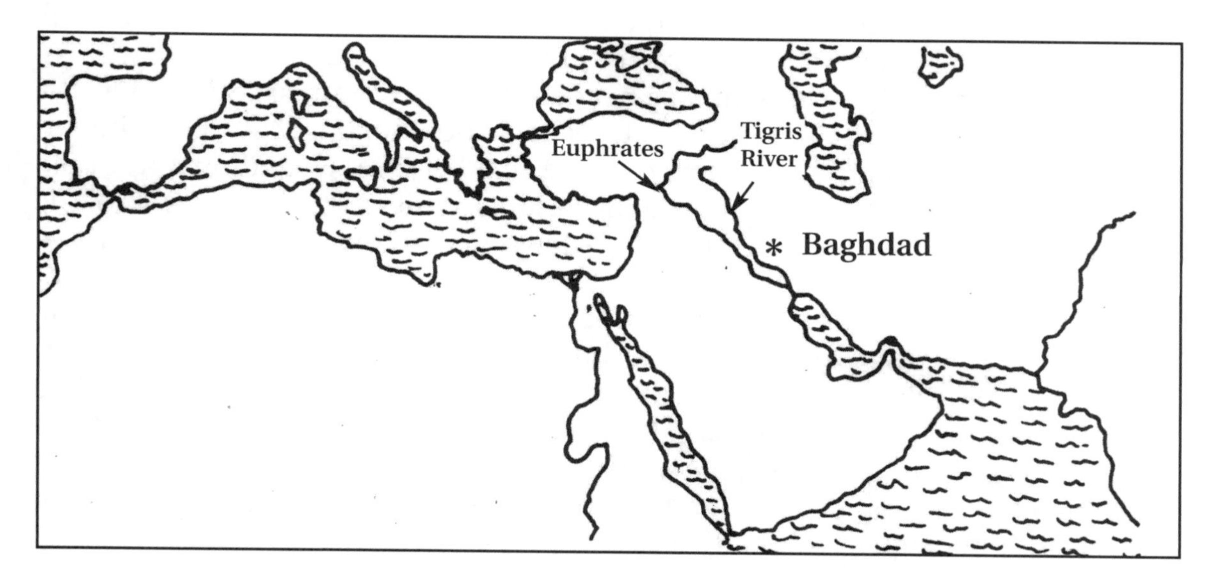


## Two Periods of Abbasid Rule

The Abbasid caliphate lasted for five centuries (from 750 to 1258). Historians divide this era into two major periods. During the first period, the caliphs completed the process begun by the Umayyads of transforming a tribal government into a centralized bureaucratic state. This was the age of great achievements in science, mathematics, medicine, and philosophy. The second period was a time of division and fragmentation. Although the Abbasid caliphs lost most of their political clout, Islamic culture became more diverse and, in many ways, richer than ever. In this chapter, we'll study each period separately.

# Part I — The Golden Age

Al-Abbas, the founder of the Abbasid dynasty, ruled for only a short time, during which he managed to restore order and stabilize the caliphate. He moved his political base east to Kufa, shifting the center of Islam from Syria to Mesopotamia. When he died (of natural causes) in 754, he was succeeded by his brother, al-Mansur. You learned in the last chapter how the Abbasids came to power with the aid of Shi'ite rebels who were disenchanted with the worldly ways of the Umayyads. After the fall of the Umayyads, Abu Muslim, the major architect of the revolution, continued to exercise power in Khurasan. Al-Mansur wanted the full support of the Sunnis, who greatly outnumbered the Shi'ites. To prevent future uprisings by the Shi'ites that might rock the ship of state, he ordered the execution of Abu Muslim, along with several of his closest supporters. The dreams of a return to the simpler times of Muhammad so closely embraced by the Shi'ites were no longer publicly discussed.

The Abbasid government was headed by a set of ministries, such as the treasury, chancery (which drew up letters and documents), army, post, intelligence, and so on. High officials, who converted to Islam, were drawn from old Persian families that had once served the Sasanian rulers. The lower levels of the bureaucracy were staffed by *dhimmis* — Jews, Christians, and Zoroastrians — and a smaller number of Buddhists. Al-Mansur established an elite corps of Khurasani soldiers as his personal guard. In time, the Persian warriors would fill the ranks of the entire army. Gradually, the old guard of Arabs who had dominated the political and military scenes since the days of the Prophet would be replaced by men born in Persia, Mesopotamia, Syria, and other parts of the growing empire. In fact, as Islamic society took on a more eastern look, the word "Arab" no longer meant someone from Arabia but simply referred to a person who spoke the language of the *Quran*.

## The Round City

Al-Mansur was not satisfied with his present capital and envisioned a new city that would reflect the power and prestige of his caliphate. He was drawn to the site of a village on the west bank of the Tigris River not far from the ruins of the old Sasanian capital of Ctesiphon. Here the Tigris and Euphrates rivers were only 25 miles apart and were connected by a series of canals. The Arabs referred to this lower region of Mesopotamia as *Sawad*, meaning "Black

Land," a reference to the rich and fertile soil. This seemed an ideal setting for a new capital. The local farmers would ensure a steady supply of wheat and barley, and the Tigris was already a busy commercial artery. Also, the location on a crossroads of land and water routes made it easily accessible from other parts of the empire. The caliph hired a staff of architects and surveyors as well as thousands of craftsmen and laborers from distant regions to build his city. Work began in the spring of 762.

Unlike most Muslim cities, which were rectangular and organized on a tribal basis, Al-Mansur's capital was round. It was about a mile and a half in diameter and was surrounded by a double brick wall and a broad moat fed by the Tigris. Four great gates were named for the places they faced: Kufa to the southwest, Syria to the northwest, Khurasan to the northeast, and Basra to the southeast. Within the wall, a series of radial streets, much like the spokes of a bicycle wheel, passed through two distinct rings of houses, shops, and government offices before reaching the inner core. Here stood the palace of the caliph, the main mosque, and the quarters of the Khurasani guards, surrounded by a wall 90 feet high.

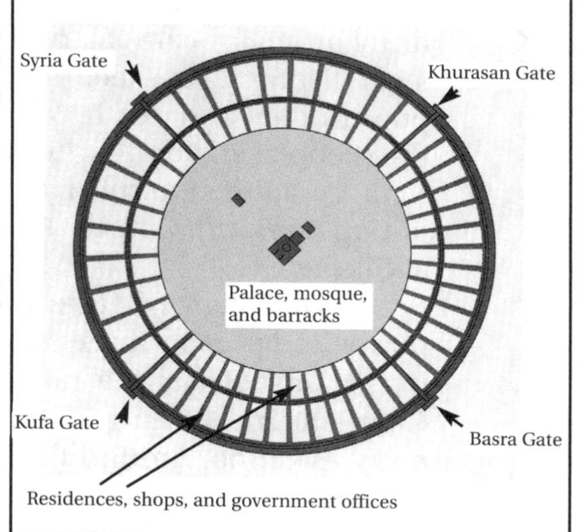


Water was brought into the city through an elaborate system of underground water channels, called *qanats*. Most buildings were constructed of sun-dried mud bricks, which could be covered with plaster or stucco and then carved. The caliph's palace, however, was built of stone, with a great deal of marble, onyx, and alabaster salvaged from the ruins of Ctesiphon. Its huge green dome rose over a hundred feet and could be seen from far beyond the city walls. Surrounding the palace was an enormous acreage of gardens, pools, fountains, and even a menagerie and aviary. The palace staff numbered more than 15,000.

Although the capital's official name was "The City of Peace" (*Madinat al-Salam*), it is better known by the name of the village that had first occupied the site — Baghdad, which in Persian means "Gift of God." Since it was mostly a government complex (the houses in the outer rings were inhabited by officials

The *qanats* were built as much as 50 feet deep to tap underground water. The channels inclined very slightly over long distances to keep the water slowly moving. Vertical shafts were built every 30 to 50 yards for ventilation and for cleaning and repair. Being underground also reduced evaporation of the water.

and staff members), a town of merchants and craftsmen quickly grew up on the east side of the Tigris. Its single-story houses had flat roofs (ideal for sleeping on hot desert nights) and stood amid walled courtyards. In time, palaces and villas would be built here as well. Al-Mansur had a pontoon bridge built to join the round city with its new suburb. (The bridge consisted of small boats tied side by side with a wooden walkway across them. Such bridges were built across the Tigris until the 20th century.)

## The Role of the Caliph

The caliph's grand and isolated palace reflected his lofty — and remote — status. Unlike the Umayyad rulers, who met often with advisory councils, the Abbasid caliph made his own decisions, which were then carried out by his bureaucracy of salaried officials. He appeared in public only on ceremonial occasions, to lead Friday prayers in the central mosque, and to command the army on major campaigns. He also represented the court of ultimate appeal in legal disputes. An executioner stood behind his throne to show that he had the power of life and death. Much of his time and energy was devoted to his court, the scene of elaborate rituals modeled upon those of the Sasanian emperors. Al-Mansur claimed to rule by divine mandate and gave himself the title of *Shadow of God on Earth.* Courtiers were required to bow before him, kissing the ground at his feet.

The reign of Harun al-Rashid (785-809) marks the height of Abbasid power and prosperity. Al-Rashid ably defended the empire's northwestern frontier against Byzantine raids and even entered into diplomatic relations with Charlemagne, the king of the Franks. He also received ambassadors from as faraway as China. Around this time the Umayyad postal system was extended to link all provinces of the empire to Baghdad. Besides relaying messages, the system became an efficient intelligence service. Postmasters in outlying provinces sent reports on every aspect of local economy and politics (in particular dissident sects) to a central agency in Baghdad.

Al-Rashid created the office of vizier to head his bureaucracy. The word "vizier" comes from *wazir,* which is Arabic for "bearer of burdens," and indeed this man bore the awesome responsibility of running the government. This is not to say that the caliph was insensitive to the needs of his subjects. According

When Charlemagne proclaimed himself Emperor in Rome on Christmas Day, 800, al-Rashid sent him a coronation gift — an elephant named Abu al-Abbas. Elephants were a Persian symbol of authority. The caliph also sent along a brass candelabra, ivory chessmen, a huge tent with silk curtains of many colors, and a waterclock that struck a bell every hour. This may have been the first clock in Europe.

to legend, al-Rashid often disguised himself at night and went through the streets and bazaars (marketplaces), listening in on conversations to discover whether the people were being treated well by their government. (The caliph had a modern counterpart: Theodore Roosevelt. Before becoming President of the United States, Roosevelt was a commissioner in the New York Police Department. A local newspaper referred to him as "Harun-al-Roosevelt" because he often took nightly walks on the streets of Manhattan, looking for police officers who were not performing their duties properly.)

## The Abbasid Economy

Unlike the Umayyads, who had grown wealthy through military conquest, the Abbasids became rich through trade. From the beginning, Baghdad profited from its strategic location on land and water trade routes. But as the population of increased and the local supply of grain became inadequate, the need arose to import wheat and barley as well as other scarce materials such as wood and metal. This led to the development of a complex trade network linking Baghdad with many parts of the world. Muslim merchants established posts in seaports around the Mediterranean and as far away as India, the East Indies, and China. Caravans of camels and donkeys plodded along the Silk Road, the major trade route connecting Chang'an, China with Baghdad, Damascus, and Antioch. This vast trade network provided Baghdad and the surrounding regions with wheat from Egypt, iron from eastern Europe, tin from the British Isles, silver from Central Asia, gold from Africa, and cedar from southern Syria. Luxury products included pearls from the Persian Gulf, furs and amber from northern Europe, silk from China, and spices (nutmeg, cloves, cinnamon, and pepper) from India.

> *Caravanserais* (lodging places for travelers and merchants) scattered along the land routes resembled forts, with towers placed at the corners of their high walls and a single gate just high and wide enough to admit a loaded camel.

Baghdad's community of craftsmen produced specialty items that visiting merchants eagerly bought to resell in distant lands. These included ceramics, jewelry, and woven cloth, but the most highly sought after product was the carpet. Carpets had been commonly used in the arid regions of Mesopotamia, Persia, and Central Asia for centuries, since most people sat on the ground or the floor for meals and other activities. Because Muslims were required to have a clean place to pray, many had small prayer rugs, which were easily folded up and

> Caliphs often took a throne name when they came to power, just as Chinese emperors did. These names described the character of the ruler, either as he was or as he hoped he would be perceived. For example, al-Abbas took the name of al-Saffah ("Bloodshedder"). Al-Mansur means "the Victorious," while al-Rashid means "the Upright."

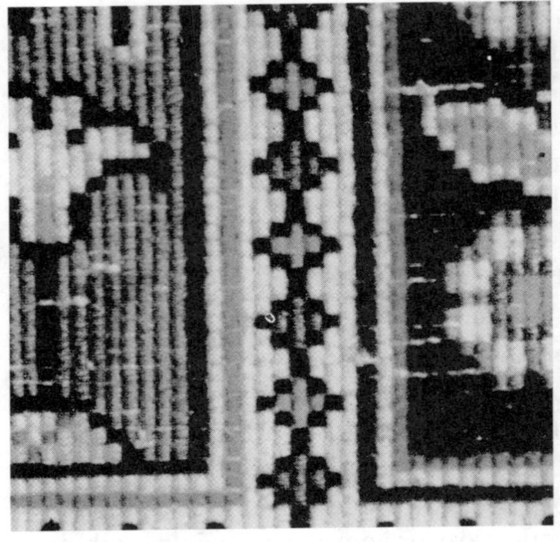

even carried around when not in use. Traditionally, nomads living in these regions had woven their own rugs on portable looms using sheeps' wool or the hair of goats and camels. The crossing of warp (vertical) and weft (horizontal) threads on the loom generated a grid. A weaver could create geometric designs by tying knots of different colors (dye was made from ground minerals and plants) onto the warp threads. After a row of knots had been placed across the width of the loom, two or more weft (horizontal) threads were woven in. Once the entire rug was knotted, the pile was shorn to make it smooth. The precision of the design and durability depended on how tightly the rug had been knotted and how short the pile had been cut.

Under the Abbasids, a number of workshops were set up in Baghdad that used very large looms. They turned out elaborate carpets for palaces, mosques, and the homes of the wealthy. These carpets were very densely knotted and had complex patterns combining stylized floral and animal motifs with geometric grids. Prayer rugs (like the one to the left) had a curved niche woven into the design, representing the *mihrab* as the worshipper faced Mecca.

The growth of trade led to the development of banking. Head offices of banks in Baghdad were linked with branches in other cities throughout the empire. A letter of credit (a check) issued in the capital could to be honored as far away as Sijilmassa, Morocco or Samarkand in Central Asia. In the port city of Basra, every merchant had a bank account and payments in the marketplace were made exclusively by check. Of course, there was a metal currency as well — the silver *dirham* and gold *dinar.* These coins had a fixed weight that seldom varied. (In the region of Baghdad, a *dirham* would buy an entire sheep, four lambs, or 60 pounds of dates.)

The duties levied on imports and exports as well as the tribute paid by distant rulers filled the coffers of the caliph's treasury. Al-Rashid easily outspent the most worldly of the Umayyad rulers on building construction and the entertainment of the members of his court. He and the lofty elite drank rosewater (water flavored with rose petals) from golden goblets and dined on highly seasoned dishes served on the finest Chinese porcelain. In a single year, the caliph and his courtiers consumed 50,000 pounds of sugar (in the form of cakes, candies, and other tasty treats), 100,000 pomegranates, 20,000 pounds of raisins, 15,000 pounds of mango jam, and 1,000 pounds of dried peaches. The caliph offered generous sums to attract the finest artists, poets and musicians to his court, and the wealthy merchants of Baghdad followed his example at their private parties.

Al-Rashid loved melons imported from eastern Persia. They were kept fresh during transport in leaden boxes packed with snow.

Baghdad's commercial activities kept it on the cutting edge of the latest technologies. One innovation that would have the most far-reaching influence upon Muslim culture as well as western civilization was the manufacture of paper. Paper was first made in China in 105 BCE, and it soon became the major writing material in that country. In the middle of the 8th century CE Umayyad warriors defeated a Chinese army in Central Asia, and among their prisoners were some papermakers. By the 9th century papermaking technology had arrived in Baghdad.

Until this time, precious books like the *Quran* had been made with parchment, while government documents were written on papyrus. Neither material was very suitable — parchment (made from animal skin) was very expensive, and papyrus (made from the Egyptian papyrus plant) decayed in climates that were damper and colder than in Egypt. Paper, on the other hand, could be cheaply produced from readily available materials — pulped rags, hemp, bark, and water. Al-Rashid was so impressed with the advantages of the new material that he ordered it used for all government documents and records. Before long, paper fell into the hands of merchants, who used it for their bookkeeping. Eventually, it was available to the general public.

There were many grades of paper. Among them was a special lightweight type known as "birds' paper" because it could be sent by carrier pigeons. It was the earliest known airmail paper.

## The House of Wisdom

Because of the importance of reading the *Quran* Muslims were already a literate society, but the introduction of paper led to the production of huge numbers of books on every subject. This, in turn, stimulated a great enthusiasm for learning. As we saw in the last chapter, much of the knowledge of the ancient world had been preserved in a number of cities of the Mediterranean world. Al-Mansur sent an envoy to the Byzantine Emperor in Constantinople asking for copies of ancient texts kept in his library. The Emperor sent him a copy of Euclid's *Elements* (a major work on geometry) and several scientific texts. Al-Rashid acquired a number of other Greek writings as booty in his raids on Byzantine territory. He assembled all the ancient texts in his possession in a large library, which he called the "Treasury of Knowledge." He sponsored the translation of many ancient writings into Arabic. Al-Mamun (ruled 819-833) was the most intellectual of the Abbasid caliphs, a poet and scholar in his own right. He sent a delegation to Constantinople to obtain copies of major works of Greek philosophy, astronomy, math, and medicine. After receiving them, he transformed his father's "Treasury of Knowledge" into a learning center known as the "House of Wisdom."

Muhammad once remarked that "the scholar's ink is more sacred than the blood of martyrs."

The new learning center was modeled upon the Academy of Jundishapur, which had been founded near the site of Baghdad by Sasanian king Shapur I in the 3rd century CE. The king employed scholars from many lands as teachers, including prominent Indian physicians and mathematicians. In the 5th century, when Nestorian scholars were forced to flee their Byzantine homelands because of their religious views (which were at variance with those of the Orthodox Church), many sought refuge at Jundishapur, bringing with them a knowledge of ancient Greek medicine and astronomy. The closing of the Athenian school in Alexandria in the 6th century by Byzantine emperor Justinian drove another flock of learned men to the Academy. Over the years, the scholars translated many ancient Greek and Indian writings into Syriac (the written language of Syria and Mesopotamia at that time). Sasanian ruler Anushirvan later founded a hospital and medical school at Jundishapur, further enriching the city's renown as a bastion of knowledge. When Mesopotamia came under Muslim rule, Jundishapur continued to function as before. In 776, a physician from the medical center, Jirjis ibn Bakhtishu, cured al-Mansur of an ailment and was made court physician in Baghdad. This brought the Abbasid rulers in closer touch with the Academy, which ultimately led to the founding of the House of Wisdom.

Al-Mamun hired Jewish and Christian scholars as well as Muslims to translate his Greek texts into Arabic. Later, the scholars would also translate works from Syriac, Pahlavi, and Sanskrit (the language of ancient India). By the

According to legend, Al-Mamun paid each translator the weight of his translated books in gold.

end of the 9th century, al-Mamun's translators and their successors had produced Arabic versions all the important books of Greek, Indian, and Persian science, mathematics, medicine, and philosophy — an enormous accomplishment. Imagine all the great works of the past being made available to scholars living throughout the Islamic realm, and even beyond. The careful study and analysis of these translations inspired many thoughtful men to further expand their horizons of knowledge, plunging into their own worlds of research. As they began to produce new books about their findings, Arabic became the international language of scholarship. It would remain so for a long time. The Arabs made more scientific discoveries during the next several centuries than in the whole of previously recorded history.

Each week al-Mamun hosted discussion sessions, where scholars sat around a table, listening to one another's views and discussing their differences.

## Mathematics

Aristotle was probably the greatest of the ancient Greek scientists and philosophers. He had inscribed above the door of his house: "Let no one enter who does not have a knowledge of mathematics." The Arabs revered Aristotle above all others, and like him, they had a great interest in mathematics. They were motivated by a need to find ways of keeping accurate records and to measure distances. While translating Indian texts at the House of Wisdom, scholars stumbled upon some strange-looking figures. After careful study, they realized that the figures represented a very efficient method of calculating numbers, which involved using the symbol of zero and a place-value system. This method (we use it today) allowed all numbers, no matter how large, to be expressed by means of nine figures (plus zero). This number system was a vast improvement over the cumbersome Roman numerals that were in use in Europe and western Asia at the time. Although they came from India, the numbers are known today as "Arabic numerals," because the Arabs adopted them and spread their use throughout much of the civilized world.

Mathematician Al-Khwarizmi was the first Arab to make calculations using the Indian numerals. He wrote a book on the subject (*Addition and Subtraction in Indian Arithmetic*). Using the new number system, he refined the

The House of Wisdom was like a modern research center. The earliest translations underwent continual revision, as new texts were found. The scholars created glossaries, made comments in margins, and compiled dictionaries of technical terms. The vast scientific library eventually included over 10,000 volumes. It was open to the public, and anyone could copy any book he wished.

Khwarizmi was born in an area called Khwarizm that lay east of the Caspian Sea. He used his place of birth in his name, as was the custom at that time in the Islamic world.

system of algebra developed by the ancient Greeks and Egyptians so that he could reduce all mathematical problems to algebraic equations with standard solutions. He wrote the first book on algebra (T*he Science of Substitution and Cancellation*). (The word "algebra" is derived from the Arabic term *al-jabr,* meaning "substitution." In algebraic equations, one substitutes symbols [such as x, y or z] for numbers in order to solve problems.)

Al-Battani worked in trigonometry, the branch of mathematics dealing with sides and angles of plane and spherical triangles. He constructed tables giving the ratios between the sides of any right triangle, noting that when two angles and the side between them are known, the remaining angle and the unknown sides can be found. The Banu Musa ("the Sons of Musa") were three brothers who excelled in the study of mathematics, astronomy and mechanics. One of their major works (*The Book on the Measurement of Plane and Spherical Figures*) demonstrated the Greek methods for determining area and volume.

## Astronomy

Muslim religious leaders needed to measure time so they could determine the hours of prayer, and they also needed to accurately calculate the points of the compass to find the direction of Mecca from any given location. To accomplish these tasks, the Arab scholars studied the ancient texts and observed the heavens.

The most important ancient work on astronomy was the *Almagest,* which was compiled by Ptolemy, a Greek astronomer and geographer, in the second century CE. Ptolemy believed that the motions of the sun, moon, planets, and stars could be explained in mathematical terms. His book was filled with tables, maps, and commentaries, as well as geometric models displaying the motion of the five closest planets. Although certainly an important work, the *Almagest* had some major flaws, which unfortunately led the Arab scholars away from some significant discoveries made by earlier astronomers. Centuries before Ptolemy, the Greeks had speculated that the earth moved around the sun. Ptolemy, however, placed the earth at the center of the universe, with the sun, moon and planets traveling around it in perfect circles. The earlier astronomers had also calculated the distance around the earth to be about 24,600 miles (very close to the actual 24,900 miles); however, a century later, another Greek astronomer, Posidonius, wrote that the

The title, *Almagest,* is a combination of Greek and Arabic terms, roughly meaning "The Greatest." Ptolemy had actually entitled his work *The Mathematical Collection.*

earth was smaller (only 18,000 miles), and his figure was used by Ptolemy to create his maps. (Because of this mistake, passed on for many centuries, Christopher Columbus greatly underestimated the distance between Portugal and the East Indies.)

Inspired by Ptolemy's work, Arab astronomers viewed the heavens from an observatory on the left bank of the Tigris. Before long, they were challenging Ptolemy's theories about eclipses, planetary orbits, and the position of the stars, although they continued to accept the smaller circumference of the earth and the concept of an earth-centered universe. Al-Khwarizmi was one of the first Arabs to compute astronomical tables to determine the positions of the stars and planets. He also made calculations to predict the time of visibility of the new moon, which signaled the beginning of a new month in the Muslim calendar. He wrote Islam's first atlas (*The Form of the Earth*), which contained maps of the heavens as well as the earth, listed the longitudes of different places, and indicated the length of daylight at many locations. (Latitude, or distance from the equator, was determined by noting the length of daylight at certain locations at the summer solstice. If the length was the same as at another place, it was assumed the two places were the same distance north of the equator.) Al-Mamun instructed the Banu Musa to measure a degree of latitude. They made careful measurements in the desert north of Baghdad, calculating the length of a terrestrial degree of latitude at 56 and 2/3 miles, which is within a half-mile of the correct value. They also measured the length of the solar year, obtaining the accurate value of 365 days and 6 hours.

Many mathematical and scientific words come from Arabic. Among them are alchemy, alcohol, algebra, almanac, aorta, arsenic, atlas, chemistry, cipher, cornea, diaphragm, elixir, monsoon, nadir, pancreas, zenith, zero, and zircon.

The charts and tables created at the House of Wisdom brought Arab astronomers closer to discovering the fallacy of Ptolemy's earth-centered solar system, but it would not be until the 16th century that the Polish astronomer, Copernicus, would reaffirm the heliocentric (sun-centered) theory.

## Medicine

Much of the medical knowledge of the ancients had been translated into Syriac at Jundishapur. Hunayn ibn Ishaq was a Nestorian physician who taught himself Greek and then set about translating almost the entire corpus of med-

*The Book of Ingenious Devices* by the Banu Musa contains descriptions, each with an illustration, of 100 clever devices. Among them are fountains that change shape at intervals, a glass enclosed hurricane lamp, a gas mask for use in polluted wells, a grab for recovering objects from the beds of streams, and a vessel having a single outlet pipe that can pour out first wine, then water, and finally a mixture of the two.

ical works at Jundishapur into Arabic. The most important Greek physicians were Hippocrates and Galen, and their works exist today only because of the translations of Ibn Ishaq.

Hippocrates lived in the 5th century BCE. He rejected the views of his time that illness was caused by evil spirits and the disfavor of the gods. He was convinced that it had a physical and a rational explanation. He believed that the body should be treated as a whole, not just a series of parts, and he promoted the healthful benefits of a good diet, adequate rest, fresh air, and cleanliness. He closely observed the conditions of his patients, accurately describing the symptoms of pneumonia as well as epilepsy. Hippocrates founded a medical school and wrote an Oath of Medical Ethics, required of all new physicians. (Until recently, the Hippocratic Oath was recited by physicians around the world upon completion of medical studies.)

Galen lived in the 1st century CE. He studied the functions of the brain, heart, nerves, and muscles. He demonstrated that arteries carry blood (not air, as was currently believed) and argued that thoughts, ideas, and feelings come from the brain and not the heart (as others claimed). However, much of Galen's understanding was flawed. He did not understand how blood circulated and concluded that veins and arteries were separate systems. Most of his knowledge of anatomy was based on his dissection of pigs, dogs and Barbary apes, and he made assumptions that did not actually apply to the human body.

Building upon these two ancient sources, Arab physicians established Muslim medicine as a science based on observation and experiment, eliminating the superstition and folk-practices common at the time. Ibn Ishaq wrote a long medical book which even included anatomical drawings (*The Introduction to the Healing Arts*). He also wrote nearly 30 treatises on medical topics and a collection of essays on ophthalmology. Physician Ali ibn Rabban al-Tabari wrote a major compendium (*The Paradise of Wisdom),* synthesizing the Greek tradi-

Health and hygiene were important in Muslim culture from earliest times. Among the sayings attributed to Muhammad were the following:

*—He who wakes up in the morning healthy in body and sound in soul and whose daily bread is assured, he is as one that possesses the world.*
*—After security of faith, nothing better is given to a man than good health.*
*—For every disease, God has given a cure.*

Public baths (*hammams*) could be found in all Muslim towns and cities, with separate areas (or times) for men and women. Admission was free. People spent at least an hour there, bathing with both hot and cold water and gossiping with their friends.

The astrolabe was a Greek invention used to compute the movement of the planets and the position of stars. Ibrahim Fazari, who helped plan the city of Baghdad, improved upon this invention. His version was a flat circular metal disk with the degrees of a circle marked on its outer edge and pointing arms that could be aimed at two different places to measure the angle between them. A ring was attached to the top of the disk. An astronomer would suspend the astrolabe by the ring and line up one pointer with the horizon, then aim the other pointer at a star. The pointers would form an angle, and by measuring the number of degrees in the angle he could determine the altitude of the star. The astrolabe later became invaluable to navigators, who determined their latitude at sea by measuring the angle of the North Star above the horizon.

tions of medicine with those of India and Persia. Al-Razi surveyed all the available medical knowledge and then provided a critical review of this knowledge on the basis of his own practice. His huge (23-volume) compendium (*The Comprehensive Book on Medicine*) described his many experiments, observations, and diagnoses. He made the connection between bacteria and infection and introduced the use of antiseptics (alcohol) in cleaning wounds. Al-Razi pioneered the use opium for anesthesia for surgery. His *Treatise on Smallpox and Measles* was the first accurate study of infectious disease. He was a compassionate physician, who brought rations to the poor and provided nursing for them. He sponsored educational seminars and lectures, as well as on-site training in his medical practice.

Caliph al-Rashid founded the first hospital in Baghdad in 809 and brought Jibrail Bukhtishu, son of his court physician, from Jundishapur to head its teaching staff. The hospital served as model for other medical centers in Baghdad and eventually throughout the Islamic realm. When al-Razi was commissioned to select a site for a new hospital, he had strips of meat hung on poles

Jabir ibn Hayyan was a pioneer in applied science. He helped develop chemistry as a science, separate from the "pseudoscience" of alchemy.

Ibn Hayyan developed techniques for making steel, dyeing cloth, and preventing rust. He also used the process of distillation to purify water, identified numerous alkalis, acids, salts, and discovered mercury. *And* he proposed that the various functions of the human body were based on complex chemical reactions.

in various quarters of the city. He then selected the site where the meat had given the least evidence of decay, reasoning that it was relatively free of contaminants.

Muslim hospitals were open to everyone, regardless of gender, religion, age, or social class. They treated men and women in separate wards, and reserved areas for the treatment of contagious diseases, surgical cases, and the mentally ill. There was no fee to patients. In fact, upon discharge a patient often received a small sum of money for a smooth transition back into the community. The hospitals were financed from the income of pious endowments known as *waqfs*. Funds were donated by wealthy men as well as the caliph himself and were used to purchase or build shops, mills, and hostels, the profits of which went directly to the hospital. *Waqfs* also supported the construction and upkeep of mosques, public baths, municipal drinking fountains, and schools.

Arab scientists learned a great deal about medicines through the works of Dioscorides, a Greek physician, pharmacologist and botanist who practiced in Rome in the first century CE. As a surgeon with the army of Emperor Nero, he had the opportunity to travel extensively. This enabled him to gather medicinal substances from many places. His five-volume book (*De Materia Medica*) contained descriptions of approximately 600 plants and 1000 different medications. Inspired by Dioscorides, many Arab scientists devoted their lives to seeking out herbs in the vast territory of the Islamic empire, experimenting with them, categorizing them, and writing exhaustive notes on their curative effects. Before long, all Muslim hospitals had herb gardens and pharmacies for preparing remedies.

The Arabs established the first apothecary shops. At one time, Baghdad had as many as 862 registered pharmacists, all of whom had passed formal examinations. The great interest in medicines led to an active trade in drugs, herbs, and spices from as far as Africa to China. Arab pharmacists produced the first syrup-based medicines (to disguise the bitter taste) as well as ointments

Al-Jahiz, a 9th century scientist, wrote the earliest Arab work on zoology — the 17-volume *Book of Animals*. It included observations on the social organization of ants, communication between animals, and the effects of diet and environment upon physical and social development. It also touched upon a number of concepts that were not fully developed until the first half of the 20th century. Among these were animal mimicry (he noted that certain parasites adapt to the color of their host) and natural selection (the transformation of animal species under different factors), a theory usually attributed to Charles Darwin. He also found time to write about 200 books on a wide range of topics, including *The Art of Keeping One's Mouth Shut* and *Against Civil Servants*. He died at the age of 92, allegedly when a pile of books in his personal library fell on top of him!

and lotions. Calamine lotion, used for itches caused by allergic reactions, takes its name from the Arabic word for zinc.

## The Philosophers

As the scholars at the House of Wisdom discovered new truths about the natural world, many began to wonder whether they could reconcile this rational approach to knowledge with their religious faith. Some went a step further, asking themselves whether they could use reason to find answers to fundamental questions about the creation of the universe, the nature of the human soul, and the existence of the unseen. Debates about the relationship between revelation, or faith, and reason created a new intellectual discipline — philosophy (*faylasafa*). Like the Greeks, the Muslim philosophers believed the world was rationally ordered and that through logical inquiry they could move beyond the visible world of nature to discover the mysteries that lay beyond it.

Al-Kindi, the first major Muslim philosopher, wrote detailed commentaries on the works of Aristotle and used the famous Greek's logic to support Islamic religious beliefs. He considered the revelations parables about divine truths (such as the creation of the universe and the destiny of mankind) and claimed that through the use of logic philosophers could discover these same truths. Therefore, rather than conflicting with religious beliefs, rational thinking reinforced them. Al-Razi, a philosopher as well as physician, also stated that the use of reason could lead to the discovery of universal principles. Al-Farabi was influenced by the Greek philosopher, Plato. He believed that a set of unchanging, absolute values (such as love and beauty) gave meaning to a person's life, and that one had only to block out the material world and look within to find these values. (This approach is not far removed from the mysticism of the Sufis.) Al-Farabi considered Islam a more reasonable religion than its predecessors because it had no "illogical" doctrines and stressed the importance of moral values. His book (*The Perfect City*) described an ideal community founded on ethical and religious principles. (His city is similar in many ways to Plato's utopia, Atlantis.) Not everyone was won over by the rational approach to understanding the mysteries of the universe, however. Many devout Muslims insisted that faith and reason were as different as apples and oranges and could not be reconciled. As you will see, the debates would rage on for centuries.

> The Arab scholars were often interested in a wide range of subjects. Besides his philosophical writings, al-Kindi produced over 250 treatises on a great variety of subjects — music, ethics, chemistry, astronomy, medicine, geography, mathematics, the manufacture of swords, and cooking. Al-Farabi wrote at least 117 books on logic, metaphysics, ethics, political science, music, medicine, and sociology.

## A Glittering Capital

Ninth century Baghdad was the world's richest and most intellectual city, with half a million people. It covered 25 square miles and stretched along both sides of the Tigris, with palaces, mosques, multi-story homes, hospitals, *hammams*, marketplaces, gardens, and parks. Fresh water was supplied through the underground system of pipes (*qanats*). The city was divided into walled neighborhoods or quarters, each under the control of an overseer, who saw that the paved streets were regularly swept and the gardens and parks were watered. No refuse was allowed to remain within city limits. (Muslim cities were the cleanest in the medieval world.) Promenades lined the river, with marble steps leading down to the water's edge. Fleets of gondolas carried citizens from one riverbank to the other. Waterside cafes served such local specialties as halva (a sesame sweetmeat), baklava (a pastry made with honey and nuts), and candy made from licorice root. (These are popular Middle Eastern desserts even today.)

Most mosques had elementary schools attached to them. At the age of five, boys and girls learned to recite simple verses from the *Quran*. After they learned to read and write, they studied the *Quran* in depth. Older students (usually just boys) studied Arabic grammar and poetry, mathematics, algebra, logic, biology, and history.

Baghdad had over one hundred bookshops, selling works on every topic imaginable — from gardening and cooking to poetry and philosophy. The bookshops, which were concentrated in certain quarters of city, became meeting places for writers, philosophers, and men of letters. They even sponsored book discussions, which were open to all interested readers. The process of publishing a book involved the writer dictating his pages every day at a certain time in a bookshop (or mosque) to a copyist. Once the manuscript was copied, it was presented to the writer for corrections and then placed in the public domain and sold in the bookshops. The writer received a royalty through the copyist, who acted like a modern publisher.

Book collections were preserved in libraries, both public and private, in cities throughout the empire. Among the most prized volumes were beautifully written *Qurans* and illuminated manuscripts of secular works. A calligrapher was one of the most highly revered members of Muslim society. He studied for many years under a master until he had perfected his skill. He prepared each

The expansion of trade led to a greater knowledge of world geography. In 848 the Postmaster General of Baghdad published *The Book of Routes and Kingdoms*, which included a detailed map of the entire Muslim world and a description of main trade routes. A hundred years later, al-Masudi would publish *Meadows of Gold and Mines of Precious Stones*, a geographical encyclopedia in which he discussed such things as earthquakes and the unique conditions of the Dead Sea.

sheet of paper by polishing it smooth with a stone and then ruling it with fine guidelines. He made his own ink from soot, henna, indigo, and gum, and wrote with a reed pen whose nib he had carefully cut. The angle at which the nib was cut depended upon the writing style he would use it for. (A calligrapher was often buried with his best pen.) Artists often embellished the pages of religious texts with interwoven leaves, geometric patterns, or flower designs like the one on the right. Secular texts contained highly detailed miniature paintings. Gold leaf was used to highlight the painted colors — red, blue, green, and yellow. A finished volume was about the size of a modern book, with writing and decorations on both sides of the paper. It was bound together by thick gilded leather covers.

## The *Sunna*

The *umma* had changed dramatically since the time of Muhammad. No longer a small community of Arabs who knew one another quite well, Muslims were fast becoming the majority group in a vast empire. As *Dar al-Islam* (the

*The Thousand and One Nights* is a collection of anonymous stories set in Persia, India, China, Egypt, and Anatolia that were translated into Arabic in the 10th century in Baghdad. It has become a classic in world literature. The stories were supposedly told by Shahrazad (Scheherazade), wife of Sultan Shahryar. Betrayed by his first wife, the sultan became distrustful of all women and began the habit of marrying and murdering a new wife every day. So every night Shahrazad told her stories, stopping at such an exciting point at daybreak that her husband's curiosity compelled him to let her live another day in order to hear how it ended. This went on for a thousand nights until Shahrazad was pardoned, her life saved by her own cleverness and imagination.

The stories offer a panorama of life in the Islamic world at this time. The best known heroes are Ali Baba, Sinbad the Sailor, and Aladdin. (The genies are derived from the jinns, spirits of the Arabian peninsula.) The glory of Baghdad at its height is reflected in descriptions of palaces and bazaars in many of the tales. Caliph al-Rashid, disguised as a commoner, appears from time to time in the streets of the city, eager to learn more about his people. He is depicted as able, just, wise, and compassionate. In one tale ("The Three Apples"), he intervenes personally to save a poor man wrongfully accused of murder.

Sinbad the Sailor appears in seven adventures in distant lands (China, Japan, and the East Indies) where he encounters strange creatures. These tales show the extent of Arabic shipping routes and knowledge of climate and geography.

abode or realm of Islam) expanded and grew more diverse, there was a need to organize and reform the religious institutions that regulated the lives of its people. The first step was to filter through the vast collection of information currently in circulation about the origins of Islam.

The lives of the first Muslims had focused upon the revelations the Prophet continued to receive. He explained and reinforced these messages through his own teaching and example. After he died, a vast number of eyewitness accounts of his words or sayings, known as the *hadith* (hah DEETH, "traditions"), were in circulation. By the 8th century there were tens of thousands of them, more than any one man could possibly have uttered in a lifetime. In order to authenticate them, a system was devised in which each remark was traced through reputable sources to the mouth of the Prophet himself. In the 9th century Muhammad al-Bukhari selected and classified what seemed to be the most authentic sayings — over 7,000 selected from the 600,000 he had gathered. They were published in a vast compendium. Another scholar, Abdul Muslim, gathered over three million and authenticated 9,200. The collections of these scholars are generally regarded today as "reliable."

The body of information about the life of Muhammad is known as the *sira*. The earliest biography, written less than a century after the Prophet's death, was *The Life of the Messenger of God* by Muhammad ibn Ishaq. He based his work on accounts that had been passed on by word of mouth from one generation to another. In some cases, he offered two versions of the same event, remarking that only God knew which one was true. Although his book has not survived, we have access to his findings through later historians. Ninth century historian al-Tabari wrote a huge (38-volume) *History of the Prophets and Kings*, a prime collection of Arabic source materials containing a great deal of important information about the life and times of Muhammad.

The *hadith* and the *sira* form the *sunna (SOO nuh*, an Arabic word meaning "habitual practice"). In pre-Islamic Arabia, *sunna* referred to precedents

The efforts to compile the sayings of Muhammad led to a study of meanings that might be attached to the actual words and phrases of the revelations and an investigation of the circumstances in which each revelation was made. Al-Tabari wrote a detailed commentary on the *Quran*, which became a standard from which later commentators drew.

During the Abbasid period, two schools of thought emerged. The traditionalists, centered mainly in Mecca and Medina, took the text literally. The rationalists, active in Kufa and Basra, sought to apply the writings to contemporary situations. Disputes about the interpretation of the *Quran* and the *sunna* would continue for centuries. In modern times, the traditionalists dominate, although rationalists are making ever stronger efforts to bring Islam into step with the times.

established by ancestors that were practiced by a tribe. In Islam, the *sunna* refers to the customs and practices of the *umma* based upon the life and words of the Prophet. It provides models of ideal behavior, enabling Muslims to imitate the way Muhammad spoke, worshiped, ate, washed, and even wound his turban so that they can reproduce the smallest details of his life in their own. It is also a practical guide to the *Quran*. For example, the *Quran* says that Muslims should pray, worship, and give to charity, while the *sunna* explains the rituals of prayer, the content of worship, and the specific acts and sources of charity. Today, the *sunna* binds together Muslims from every walk of life as they perform daily rituals in exactly the same way around the world.

## Islamic Law

Islamic law is known as *sharia* (shah REE ah), which literally means "the path leading to the watering place." It has come to be associated with "the straight path," the morally responsible way of life referred to in the *Fatiha* of the *Quran*. (See page 29.) The law provides the guidelines for living according to the teachings of Muhammad. *Sharia* differs from the traditional legal systems of western societies in its emphasis upon religious and ethical behavior. It has its roots, as you would expect, in the *Quran* and the *sunna*. Rules about nearly

It was customary for a Muslim to cover his head as a way of showing respect to God. Muhammad once said, "What differentiates us [in appearance] from the [pagans] is the turban." The art of winding a turban required skill, the wearer fitting a skullcap over his knee and winding a long piece of cloth around it. (The cap then kept the folds of the turban in place.) A head covering was always worn in the mosque and even when praying outside the mosque. Poor men simply wore caps or small pieces of cloth. Women wore scarfs or other head coverings whenever they left their homes. Footwear was removed upon entering a mosque for fear of defiling the interior with impure substances that may have adhered to the sole of the shoe.

The *ulama* (religious scholars) wore a long, wide-sleeved, dark colored robe buttoned halfway down over a striped caftan and a white turban. Among the Shi'ites, clerics always wore black as a symbol of mourning for Ali and Husayn.

Members of the Abbasid elite wore richly embroidered caftans (long flowing gowns.) Al-Rashid had a wardrobe of 10,000 caftans, 8,000 robes, and 4,000 turbans! The wearing of gold or silk was forbidden for all Muslim males, although the caliph tended to ignore this rule.

*Tiraz* was a special type of cloth used to make ceremonial robes, which were granted as marks of favor to high officials, army commanders, and foreign ambassadors. They were embroidered with Arabic writing — praises of the person wearing the robe, quotations from the *Quran*, the date the robe was made, its place of origin, and the name of current caliph. Since the late Umayyad period, the government had maintained workshops for the production of *tiraz*.

every aspect of living were passed down from one generation to another after the time of Muhammad and were enforced by religious judges (*qadi*). In the 8th century Malik ibn Anas compiled *The Beaten Path,* the first written account of the legal traditions and religious practice of Medina, originating with the first *umma.*

But as the empire expanded into regions where the culture was very different from that of Arabia, new legal and social issues arose that were not covered by the religious writings. The early Abbasids dealt with the problem by appointing members of the *ulama* (the religious scholars) as jurists in the courts. The jurists had the power to interpret the laws, and over the years they developed a comprehensive system of law based upon the principles and values of the *Quran* and the *sunna* that were to govern Muslim life up to modern times. Their intent was to create a devout and morally responsible society, emphasizing the rights and responsibilities of individuals towards each other and within the community. The *fiqh* ("understanding") refers to the legal rulings of the Muslim scholars. It deals with religious duties (cleanliness, ritual prayer, fasting, pilgrimage, alms, and *jihad)* on the one hand, and social duties (marriage, laws of inheritance, property law, and so on) on the other. Nearly every important activity in a Muslim's life is classified in a scale of five values: obligatory (such as adhering to the Five Pillars of Islam), recommended (like making an extra pilgrimage), permissible or indifferent (bathing with hot or with cold water), discouraged (divorce), and forbidden (drinking alcohol). Once it had been established and set down in legal manuals, Islamic law became permanent and inflexible. The decisions made during the early Abbasid period still apply to Muslim society today. Whether the law should be reformed to meet the needs of modern times is a major issue in contemporary Islam.

According to Islamic law, women had the right of inheritance, although they received less than men. This was because they were entitled to receive a dowry at the time of marriage in addition to their inherited share.

## A Change of Venue

When al-Mu'tasim became caliph in 833, he decided to create a personal guard by hiring Turkish mercenary troops from Central Asia. As the numbers of Turkish guardsmen increased, clashes broke out between them and the Persian

Although in principle the caliph was subject to the rules of the *sharia,* in practice these rules did not prevail at high levels of the Abbasid government. The caliph, his court and high officials followed the more autocratic norms of the pre-Islamic period and were in this sense "above the law" of the rest of Muslim society. This was a far cry from the egalitarianism prescribed by Muhammad.

soldiers. Even the native population became resentful of the new alien corps. So in 836 the caliph, hoping to free himself from the growing unrest in Baghdad, shifted his capital — and his guard — 60 miles north up the Tigris River to Samarra, where he built a new imperial city.

Samarra consisted of a series of walled districts stretching along the riverbank. The original palace was huge — over six times larger than al-Mansur's palace in Baghdad's round city. It was a vast complex of rooms, passageways, and interconnected courtyards. Its sunken apartments had double walls, with water running through the cavities to keep them cool. (This was an ingenious early version of air-conditioning.) A round sunken pool, fed by a stream, also provided the caliph with welcome relief from the desert heat. Gardens filled with the fragrant scents of roses and jasmine led down to the river's edge. High government officials and army commanders built themselves palaces that were nearly as impressive, with high domes and vaulted halls adorned with marble. The wealthy elite spent much of their leisure time in the two enclosed game reserves (where the supply of game animals was constantly replenished), twelve polo grounds, and four race courses. The colossal Great Mosque was for many centuries the largest in the world. Its spiral minaret (shown to the right), modeled upon an ancient Babylonian temple (a *ziggurat*), reached a height of more than 150 feet.

The move to Samarra isolated the caliph from the people more than ever, while the Turkish soldiers grew more powerful with every decade. Before long, they had completely displaced the Persian army. In 861 Caliph al-Mutawakkil was assassinated by his unruly troops, and for the next nine years the soldiers made and deposed rulers virtually at will. In 870 stability was restored, with Caliph al-Mutamid residing in Samarra as official ruler and his brother (with military backing) exercising real power back in Baghdad. In 892 al-Mutamid returned to Baghdad, which became once again the Abbasid capital. He and his successors largely abandoned the round city and moved the center of government to the east bank of the river. A magnificent caliphal palace replaced that of al-Mansur, which was transformed into a prison.

The glorious palaces and mosques of Samarra, being mostly built of mud-

Hubshiyya, the mother of Caliph al-Muntasir, built an octagonal funeral shrine for her son across the Tigris from Samarra. Inspired by the Dome of the Rock, it had a vaulted ambulatory and a dome. It is the earliest surviving Islamic mausoleum, marking the beginning of new tradition that offended many devout Muslims. Such an elaborate funerary monument violated the egalitarian principles of early Islam, when Muslims preferred to be buried in unmarked graves. Later rulers would enshrine their tombs by placing them inside mosques.

brick, gradually crumbled and over the centuries the entire city melted away. Today nothing remains, apart form the minaret (which was built from stone) and faint traces of the streets and building foundations.

The later caliphs continued to live a lavish lifestyle, secluded in their palace and practicing their elaborate court rituals. An account of the Byzantine mission of 917 to Caliph al-Muqtadir describes a lengthy palace tour designed to impress any visitor. Having entered by a gateway on the river, the ambassadors were conducted through a succession of buildings, courtyards, and corridors before arriving in the caliph's presence. Along the way, they were dazzled by marble-columned stables, where they observed horses with golden saddles and elephants adorned with brocade and satin; they entered a lion house with a hundred animals, each standing quietly with its trainer; they passed by ornate pavilions, gardens of melons, oranges, lemons, and limes, a glittering artificial pool of liquid white lead upon which floated boats of silver and gold, a bejeweled silver tree bearing mechanical birds that sang at certain hours, thousands of beautifully woven carpets and wall hangings, and a huge hall filled with thousands of suits of armor and a spectacular array of weapons. They finally arrived in the presence of the caliph, who sat upon an ebony throne, dressed in silk brocade embroidered with gold. This ostentatious display of wealth reflected the splendor of the Abbasid dynasty. It would have shocked Muhammad. And it was not to last.

**Review Questions:**

1. How did al-Mansur's government differ from that of the Umayyads?
2. What was unique about the new Abbasid capital?
3. What were the major products imported by the Abbasids?
4. What were the major exports?
5. How did the manufacture of paper influence Muslim culture?
6. In what ways did the House of Wisdom resemble the Academy at Jundishapur?
7. What were some of the major ancient Greek texts translated at the House of Wisdom?
8. Describe a major advance made in mathematics.
9. What discoveries were made in astronomy?
10. Describe al-Razi's major work in medicine.
11. How were Muslim hospitals financed?
12. How did the philosophers relate reason to faith?
13. What was the process for publishing a book in Baghdad?
14. What is the *sunna*?

15. How did the *ulama* update the Muslim legal system?
16. Why was it a major mistake for al-Mutasim to hire Turkish mercenaries?
17. What happened to Samarra?

**Questions for Discussion:**

1. Muslim scholars preserved through their translations the scientific legacy of ancient Greece, India, and Persia. Certain modern scholars have proposed that the scientific spirit of the Renaissance would never have sprung to life if the Muslims not not passed on this legacy enriched by their own contributions. Do you agree or disagree? Give reasons for your answer.
2. In what ways did the teachings of Muhammad inspire Baghdad's Golden Age? What aspects of 9th century Baghdad might have shocked the Prophet?
3. In what ways might Islamic law, as it was written in the 9th century, discourage social change?

# Part II - The Empire Fragments

Despite the wealth and prosperity of the Abbasid caliphate, the government had difficulty running the vast and unwieldy empire. As early as the 8th century, distant provinces began to break away — Spain in 756, Morocco in 786, and Ifriqiyah (present-day Tunisia) in 800. During the 9th century, the financial strain caused by the expenses of the bureaucracy and the luxury of the court forced the caliphs to grant large outlying regions of the empire to local governors (emirs). These governors collected taxes and sent a percentage to Baghdad. Eventually, many of them established semi-independent states, which competed with one another militarily while continuing to acknowledge the Abbasid caliph as head of the *umma*. By the early 10h century, more provinces had broken away and it had become clear that *Dar al-Islam* could no longer function as a single political unit.

## The Buyids

In 945 Baghdad was invaded by the Buyids, tribesmen from the coast of the Caspian Sea, who had established an independent Shi'ite dynasty in western Persia. Once in control of Baghdad, the Buyids destroyed the last shreds of the caliph's independence, making him their puppet. Although a captive in his own palace, he remained the titular head of the Abbasid Empire and leader of the *umma*, lending a certain legitimacy to the regime of the new overlords. As Shi'ites, the Buyids promoted the observance of public rites on the anniversary of the death of Husayn, and they encouraged pilgrimages to the shrines at Karbala and Najaf (the burial site of Ali). Tensions soon arose between the Turkish soldiers and the Buyids, while local Sunnis protested the new authority of the Shi'ites. Baghdad itself was soon divided into a number of small walled communities that were either Sunni or Shi'ite.

The Buyids controlled lower Mesopotamia and all of present-day Iran. However, they quickly diluted their power by dividing up this territory among the three brothers of their ruling family. The region was reunited briefly during the reign of Adud al-Dawlah, the most enlightened of the Buyid rulers. He built the al-Adudi Hospital in Baghdad, rekindling the city's commitment to medical treatment and research. A patron of learning, al-Dawlah invited creative men to his court in Isfahan (in central Persia) and even wrote poetry himself. A prominent member of his court was Persian astronomer Al-Sufi. After making a number of careful estimates of the brightness and magnitude of stars from his own observations, he corrected many entries in Ptolemy's *Almagest*. In his *Book of Fixed Stars* he attempted to relate the constellations of the ancient Greeks with those traditionally observed by the Arabs. For example, he changed the centaur of classical mythology into a turbaned man-horse. Al-Sufi also described the Andromeda galaxy (our closest neighbor) and called it "little cloud." This was the first record of a star system outside our own galaxy.

## Samanids and Ghaznavids

While the Buyids controlled the heartland of the faltering Abbasid Empire, other groups gained power in nearby provinces. The Samanids were provincial governors who had been appointed a century earlier to govern the provinces of Khurasan and Transoxania (located northeast of Khurasan). In 892 they established semi-independent rule with their capital at Bukhara. They were the first native dynasty to arise in Persia since the Arab conquest. With the weakening of the caliphate, they promoted a modified form of the Pahlavi language (known as New Persian), which was simplified in grammatical structure but enriched by a large infusion of Arabic words. Court poet Rudaki was the first to write verse in the new tongue. His many odes and epigrams expressed an optimistic view of life and glorified the pleasures of romantic love and good wine.

The Ghaznavid dynasty began in 977 when the Turkish governor of Ghazni (a region in the mountains of modern Afghanistan) claimed independence. His eldest son, Mahmud, was the first Muslim ruler to take the title of *sultan*, an Arabic word meaning "power"or "dominion." He defeated the Samanids, laying claim to Khurasan. Then he turned south and invaded the Punjab (modern Pakistan). He destroyed many Hindu temples, having taken offense at the idols displayed in them, and plundered the Indian cities. His troops returned home laden with rich booty that helped make Ghazni one of the most brilliant cities of the Islamic world. Mahmud built a magnificent mosque faced with marble that rivaled the Great Mosque of Damascus. He promoted Persian culture

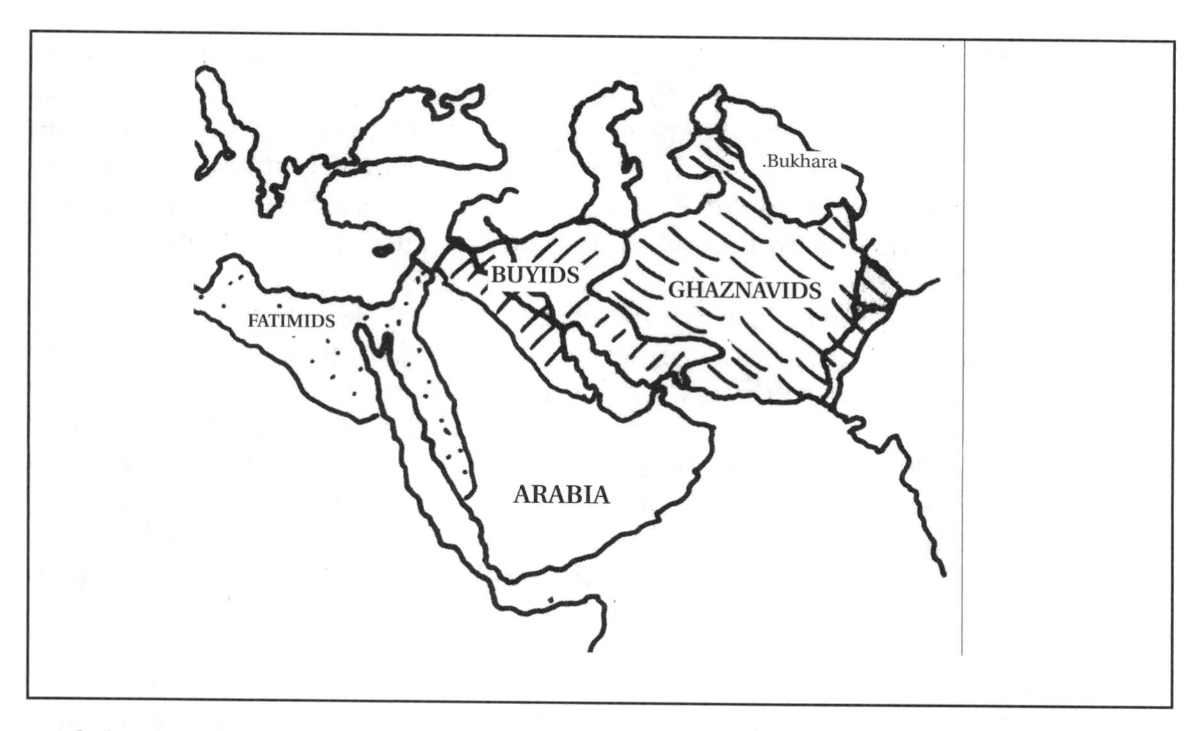


and the revised Persian language, and he drew to his court the era's most illustrious poets, artists, architects, philosophers, musicians, historians, artisans, and craftsmen. One historian, Bu'l-Fazl-i Bayhaqi, wrote a colorful portrait of life at the center of power in Ghazni. This was the first major work in prose written in New Persian.

Firdawsi was a poet living in Khurasan in the late 10th and early 11th centuries. He wrote a great epic of Persian history and legend entitled *The Book of Kings* (*Shahnama*), tracing the reigns of Persian kings from earliest times to the death of the last Sasanian ruler in 651. It was written entirely in New Persian, based on an earlier, shorter work in Pahlavi. With nearly 60,000 couplets, it is one of the longest poems ever composed. *The Book of Kings* became Persia's national epic, and modern Persians consider Firdawsi their greatest poet.

According to legend, Firdawsi was a landowner who made a comfortable living from his estates under the Samanids. He wrote his vast epic in hopes of selling it to the emperor to provide his one daughter with a dowry. By the time he finished in 1010 after 35 years of work (surely too late for his daughter's dowry!), the Samanids had been defeated by the Ghazanids. So he dedicated and presented his work to Sultan Mahmud. But when he was paid less than half of what he expected, he was so angry he took all the money to a bath, had some beer, and then gave the money to the bath attendants and the waiter. But now he was worried about Mahmud's anger, so he fled to the court of a minor local ruler. There he wrote 100 verses of satire about the sultan and inserted them in the preface of his poem. He then offered to dedicate the epic to his host, but the offer was refused. (The satiric verses were later expunged.) Many years later Mahmud sent 60,000 dinars' worth of indigo to the poet to compensate him for his earlier disappointment. But Firdawsi died before it arrived. His daughter refused the gift and the money was spent on repairing a rest house on the boundaries of the family property.

Ibn Sina was one of Islam's greatest physicians. He was born in Bukhara in 980, the son of a Samanid government official. By the age of ten he had memorized the entire *Quran* and most of the Arabic poetry he had read. He had a thirst for knowledge and studied every scientific work he could find. By the time he was 16 he had learned enough about medicine to begin treating patients. A year later, he cured Samanid Sultan ibn Mansur of a digestive problem. Upon his recovery, the sultan wished to reward him, but the young scholar asked only for permission to use the extensive Samanid royal library. When Bukhara was conquered the Ghaznavids, he began a life of wandering, serving as a physician by day and gathering students round him for philosophical and scientific discussion in the evening. He became court physician to a Buyid prince, but when the prince died, he traveled to Isfahan and finally settled there. Ibn Sina wrote over a hundred books in his native Persian and in Arabic. His two most important works were *The Canon of Medicine* and *The Book of Healing.*

*The Canon of Medicine* was a multi-volume work that surveyed the entire scope of medical knowledge that was available from ancient and Muslim sources, plus the author's own observations. It identified 760 drugs and commented upon their application and effectiveness. Among the personal observations were descriptions of the use of oral anesthetics in surgery, advise to surgeons to treat cancer in its earliest stages and to remove all the diseased tissue, and recommendations to test new drugs on animals and humans prior to general use. In those times, these were revolutionary ideas. Ibn Sina was the first to document the contagious nature of tuberculosis and to describe the symptoms of meningitis. He diagramed the parts of the eye and the heart valves, and he proposed that nerves were responsible for muscle pain. He also noted the close relationship between emotions and the physical condition, once diagnosing a melancholy prince as having "love sickness" because he was separated from his beloved.

*The Book of Healing* was a 20-volume work covering the entire range of human knowledge. It was the largest (and most ambitious) book of its kind ever written by one man. This vast subject matter was divided into theoretical knowledge (logic, physics, mathematics, astronomy, music, psychology, and metaphysics) and practical knowledge (ethics, economics, and politics). Like al-

Kindi, Ibn Sina sought to harmonize the rational philosophy of Aristotle and Plato with the religious teachings of Islam. He believed that God was pure intellect and that scholarship brought a person closer to Him.

Al-Biruni was another man with a thirst for scientific knowledge. He once served the Samanids and was later summoned to the court of Mahmud of Ghazi. The sultan had heard stories about the natives of the far north (Eskimos) who dressed in fur and fished through holes in the ice, and he wanted to know if this could be true. He also wondered whether it was possible that the sun could shine for three months at a time. Al-Biruni had read about the sunlit Arctic summers, and he explained to the sultan that the earth's axis was tilted and the sun struck at a different angle farther north than in places like Persia, causing the sun to shine for months in the summer, and not to come out at all during the winter. Mahmud was so impressed with this explanation that he made the scientist a permanent member of his court.

> The Arab scholars were extremely productive, writing huge numbers of books as well as multi-volume texts. While they were indeed prolific, it's important to realize that many of the books were, in fact, more like booklets, and that a volume was most likely less than a hundred pages.

Al-Biruni followed Mahmud on his conquest of India and kept a detailed journal of the geography, the plants and animals, and the local people and their customs. (He even learned Sanskrit.) He estimated the latitude and longitude of cities, rivers, and mountains, which he mapped along the way. His many notes formed the basis of his 700-page *Book of India*. He continued to travel and take notes on his surroundings until he was past 70. He wrote 146 different works on such subjects as astronomy, botany, mathematics, physics, geography, and pharmacology. He is credited with many forward-thinking observations. For example, he proposed that the speed of light was faster than the speed of sound, and that the Milky Way was a collection of countless fragments of nebulous stars. He took sightings near modern Islamabad on which he based calculations of the radius and circumference of the earth that are very close to modern estimates. (He was also quite certain that the earth circled the sun.) And he described roughly five times as many medicinal plants as had the Greek botanist Dioscorides.When the sultan sent him three camel-loads of silver coins in appreciation of his work, he returned it, remarking, "I serve knowledge for the sake of knowledge and not for money."

## The Seljuk Turks

During the 10th century a group of Turkish tribes, the Orghuz, settled just east of the territory of the Samanids and Ghanavids under their leader, Seljuk. They gradually abandoned their pagan beliefs and embraced Sunni Islam.

Known as the Seljuks after their leader, they were formidable warriors, greatly feared for their deadly skills as mounted archers. After the death of Seljuk, power passed to his son Arslan. He began to push into the land controlled by Mahmud of Ghazna. His nephews, Tughril and Chaghri Beg, conquered all of northeastern Persia. (The Ghaznavids were left in possession of eastern Afghanistan and northern India, where they continued to rule until 1186.) The brothers then divided their territory — Chaghri took over Khurasan while Tughril established himself at Nishapur in western Persia.

In 1055 Tughril captured Baghdad, overthrew the Buyids, and founded the Seljuk Sultanate, assuming leadership of the heartland of the Islamic world. The Abbasid caliph continued in his role as puppet ruler of his diminished realm and leader of the *umma*. Tughril made Isfahan his capital and adopted Persian culture. In 1071 Seljuk warriors defeated a Byzantine army at Manzikert (just south of the Black Sea), captured the Byzantine emperor, Romanus Diogenes, and forced him to accept a peace treaty that opened the door for Muslim expansion into Anatolia (Asia Minor). The Seljuks now controlled all the territory from the Oxus River (the eastern boundary of Persia) to Anatolia. For the first time, a Turkish people dominated most of western Asia.

Seljuk vizier Nizalmulmulk built the first *madrasas*. These were schools of higher learning attached to certain large mosques. Students concentrated on religious texts and dogma as well as languages, literature, and science. Future religious scholars and administrators would now be taught in a uniform way. The *madrasas* were supported by *waqfs* (the endowements set aside for the upkeep of these and other public institutions, see page 64).

Jerusalem fell to the Seljuks in 1076. The holy city had been in Muslim hands since Umar conquered it in 637. The Abbasids had continued a policy of tolerance towards the Christians and Jews visiting or residing in the city until 969, when control of the city passed the Fatimids, a Shi'ite caliphate based in Egypt. (You'll learn about them in Chapter 6.) The Seljuks drove out to the Fatimids, and, unlike Umar and his successors, they staged vicious attacks on the Christian pilgrims, degraded the holy sites, and even kidnapped for ransom the city's patriarch. It was only a matter of time before Christian leaders in Europe would respond.

The Ghaznavids introduced Persian culture into India. The Persian language and poetry became the vogue among the ruling classes. At the court of Moghul emperor Akbar New Persian was adopted as the official language. It later spread and fused with Hindi, giving rise to the Urdu tongue.

## Al-Ghazali and the Sufis

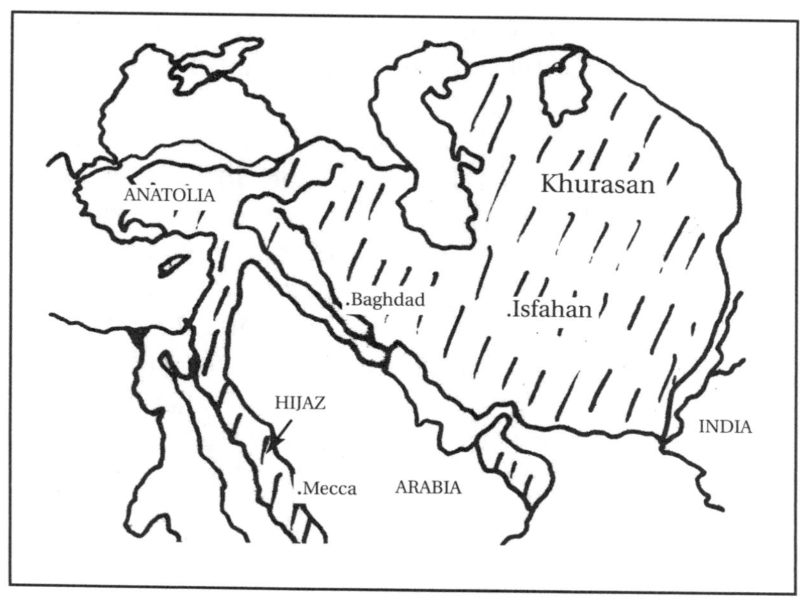


**The Seljuk Sultanate at its Peak**

The Seljuks did not have an extensive bureaucracy. Order was imposed at the local level by the emirs and the *ulama*. The emirs, being military men, had little interest in civil activities and served fairly short terms. It was the *ulama*, the religious scholars and teachers, who provided a sense of unity and support. The sense of religious community was strengthened by the Sufis. Under the Umayyads, Sufism had been limited to individuals who lived on the fringe of society, but by the 9th century the mystical movement was beginning to find acceptance among the general public. With the fragmentation of the empire, the Sufis began to play a key role in transmitting the message of Islam.

Under the Seljuks, a Persian Sufi named al-Ghazali brought Sufism into the mainstream of Sunni religious life. As a young man, al-Ghazali had been a scholar of religion, philosophy, and law. In 1091 he was appointed head of the prestigious Nizamiyah Madrassa in Baghdad. But he felt torn apart by a personal religious struggle — he felt that although he knew a great deal *about* God, he did not know Him. So in 1095 he left Baghdad and became a wandering ascetic. By meditating and practicing Sufi exercises, he was finally able to sense communication with God. He returned to Nishapur (his hometown) ten years later and began writing a critique of rational philosophy, *The Incoherence of the Philosophers*. In this work he rejected all philosophical claims to knowledge, attacking the views of al-Farabi and Ibn Sina. Reason, he said, was useful in the search for knowledge in disciplines such as mathematics or medicine, but only ritual and prayer could lead to a knowledge of God.

In one of his books, *The Alchemy of Happiness,* al-Ghazali described a competition between two artists, one Chinese and the other Greek. The Chinese artist painted an elaborately realistic scene on one wall, while the Greek merely polished the opposite wall so that it reflected the Chinese scene. This was a parable for the Sufi's endeavor to purify himself so that he became a mirror for the Divine Light.

In his other major work, the four-volume *Revival of the Religious Sciences*, al-Ghazali blended Muslim religious traditions with mystical beliefs and rituals to create a comprehensive guide for the devout Muslim. Al-Ghazali felt that one should be conscious of God's presence in every moment of life, even during non-religious activities. His book covered every aspect of religious and daily life, taking all the rules about eating, sleeping, washing, hygiene and prayer found in the *sunna* and giving them a devotional interpretation. Al-Gazali urged the *ulama* to practice the contemplative rituals that the Sufi mystics had developed and to promote this interior spirituality at the same time that they followed the rules of Islamic law.

Sufis believed that particularly pious individuals, whom they call "friends of God," had extraordinary powers, which permitted them to perform miracles, such as healing the sick, reviving the dead, or even flying.

Sufi orders (*tariqas*) headed by masters (*shaykhs*) began to form around the late 12th and 13th centuries. (*Shaykh*, an Arabic term that simply means "an old man," was used to refer to the chief of a tribe, a religious leader, or even the head of a guild. The Persian word for a Sufi master is *pir*.) Members of a Sufi order were expected to obey their leader, attend meetings, and live a pious life. A new member was sent off for forty days' seclusion, during which he would meditate and repeat a formula of words from the *Quran*, usually the 99 names attributed to God (see the box on the left). Each order traced its lineage to a particular master, who codified the order's distinctive teachings and practices. Members of various orders were initiated with a ritual handshake (*baya*) with the *shaykh* in a ceremony resembling the one performed in the installment of the Rightly Guided Caliphs. The Sufi convent (*khanqa*) had a prayer hall, a kitchen, and cells for the individual residents. By the 12th century every good-sized town had a *khanqa* as well as a mosque and *madrasa*. Muslims living nearby came to the Sufi communities for supplementary worship, spiritual consolation, healing, charity, and even for political mediation of problems with the government.

There are 2,700 references to God in the *Quran* and 99 attributes, which include God the Merciful, the Compassionate, the King, the Most Holy, the Almighty, the Creator, and the Bestower. Repeating the 99 attributes or names of God (a practice known as *dhikr*) was a group chanting activity that propelled Sufis into a trance-like state.

The new emphasis upon faith over reason fostered by the growth of Sufism and promoted by al-Ghazali brought an end to the golden age of scholarship begun three centuries earlier at the House of Wisdom. The spirit of

At first most Sufis lived in the heartland of the Islamic world, but over the centuries they spread out to distant regions in Africa, Asia, and Europe. Because Sufis preached in the vernacular languages of the lands where they were based, they converted to Islam many non-Muslims living thousands of miles from Baghdad.

inquiry and experimentation that had led to such great advances in science was now regarded with distrust. Schools began to limit their teaching to matters of theology. The free and open discussions of the natural world and the human spirit were becoming phenomena of the past in much of *Dar al-Islam*.

## The Crusades

The Seljuks' capture of Jerusalem and their advance into Anatolia had produced great anxiety in Europe. Byzantine Emperor Alexius I called upon other Christian leaders to oversee a "pilgrimage" to free the holy city and its environs from Muslim rule. At the Council of Clermont in 1095, Pope Urban II gave a rousing speech urging Christian rulers to unite to recover the "Holy Land." Before long, armies of European knights, driven by a combination of faith, a desire for adventure, and visions of booty, set off for Jerusalem. Their expeditions became known as "Crusades," since they were made on behalf of the Christian cross.

Three years after the Pope's speech, the Crusaders took the cities of Edessa and Antioch in Syria. In July of 1099 they captured Jerusalem. They showed no mercy to the city's Muslim and Jewish inhabitants, filling the streets with blood. The Dome of the Rock was converted into a church and the al-Aqsa mosque became the residence of the army commanders. Crusader armies gained control of a narrow strip of land along the eastern Mediterranean coast

Omar Khayyam was a Persian mathematician and astronomer who lived between 1048 and 1131. He was famous in his own times for writing a treatise on algebra. Sultan Malik-Shah summoned him to undertake the astronomical observations necessary for the reform of the solar calendar. He built an observatory in Isfahan and for 18 years he worked with other scientists compiling tables. He measured the length of the year as 365.24 days and developed a reliable calendar based upon making 8 of every 33 years leap years.

Khayyam's fame in the West rests upon the collection of *The Rubaiyat* (*Quatrains*) attributed to him. (A quatrain is a piece of verse complete in four rhymed lines, although in Khayyam's poems the third line often does not rhyme.) He wrote nearly 600 brief, lyrical pieces, each composed on a particular occasion and forming a complete poem. They expressed his personal philosophy: rather than worry about questions of faith or the impermanence and uncertainty of life, one should joyfully appreciate the fleeting and sensuous beauties of the material world.

The quatrains had attracted comparatively little attention until in 1859 they inspired Edward FitzGerald to write his celebrated *The Rubaiyat of Omar Khayyám*. FitzGerald combined the verses into a continuous unified elegy. The quatrains have been translated into almost every major language and contain such famous phrases as "A Jug of Wine, a Loaf of Bread, and Thou," and "The Flower that once has bloomed forever dies."

and set up four states, collectively known as Outremer ("Across the Sea").

These military actions forced the Turks living in Anatolia to migrate into the region's interior. At the beginning of the 12th century, the Sultanate of Rum was established between Byzantine territory and the Crusader states. (It was called "Rum" after ancient Rome, which had once ruled the region.) Its capital city of Konya became a flourishing center of trade and the arts, where Christians and Muslims lived and worked together.

The Muslim response to the sacking of Jerusalem was at first limited. The emirs, used to fighting one another, found it difficult to band together against an external foe. Finally, forces led by Nur al-Din of Syria recaptured Edessa in 1144 and Damascus in 1154. You'll learn about the Muslim recapture of Jerusalem in Chapter 6. The Crusades were a marginal event for Islam. More significant was the dissolution of the Seljuk Empire. The practice of dividing provinces among a deceased ruler's sons created many independent and unstable principalities. By the second half of the 12th Century, Seljuk rule had given way to the local dynasties.

Nur al-Din founded An-Nuri Hospital in Damascus in 1156 to express thanks for his victories. The hospital included a medical school and served the public for seven centuries. Parts of it still exist today.

## The Mongols

By the 13th century, the Islamic world was a sprawling, fragmented commonwealth of semi-autonomous states, each with distinct political and religious divisions. In a weakened condition, the lands of the Middle East faced another invasion of nomads from the steppes of Asia — one more terrible than anyone could have envisioned. The invaders were the Mongols, warlike tribesmen from north of China who had been unified under a single leader, Genghis Khan. Intent on creating a world empire, Genghis had turned his warriors into an invincible fighting machine. After subjugating China and much of Central Asia, he moved west. In 1220 his armies entered Persia and sacked several cities before withdrawing.

After Genghis died in 1227, a new invasion was launched by his grandson, Hulago. As the Mongols moved through present-day Afghanistan, they encountered the Assassins, an extreme Shi'ite sect that specialized in suicide missions against their enemies. They gained courage through use of the drug hashish (which is the source of the word "assassin") and from the belief that their acts would win them admittance to Paradise. Members of the sect had assassinated the very enlightened Seljuk vizier, Nizalmulmulk, in 1092. Hulagu drove the Assassins out of their mountain camps and decimated them. In this one respect, the Mongols did something beneficial for Muslim society.

In February, 1258, the Mongols captured Baghdad. The city fell after a single battle, and the caliphate with it. The last Abbasid caliph, al-Musta'sim, was trampled to death by enemy horseman, the traditional Mongol way of executing a conquered leader. Hundreds of thousands of inhabitants were slaughtered, making the Tigris run red with blood. The city, after being looted for several days, was burned to the ground. The research centers and laboratories, schools, libraries, mosques, palaces, and even the roads and waterways were destroyed. So many books were thrown into the river that it was said a horse could walk on them from one bank to the other. Many of the scientific discoveries made by Muslim researchers, such as the use of antiseptics and anesthesia in surgery, were lost and would have to be rediscovered independently by others in future centuries. Beyond the capital, the countryside was laid waste and the ancient systems of irrigation were destroyed. The devastation was so complete that in many areas agricultural recovery is still incomplete.

After the onslaught, Baghdad rapidly sank to the level of a small provincial town. Trade routes throughout western Asia became unsafe, urban life broke down, and those individual communities that survived drew in upon themselves. Islamic culture was in danger of loosing its essence.

## Review Questions:

1.What factors led to the breaking up of the Abbasid empire?
2. What religious changes did the Buyids bring to Baghdad?
3. How do you explain the revival of the Persian language?
4. What contributions did Sultan Mahmud make to Persian culture?
5. What was the subject of Firdawsi's great epic?
6. What were the titles and subjects of Ibn Sina's two greatest works?
7. Give an example of how al-Biruni was ahead of his time.
8. What actions of the Seljuk Turks motivated Christian Europe to launch the First Crusade?
9. In what major way did al-Ghazali differ with Ibn Sina?
10. Describe a Sufi community of the 12th century.
11. What was the Sultanate of Rum?
12. What was the goal of Genghis Khan?
13. Describe the Mongol conquest of Baghdad

## Questions for Discussion:

1. The Crusades are considered a major event in European history. When, then, are they considered a minor episode by Muslim historians?
2. Firdawsi's *The Book of Kings* is a magnificent tribute to Persian nationalism. Did the poet just happen to write his great epic at a time when it would be most gloriously received, or was he inspired by particular events?
3. The *Quran* forbids forced conversion of Islam. Yet, the religion spread at a dramatic pace throughout a vast region on three continents. How do you explain this? What role did mer chants, missionaries, and Sufis play in the conversion of non-Muslims to Islam?

Jalal al-Din Rumi (1207-73) was the greatest mystic poet and thinker to write in Persian. He fled as a child with his family from Khurasan as the Mongols approached. They ended up in Konya, capital of the Sultanate of Rum. (Rumi means "of Rum.") He eventually got a job teaching at a *madrasa* there. His life changed dramatically when he met a wandering mystic, Shams of Tabriz, and was so drawn to his views that he became a mystic himself. Rumi soon had a number of followers. They referred to him as *Mevlana* (Turkish for "our master") and their order became known as the *Mevlevi*.

Rumi used music as a means of drawing closer to God. He and his followers would often form two circles, one inside the other, and spin around and around to the rhythm of tambourines and the haunting melodies of a flute. The spinning dance induced a trance. The Mevlana are often referred to as the Whirling Dervishes. (The word "dervish" is derived from *darvish*, the Persian word for Sufi.)

Rumi used poetry and fable to teach mystical truths. During a period of 25 years, he composed over 70,000 verses of poetry about divine love, mystic passion and ecstatic illumination. It is the largest corpus of lyric poetry in the Persian literature. His masterpiece (26,000 couplets long ) is *The Rhymed Discourses* (*Mathnavi*), an explanation of Sufi doctrine explained through fable, stories, and reflection. It opens with an evocation of a reed being cut to make a flute. This is a metaphor for the soul, emptied of self and filled with the divine spirit.

Rumi's verses called upon one to live beyond himself, to transcend the routines of daily life, and to rebel against injustice and weakness, not only those of others but more particularly against his own. (This is the greater *jihad*.) By divesting himself of egotism and selfishness, he would find that God is all that remains.

After Rumi's death, *The Rhymed Discourses* became the standard mystical work of the Persian world and was translated into Turkish and the local languages of Muslim India. Barely known in the West until recently, Rumi is now one of the most widely read poets in America. Here is an example of his verse:

*Dance, as though no one is watching,*
*Love, as though you've never been hurt before,*
*Sing, as though no one can hear you,*
*Work, as though you don't need the money,*
*Live, as though heaven is on earth.*

# Chapter 5 — CORDOBA

Cordoba lies at the foot of the Sierra Morena Mountains on the banks of the Guadalquivir River in southern Spain. The weather in the river valley is pleasant and dry, with summer temperatures rising only into the low 90's (F). Olive trees, poplars, and cypresses cover the surrounding hillsides, while orange and lemon trees grow in courtyards and parks throughout the city.

In the 2nd century BCE the Romans founded the city of *Corduba* here, and it became the capital of the province of Hispania Baetica. Wheat, olives, and grapevines were introduced into the region, and Corduba became an important center for shipping the grain, olive oil, and wine to other parts of the empire. In the 3rd century CE all Roman provinces became Christian. After the fall of Rome, Spain was overrun by hordes of Germanic tribesmen. Among them were the Vandals, who stayed briefly and gave the region a name — Vandalusia ("land of the Vandals"). Another group, the Visigoths, settled here and established a Christian kingdom.

The Muslims entered Spain in the 8th century. Under their rule, the old Roman city of Corduba was rebuilt and expanded. Known as Cordoba, it became the center of Islamic culture in western Europe.

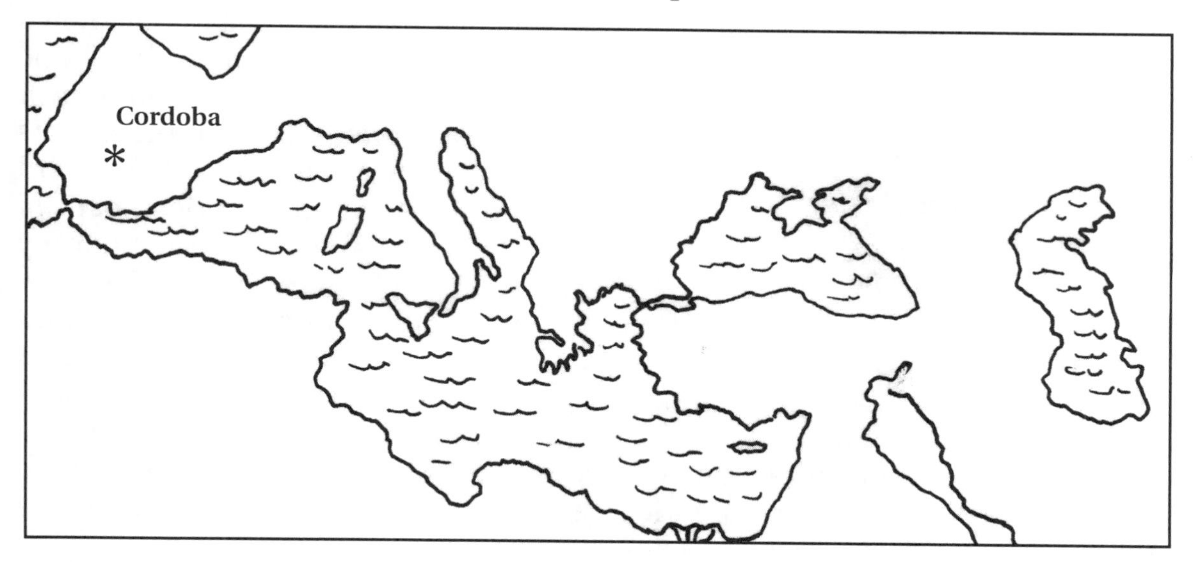


## Islam Spreads to Spain

During the early years of Muslim expansion under Umar, the second of the Rightly Guided Caliphs, Arab armies spread across North Africa and established their first important base at Kairouan (in present day Tunisia). From there they continued westwards until by 705 they had reached the Atlantic coast of Morocco. Many Berbers (local tribesmen of North Africa) converted to Islam and became Muslim soldiers.

Around this time, the Visigoths ruled most of Spain. A small number of wealthy families owned most of the land that was not already in the hands of the Roman Christian Church. The majority of the people were hard-working peasants. Life was difficult for the Jewish families, who were frequently persecuted by the Church officials. In 710 King Witiza died and an army general named Roderick seized power. Witiza's family appealed to the Arab governor in Morocco, Musa ibn Nusair, to help them regain the throne. In response, the governor dispatched his lieutenant, Tariq ibn Zijyad, and some 7,000 Berber infantry soldiers.

A narrow strait separates Morocco from Spain at the point where the Mediterranean Sea meets the Atlantic Ocean. Tariq and his troops crossed the strait in the spring of 711, landing on a sandy peninsula near a rocky ridge that rose over a thousand feet above the sea. Today it is known today as Gibraltar (from the Arabic *Jabal Tariq,* "Tariq's Mountain"). Tariq waited for reinforcements and then advanced inland toward Cordoba. When Roderick heard of the invasion, he amassed an army to defend his kingdom. Roderick was not a popular leader, and although his army was larger than that of the invaders, few of his soldiers felt loyal to him. Many deserted before any fighting began, and others switched allegiances mid-way through the battle that ensued. After Roderick was defeated and killed, Tariq marched to the Visigoth capital of Toledo to set up headquarters.

The following year Musa himself crossed the strait with a large army and proceeded inland to Toledo. He took over command from Tariq and made it clear that he had no intention of restoring King Witiza's dynasty to the throne. To signify the Muslim conquest of the region he ordered a new coinage to be struck, engraved in Latin (the language of the Christian Church) with the words,

"There is no god but God." His armies later moved north, and by 714 the Iberian (Spanish) peninsula was under his control except for a few Christian enclaves.

The Muslims called their new territory al-Andalus (the Arabic version of Vandalusia).* It became the most westerly province of the Umayyad Empire. Al-Andalus was governed by an emir sent from Damascus. The old ruling class of nobility and clergy was eliminated and their lands were redistributed, creating a new class of small landowners. As in other parts of the Islamic world, Christians and Jews (*dhimmis*) were free to practice their religions in exchange for paying a poll tax.

In 732 Muslim armies crossed the Pyrenee Mountains that separate Spain from France. Their defeat by Frankish king Charles Martel at the Battle of Poitiers ended any further extension of Islam into Europe. From then on, the Muslims would focus their attention on al-Andalus.

## The Cordoba Emirate

We learned at the end of Chapter 3 that after the Abbasids seized power in 750 they executed all members of the Umayyad ruling family — except one. Abd al-Rahman, a tall, red-headed prince, made a miraculous escape. He fled to North Africa and then to al-Andalus, where he contacted those Arabs who had remained loyal to his family. With their help, he defeated the Abbasid emir, seized Cordoba as his home base, and gained acceptance among the local factions as the new governor.

In 756 al-Rahman set up the independent Umayyad Emirate of Cordoba. This was the first example of a province formally separating from the Abbasid caliphate. Al-Rahman formed an administration modeled on the one he had known in Damascus. Many officials who had once served the Umayyads came to al-Andalus to work for the new rejuvenated dynasty. The Abbasids, of course, did not accept the new regime, and al-Rahman had to cope with political intrigues for more than 20 years. In 763, for example, his soldiers seized a mob of rebels backed by the Abbasids at the very gates of Cordoba. He ordered the leaders beheaded, had the heads filled with salt and camphor, and then sent them back to Baghdad. Al-Rahman had his problems to the north as well. When Charlemagne, king of the Franks, crossed the Pyrenees into Spain, Muslim forces had to be dispatched to drive him back. The Franks would never return to Spain.

Al-Rahman built a Syrian-style palace to the northwest of Cordoba and named it *al-Rusafa,* after his grandfather's villa on the Euphrates. He ordered Syrian fruit trees, jasmine, and roses for its gardens to remind him of his childhood home. In 785 work began on Cordoba's Great Mosque, known in Spanish as *La Mezquita* ("the Mosque"). It was built on a site where a Roman temple and,

*Today southern Spain is known as Andalusia.

later, a Christian church had stood. The builders collected marble columns and capitals from nearby Roman ruins. However, most of these columns were only seven or eight feet high, not high enough to support the ceiling of such an important building. So an ingenious architect placed rectangular piers on top of the columns and constructed two tiers of horseshoe-shaped arches on the piers. The lower tier of arches connected the columns, while the upper tier supported the roof. The alternation of red brick and white limestone in the arches created a striking "candy-stripe" pattern, which you can see in the photograph on the opposite page. *La Mezquita* was modeled on the Great Mosque in Damascus, with aisles arranged perpendicular to the *qibla* wall. While this worked well as a design for the prayer hall, the architect followed his model a bit too closely: the *qibla* of *La Mezquita* faced south, which was the correct orientation towards Mecca for Damascus, but not for a city in Spain!

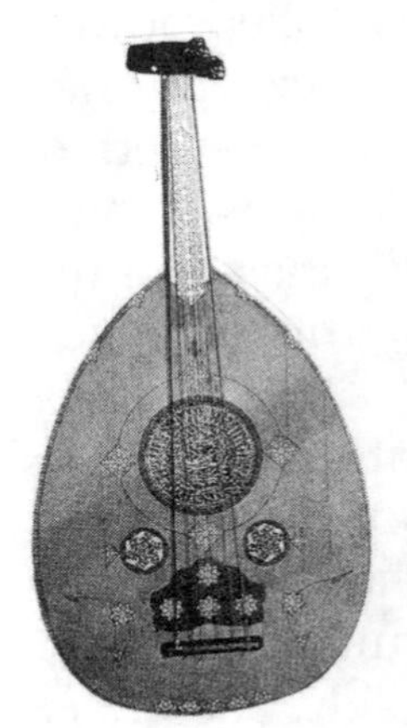

The 4th emir, Abd al-Rahman II, was a well-educated man who loved poetry and music. He presided over a splendid court, which was greatly enriched by the efforts of one man — a Persian musician named Ziryab. He had been a member of the court of al-Rashid but was forced to flee from Baghdad to escape the jealousy of the head musician. As he traveled across North Africa, Ziryab was entranced by the melodies and rhythms he heard. After being welcomed to al-Rahman's court, he began experimenting with musical forms, blending elements of Greek, Persian, and Arab music with what he had heard in North Africa. This led to the creation of a distinctive new type of music, known as Andalusian. Ziryab introduced into Spain the Arabic *ud* (ancestor of the lute), to which he added a fifth string. This became a major instrument for accompanying singers of the new Andalusian melodies. Ziryab also took it upon himself to bring the members of the Cordoba court up to date on the latest Abbasid fashions. Courtiers were soon wearing the brightly

Ibn Firnas, a scientist living in Cordoba, came up with a formula for making glass crystals from sand and stone. This led to the popularity of crystal goblets among the wealthy. He also constructed a mechanized planetarium with a series of rings depicting the motions of stars and planets. In 875 he built a primitive flying machine, consisting of a pair of feathered wings on a wooden frame, and invited the people of Cordoba to witness his flight from a nearby hilltop. After gliding some distance, he plummeted to the ground. This is the first known instance of man in flight.

colored silk robes popular in Baghdad and eating asparagus, a new delicacy imported from the East.

Islam gradually spread throughout al-Andalus. The native people who converted were referred to as *muwallads* (roughly meaning "adopted"). Arabic was spoken by nearly everyone, including Christians and Jews. As early as the middle of the 9th century, the Archbishop of Seville found it necessary to translate and annotate the Bible into this language. The Spanish Christians were called *mozarabs* (from the Arabic *musta'rib* meaning "Arabicized").

A forest of pillars in *La Mezquita*

As Islam melded with local traditions, a distinctive Hispano-Arab culture evolved, which is known as Moorish. (The term "Moor" derives from the ancient Berber kingdom of Mauretania, which lay in present-day Morocco and Western Algeria. A Moor was a Muslim who entered Spain from that region.)

## The Cordoba Caliphate

Abd al-Rahman III came to the throne in 921, a time when there was great tension among the Arab leaders, the Berber soldiers, and the *muwallads.* Making matters worse, three Christian kingdoms in northern Spain — Navarre, Castile, and Leon — threatened the Muslim borders. After resolving the internal conflicts, al-Rahman defeated the Christian armies and imposed an annual tribute on their rulers. From then on, al-Andalus enjoyed a long era of stability and peace. In 929 al-Rahman declared himself caliph, making himself religious leader as well as political head of al-Andalus. He began issuing gold and silver coins (*dinars* and *dirhems*) with his name and titles printed on them. His Cordoba Caliphate would flourish for more than a century.

The emirate had many rulers, but the three greatest all happened to share the name of Abd al-Rahman.

In 936 construction began of a vast new palace complex, *Madinat al-*

*Zahra* (named after the caliph's favorite wife, Zahra), on a spit of land between two deep ravines three miles west of Cordoba. This spot, with its commanding view of the countryside, had been a favorite setting for the country estates of the wealthy since Roman times. The new complex was inspired by the grand palaces of Samarra and was built on three levels, or terraces. It took decades to complete and cost, annually, 300,000 gold coins (a third of the state revenue). At the highest level stood the caliph's residence and audience chambers, with more than 4,000 marble columns collected from ancient Roman ruins. The middle level held the government buildings, the homes of senior officials, and accommodations for important visitors. The mosque stood on an artificially created mound between the middle level and the lowest level, where soldiers and staff workers had their homes. All buildings were equipped with running water provided by an aqueduct. Nearly 14, 000 people lived in the complex when it was completed.

The principal reception hall of the complex featured a green marble basin from Constantinople encircled by 12 golden, jewel-encrusted animals and mythical creatures spouting jets of water. Light flowed in through "windows" of translucent alabaster. Facing the throne room was a large square garden, with arbors of cypress trees, flowerbeds, fishponds, an aviary, and a menagerie (zoo). In the center of the garden stood a royal pavilion surrounded by four pools with spouting fountains. Such a garden was called a "paradise," a representation not only of the Paradise described in the *Quran* but also the biblical Garden of Eden with its four rivers of water, milk, wine, and honey. It was a microcosm of the two kingdoms of living things: the plant world (flowers and trees) and the animal world (fish, birds, and wild beasts). This was the origin of our modern botanical and zoological gardens.

*Madinat al-Zahra* drew ambassadors from the Christian kingdoms of northern Spain as well as from Byzantium, Germany, and even the Vatican. One group of visitors, which the caliph wanted to particularly impress, was escorted from the city along a three-mile corridor beneath a canopy of swords, held by soldiers standing shoulder-to-shoulder on either side all along the way. After entering the gates of the complex, they proceeded along a carpet of silk brocade to the highest level, where they met the caliph in his magnificent reception hall.

Cordoba itself was alive with commercial activity, the likes of which had not been witnessed in Europe since Roman times. Huge mills manufactured

Muslim engineers turned the arid countryside of al-Andalus into fertile fields by introducing the irrigation systems used in Syria and Mesopotamia. The technology of the windmill was brought from North Africa to grind the wheat into flour. The Muslim farmers introduced a number of new foods into Europe — rice, pomegranates, oranges, lemons, eggplants, almonds, artichokes, figs, dates, peaches, plums, and apricots. They were also the first to grow sugarcane and cotton in European soil.

great quantities of paper for book production, weavers produced luxurious cloth from fibers spun by locally raised silkworms, and potters turned out dishes and vases with a glittering sheen like that of Chinese porcelain. Cobblers fashioned the soles of sandals from the bark of cork oak trees — a lightweight, durable, and inexpensive footware first developed by the Romans. Tanners transformed animal hides into a soft leather that an English merchant described as "pliable as wool and as tough as horsehair." The Cordoban products were loaded onto boats and taken to the mouth of the Guadalquivir River, where they were put on larger vessels and delivered to ports around the Mediterranean Sea.

Fields just outside of Cordoba were used as pastures for Andalusian horses, a cross between native Spanish horses and Arabian steeds. They were bred for the caliph's cavalry. Today, the high-stepping Andalusian, like the above, is often seen in the dressage show ring.

Al-Rahman actively recruited scholars, poets, philosophers, historians, and musicians to his court, and he collected books for his library. In 949 he received an illustrated manuscript of Dioscorides' *Materia Medica* (the ancient work on botany, see page 64) as a gift from the Byzantine emperor. The book had already been translated into Arabic in Baghdad, but the translation had not yet made its way to al-Andalus. Since there were no scholars in Spain who knew Greek, an appeal was sent back to Constantinople. A learned Greek monk named Nicholas soon arrived in Cordoba, where he was joined by a Greek-speaking Muslim scholar from Sicily. Together they translated the text, setting off a flurry of interest in botany and pharmacology as well as an eagerness to learn more about the legacies of the ancient world.

In Cordoba, learning was considered the sign of a gentleman. But there were also opportunities for women. Among the population were female poets, librarians and book copyists. Other women were involved in teaching law and medicine.

Al-Hakam II, the most scholarly of the caliphs, created a vast library at Cordoba with over 400,000 books, mainly about mathematics, astronomy, and medicine, which were carefully indexed in 44 catalogues. As in Baghdad, men of learning were drawn to the library. Christians and Jews gathered with Muslim scholars, sharing their views and perspectives in a zealous spirit of inquiry matching that of the House of Wisdom a century earlier. This open-minded co-mingling of intellectuals from different faiths came to be known as the *Convivencia,* a Spanish word meaning "living together". New avenues of scholarship were opened.

Astronomer al-Majriti elaborated upon the Arabic translation of Ptolemy's *Almagest* and revised many of the astronomical tables of al-Khwarizmi. Al-Zahrawi, al-Hakam's court physician, wrote a medical encyclopedia (*Manual for Medical Practitioners*), which was a synthesis of medical knowledge available in al-Andalus at the time. It included 200 illustrations of surgical instruments, most of which the author designed himself. Ibn Juljul compiled a commentary on the work of Dioscorides and wrote a treatise on herbal medicines. He traveled widely, collecting herbs and plants which he used to make pills and tablets. His *Categories of Physicians* was a history of the medical profession from ancient times to his own day.

Tenth century Cordoba was one of the cultural centers of the Mediterranean world. It was the richest and most sophisticated city in Europe apart from Constantinople, with a population of nearly 500,000 (compared to about 38,000 living in Paris). A medieval chronicler enthusiastically described the city as "the jewel of the world," with its wide paved streets (lit at night by Europe's first streetlights), fountains and gardens, mosques, *hammams*, schools, libraries, hospitals, shops, and bustling marketplaces. The houses were typical of those found in the region since ancient times, each with its outer brick wall and inner courtyard leading to bedrooms, sitting rooms, and storage areas. As in other Muslim cities, the gates of the walls surrounding each of the many neighborhoods were locked at night after evening prayers.

When Hisham II inherited the throne in 976 at the age of 11, the royal vizier, al-Mansur, became regent. For over 20 years, this ambitious and ruthless man ran the caliphate, isolating the young caliph from his subjects. He introduced a secret police and expanded his army with mercenary (hired) European troops. He led annual campaigns against the Christian states in northern Spain, sacking the cities of Castile, Leon and Barcelona. In 997 he attacked Santiago de Compostela, a center of Christian pilgrimage. (This was believed to be the bur-

*La Mezquita* was enlarged several times over the years. Al-Rahman II and al-Hakam II both added southern extensions, each of which required building a new *qibla* and *mihrab*. Al-Hakam brought craftsman from Constantinople to teach the local artisans how to decorate his *mihrab* with glittering gold, blue, and red mosaics. Above it was a single block of white marble carved in the form of a seashell.

A major expansion by al-Mansur doubled the size of the original mosque. It became the third largest structure in Islamic world. (It is just a little smaller than St. Peter's Cathedral in Rome.) The windows in the four cupolas and the thousands of small oil lamps suspended from chains in the ceiling flooded the interior with light.

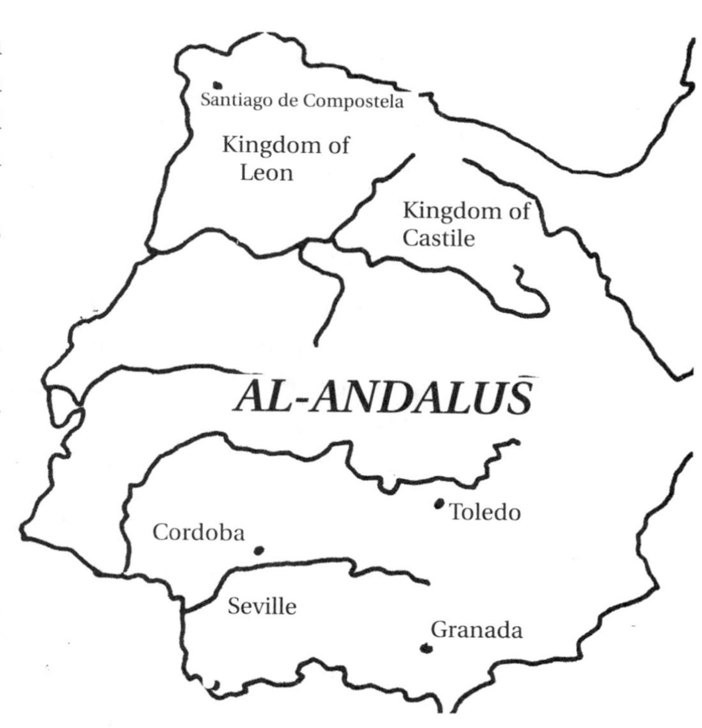


ial site of St. James the Apostle, whom Spanish Christians considered the twin brother of Jesus.) Al-Mansur destroyed the church, and even stole the church bells. However, he left the tomb alone.

When al-Mansur died in 1002, his sons succeeded him as ruling viziers, while the caliph remained a figurehead. But they lacked their father's ability, and the caliphate began to flounder. Quarreling soon arose among the major groups of society — the Andalusians (the local Muslim population), the Berbers who had recently immigrated from Africa, and the European mercenaries in the army. Civil war gradually engulfed Cordoba, with riots and pillaging that caused many of the educated and wealthy to flee. The magnificent buildings of *Madinat al-Zahra* were destroyed. In 1031 Hisham II abdicated. The Cordoba Caliphate had come to an end.

## The Taifas

Some of the most powerful men in al-Andalus took advantage of the power vacuum by carving out for themselves little kingdoms, which were called *taifas* (Arabic for "faction" or "party"). Known as the "party kings," they fought continuously with one another. There were up to 21 *taifas* at a time; some lasted only months, others till the end of the century. Among the most prominent were Seville and Granada. When they were not fighting, the party kings competed among themselves for the most brilliant court, drawing artists, scientists, and scholars from distant lands. So despite the political disunity, it was during this period that Moorish civilization reached its height.

Ibn Hazm was a philosopher who was born in Cordoba. After holding various jobs in local governments, he withdrew from public life to devote himself to his scholarship, writing 400 works on various subjects. He was the leading

> Although the *muwallads* learned Arabic, they also continued to speak Spanish. Gradually, many Arabic words entered the Spanish language. More than 4,000 words of Arabic origin are used in modern Spanish.

Spanish exponent of the conservative Zahiri school of jurisprudence, which followed the literal meaning of the *Quran* and *sunna*. Al-Bakri was a minister at the court of Seville. He was sent on many diplomatic missions, where he took time to study the local landscapes. His *Book of Highways and of Kingdoms* was an encyclopedia of the entire world arranged by country. Each entry was preceded by a short introduction with descriptions of the people, customs, and climate of the country, the principal features, the major cities, and even interesting anecdotes. Al-Zarqali was a mathematician and astronomer living in Toledo. He built numerous precision instruments, including a waterclock capable of determining the hours of the day and night and indicating the days of the lunar month. He contributed to the compilation of the Toledan Tables, a highly accurate set of astronomical data that gave the position of the various planets at any given time and predicted solar and lunar eclipses.

Cordoba, having recovered from the period of riots, became a center of Andalusian poetry — courtly verses about love and friendship set in shady palace gardens. Poet Ibn Zaydun developed intricate forms of verse and was the forerunner of the French troubadours (from the Arabic *taraba* meaning "to be transported with joy and delight."). He is also known for his great love for Princess Wallada, the beautiful daughter of Cordoba's last caliph. Wallada inher-

In 827 the Islamic Aghlabid dynasty of Tunisia seized the island of Sicily from its Byzantine rulers and began a 250-year period of artistic and scientific enlightenment. The Muslims coexisted peacefully with the Christians. Crusaders returning from Palestine reconquered the island in the late 11th century. However, in the years between 1060 and 1091 Christian kings Roger I and II continued to champion Islamic art, architecture, and culture. Like Al-Andalus, Sicily was a bridge between the Arab and European worlds

Al-Idrisi was a Moroccan geographer, who, after traveling through Spain, North Africa, and Anatolia, eventually settled in Sicily. He was employed by Roger II to write a systematic geography of the world. He consulted the geographic works of the ancient Greeks and of the Arabs, then combined these with first-hand observations and the reports of "eye witnesses" who were sent to other lands to record what they saw. This information was used to write *The Book of Roger*. In the book Al-Idrisi divided the earth north of the equator into seven equal "climes," with each clime divided into ten sections. Using lines of longitude, he mapped each clime in a manner that was highly accurate for the time. The book included the distances between major cities and descriptions of the customs, people, products and climate of each section. The data was also used to engrave a silver planisphere, a disc shaped map of the world.

ited enough wealth to guarantee her independence. She refused to cover her face in public with a veil, a practice that had become prevalent among Muslim women, and she was very outspoken and free in her dealings with men. She hosted literary gatherings for both genders, attracting the finest poets and musicians. They sat around on cushions, improvising ballads and epics that were accompanied by the lute and zither. Wallada and Ibn Zaydun wrote many poems to each other, alluding to their passion quite openly. When a city judge accused Wallada of having no morals, she had one of her poems embroidered on her gown and wore it in the street for all to read. It included the following words:

*I deserve nothing less than glory*
*I hold my head high and go my way*
*I will give my cheek to my lover and my kisses to anyone I choose.*

The Christian kingdoms of northern Spain took advantage of the military rivalries of the party kings by backing one or the other with their own soldiers. In exchange for this service, they demanded great sums in annual tribute, making the Muslim rulers their vassals. In the late 11th century, the Christian kings became more aggressive, launching a movement to expel the Muslims from Spain. This is known as the Reconquest (*Reconquista*).

In 1085 King Alfonso VI, ruler of Leon and Castile, captured Toledo, which was then a flourishing center of learning. This turned out to be a boon for Western scholarship, as Christians from many parts of Europe soon flocked to study the great works preserved there — Greek philosophy and science in Arabic translation with commentaries from Baghdad's great thinkers as well as the books produced by generations of Muslim scientists. These writings were gradually translated from Arabic into Latin (the language of Christian scholarship). The translation of al-Khwarizmi's *Addition and Subtraction in Indian Arithmetic* introduced Arabic numerals to the West and gave us the word "algorithm," the Latin version of his name (Algorithmi), to define any system of arithmetic based on the use of decimals. Al-Khwarizmi's work now only survives in a translation made in Spain. As the achievements of Arabic scholarship spread throughout Europe, they inspired the great Western intellectual and scientific revival known as the Renaissance.

Popular Arabic stories of Muhammad's Night Journey were translated into Castilian and then into Latin as *The Book of Muhammad's Ladder.* The book attracted great attention in late medieval Europe, ultimately inspiring Dante to write his *Divine Comedy.*

## The Berbers Take Charge

After the fall of Toledo, the rulers of the other *taifas* worried that they would be next. Since they were too divided to decide upon a single leader among themselves, they turned for help to Muslims living in Morocco. The major power there was the Almoravid dynasty. Founded by a conservative groups of Berbers, this was a puritanical and intolerant sect that today would be called fundamentalist Islamist. The Almoravids controlled an empire with a capital at Marrakesh. It was to their leader, Yusuf ibn Tashfin, that the party kings appealed. In response, Yusuf led his army into al-Andalus in 1086 and defeated King Alfonso, putting a temporary stop to the Reconquest. But then he turned on the party kings themselves, exiling those he did not kill outright and taking over their kingdoms. (He was insensed that the Andalusians should have let themselves become vassals of the Christian rulers.) Al-Andalus was united once more, but under a rigid and inflexible regime.

The Almohads were another North African sect intent on purifying Islam. In 1147 they crossed into al-Andalus and drove out the Almoravids. The Almohads demanded that all Christians and Jews either convert to Islam or leave. (This, of course, ran counter to Islamic law, since forced conversion was forbidden in the *Quran*.) The new overlords chose as their Andalusian capital Seville, a city on the Guadalquivir River southwest of Cordoba. They built a central mosque with a spectacular 300-foot minaret, which was decorated with patterns of yellow brick and stone paneling. When Seville was later conquered by Christian armies, the mosque was destroyed to make room for a cathedral. The minaret was transformed into a bell tower, where 25 bells still ring out the hours of the day. A statue at the top of the tower acts as a weathervane. Its nickname, *Giraldillo*, gives the tower (shown on the opposite page) the name by which it is known today, the Giraldo.

Al-Mutamid, the king of Seville, was a talented poet. He often rode through the countryside with his friends, disguised as travelers. They would stop at scenic places, have a picnic, and make up poems, sometimes finishing one another's lines. One day, the king encountered an attractive young washerwoman along the Guadalquivar River. She interrupted and finished his poem with an inventive line of her own. He immediately fell in love with her, and they were soon married.

The king hoped to spend the rest of his life writing poems about his clever and beautiful wife. But after the fall of Toledo, he joined with other party kings in summoning the Almoravids. After the "liberators" took over Seville, Al-Mutamid and his family were sent into exile in Morocco's Atlas Mountains. His wife soon died, and his only consolation was the verses he had written about her.

Despite their rigidity in religious matters, several of the Almohad leaders took an interest in scholarship. One man who benefited from this was Ibn Rushd. He was born and educated in Cordoba, where his father and grandfather were prominent judges. At the age of 27 he was invited to the Almohad court. One evening, he entered into a discussion with Almohad leader, Abu Yaqub Yusuf, about the origin of the world and the nature of the mind. His descriptions of Aristotle's views on this topic so impressed Yusuf that he (Yusuf) commissioned him to write an entire set of commentaries on the Greek's writings. Ibn Rushd would spend the rest of his life on this project. His careful readings helped to eliminate the additions and false interpretations made by earlier scholars. Like Aristotle, Ibn Rushd believed that the mysteries of the universe could be understood through observation and experimentation. And like Ibn Sina, he saw no contradiction between religion and philosophy. For him, they were different ways of arriving at the truth. He devoted great energy to defending philosophy against the attacks of those who condemned it as contrary to Islam, particularly al-Ghazali (see page 79). In the long run, the views of al-Ghazali would prevail in *Dar al-Islam*. However, Ibn Rushd's commentaries, translated into Latin, helped lead Europeans to the rediscovery of the classical Greek thinkers.

Other important Andalusian scholars included Moses Maimonides, a Jewish physician and philosopher. He was born in Cordoba and fled after the invasion of the intolerant Almohads. He settled in Fez (in Morocco) in 1158, later traveling east to Palestine and then Cairo, where he became court physician to the Ayyubid ruler. His most famous work, *Guide of the Perplexed*, was an attempt to bring together elements of science, philosophy, and religion. Ibn Arabi was a mystic philosopher educated in Seville, who traveled widely before eventually settling in Damascus. He wrote a huge (37-volume) encyclopedia of Sufi beliefs and doctrines entitled *The Meccan Revelations*. He still found time to write *Bezels of Wisdom*, a description of the teachings of all 28 prophets from Adam to Muhammad.

Ibn Zuhr was the court physician of the Almoravids and, later, the Almohads. His book, *The Practical Manual of Treatments and Diet,* described such advanced surgical procedures for tracheotomy and the removal of cataracts and kidney stones. He studied human parasites, such as mites, and was among the first to test different medicines on animals before giving them to humans. Biologist Ibn Baytar spent a lifetime gathering plants in regions around the Mediterranean. His *Collection of Simple Medicines and Food* was an alphabetically arranged compendium of medicinal plants and vegetables, most of which were native to Spain and North Africa. He listed more than 2,000 simple (noncompound) drugs and gave information about the preparation of each drug and its administration, purpose, and dosage. It was the most complete treatise of applied botany produced in the Middle Ages

Al-Razi's multi-volume *Comprehensive Work on Medicine* was translated into Latin in 1279. It served as a standard medical textbook in the Western world until the 1700s, along with Ibn Sina's *Canon of Medicine.*

Early in the 13th century, the Christian kings of Aragon, Castile, and Leon defeated the Almohads at Las Navas de Tolosa, driving them back to North Africa. Ferdinand III of Castile captured Corboba in 1236 and made it a Christian city. Other cities later fell to the Christian armies — Valencia in 1238, Seville in 1248, Cadiz in 1262, and Murcia in 1266. The occupation of these centers of learning led to another great wave of translation of texts from Arabic to Latin, especially during the reign of enlightened patron Alfonso X, King of Castile and Leon. By the late 13th century most of the writings of the ancient Greeks along with their Arabic commentaries as well as the major works of Arab scientists and philosophers had become available to scholars throughout Europe.

## Granada

By the end of the 13th century, the Christian kingdoms controlled nearly all of Spain. Al-Andalus had shrunk to include only the city and province of Granada. The Nasirid dynasty had been established in Granada in 1238. When King Ferdinand of Aragon laid siege to the capital city, Nasirid ruler al-Ahmar offered to become his vassal, ensuring Granada two and a half more centuries of peace. But it also put al-Ahmar in a difficult position when Ferdinand called upon him to provide troops for the siege of Seville. He dutifully although reluctantly complied, and Seville was taken.

The kings of Granada patronized artists and scholars, attracting refugees from other formerly Muslim cities. Ibn al-Khatib, a high-ranking minister, wrote more than 50 works on travel, medicine, poetry, music, history, politics, and theology. He was the author of an outstanding history of Granada, which provides detailed descriptions of the final years of al-Andalus. Ibn Khaldun was a historian who lived for a while in Granada. His great innovation was to apply the principles of science and philosophy to the study of history. In 1375 he began his masterpiece, *An Introduction to History* (*Al-Maqaddima*). In his prologue (which became the most important part of his book), he explained that he approached history as a comprehensive study of the human experience, one that went beyond political events and considered the environmental, sociological, psychological and economic aspects as well. He was intrigued by the rise and fall of cultures and societies and concluded that history was cyclical. The cycle began when a strong community was formed and began to subjugate others. The dominant group absorbed the resources of the subject peoples, then developed a culture and a complex urban life. But as the ruling class became accustomed to a luxurious lifestyle, complacency set in. The rulers no longer took sufficient heed of their subjects, jealousy and infighting became common and the economy began to decline. Under these circumstances, the society became vulnerable to an invading group, and the whole cycle would begin again. Ibn Khaldun's historical method formed the basis of a new science of culture, known today as social science. His theory of the cyclical nature of history is accepted by most Western historians.

Granada's citadel was built on a rocky spur at the foot of the Sierra Nevada on the bank of the River Darro. It was known as the *Alhambra* ("Red Fortress") because of the reddish tint of its brick outer walls. Over the years it was gradually transformed into a royal compound of palaces and courtyards of extraordinary beauty. The walls and ceilings of the buildings were carved in intricate yet delicate patterns, like the one picture to the right. Interwoven stems, tendrils, leaves, and flowers (a style known as arabesque) and an interlacing pattern formed from little niches, bracketed out one above the other (honeycomb style) covered nearly

every surface. The stone appeared to have been magically transformed into lace. Thin columns and narrow arches enhanced the sense of airy fragility, while tall windows filled the rooms with light. The domed ceiling in one vast hall seemed to rotate slowly, an illusion caused by the interplay of light and shadow on its multifaceted carvings. Many of the courtyards had bubbling fountains and tranquil pools that reflected the sunlight. Graceful cypress trees offered the promise of shade, while rose gardens filled the air with sweet scents. Here was indeed an earthly version of Paradise.

Arabic calligraphy appeared on nearly every wall of the Alhambra. The words, "There is no victor but God," appeared again and again, forming a pattern of great aesthetic as well as religious appeal. The wall of one tower boasted, "Nothing can match this work." A twelve-sided marble fountain rested upon the backs of twelve lions in one courtyard (appropriately known today as the Courtyard of the Lions, see above). Around the rim of the basin were these lines: "Incomparable is this basin. God the exalted one desired that it should surpass everything in wonderful beauty." A garden wall was carved with the lines "I am a garden adorned with beauty. Gaze upon my loveliness and you will know this to be true." And the wall of a large hall was emblazoned with the words, "The stars would gladly descend from their zones of light and live [here] instead of in heaven."

After two centuries, Granada, the last of the great Muslim cities of al-Andalus, fell to the armies of Aragon and Castile (kingdoms now joined by the

In an arabesque design, the tendrils of a plant do not branch off from a single continuous stem as they do in nature, but grow unnaturally from one another. The design can be extended infinitely in any direction. The word "arabesque" means "in the Arab fashion" in French. It was coined in the 16th century when Renaissance artists incorporated Islamic designs in book ornament and decorative bookbindings.

marriage of Ferdinand of Aragon and Isabel of Castile). The city surrendered on January 2, 1492. According to legend, the deposed ruler, Boabdil, stopped on a small hillside just outside the city on his way to exile and gazed for the last time at the Alhambra. He wept at its beauty. The hillside is still identified with "the Moor's last sigh."

The Reconquest was now complete. Thousands of mosques throughout al-Andalus were converted into churches, and mountains of books written in Arabic were burned. (Unlike the scholars, the soldiers had no interest in preserving the "foreign" writings.) After the fall of Granada, the Muslims were told to choose between conversion to Christianity, emigration, or death, while all Jews were ordered to leave immediately. (In August 1492 Christopher Columbus set sail for the East Indies from one of Spain's smaller ports because the main port of Cadiz was packed with Jewish families leaving for new homes.) And yet, the Moorish legacy remained — its distinctive styles of architecture, innovations in farming and crafts technology, and rich heritage of scholarship contributed much to Westerm civilization.

*La Mezquita* remained relatively intact until the 16th century, when Holy Roman Emperor Charles V permitted the erection of a church in its very center. The minaret was encased within a belfry. When he visited the site, he regretted his decision, lamenting to the builders, "You have taken something unique and turned it into something mundane."

## Review Questions:

1.Under what circumstances did the first Muslims enter Spain?
2. What is the origin of the name "al-Andalus?"
3. What was the first government of al-Andalus?
4. What is most unique about *La Mezquita*?
5. Describe the court of al-Rahman II.
6. What was the function of *Madinat al-Zahra*?
7. What were some of the major crafts of 10th century Cordoba?
8. What was the *Convivencia* and how did it promote learning?
9. What caused the fall of the Cordoba Emirate?
10. What contributions did the "party kings" make to Moorish culture?
11. How did the Christian conquest of Toledo affect European civilization?
12. What is the Giraldo?
13. What was the major project of Ibn Rushd?
14. How did Granada manage to survive as a Muslim city after other parts of al-Andalus had been taken over by Christian armies?
15. What is arabesque?
16. What is unique about the decoration and style of the Alhambra?
17. What happened to the cities of al-Andalus after the fall of Granada?

## Questions for Discussion:

1. Compare and contrast the Umayyad dynasty of Damascus with the rejuvenated Umayyad regime in al-Andalus.
2.In the ninth century the caliph's library in Cordoba contained over 500,000 volumes. In later centuries, libraries in cities like Toledo and Seville were equally impressive. With the fall of Granada, countless volumes were destroyed, and with them the achievements of a great many Muslim scholars and scientists. How might the course of history have been changed if the Reconquest had not taken place? (Be specific.)
3.The Muslims entered Spain as conquerors, but they left it a richer place than it would otherwise have become. Discuss.

# Chapter 6 — CAIRO

Cairo, the capital of Egypt, has a population of 16 million people, making it the largest city in Africa and the Middle East. It is perched on both banks of the Nile River, just south of the point where the river leaves its desert valley and breaks into several branches to form a wide delta. One hundred miles north lies the Mediterranean Sea. Cairo is a city of wide boulevards lined with date palms, green parks (thanks to the magic of underground sprinkling systems), and tall government buildings. The oldest quarters of the city, however, have narrow, winding streets and crowded tenements interspersed with eye-catching historical structures.

Two thousand years ago, the Romans built a fortress near the present site of Cairo on the eastern side of the river. It was named Babylon (not to be confused with the ancient city in Mesopotamia). Roman Emperor Trajan reexcavated a canal dug by the pharaohs of ancient Egypt that linked the Red Sea with the Nile. This made Babylon a prosperous hub of commercial activity.

After the decline of Rome, Egypt was ruled by the Persians and then by the Byzantines. In the 7th century, it fell into the hands of the Muslims. Cairo was built as the capital of the Fatimid caliphate. In time, the city would become a major center of Islamic scholarship.

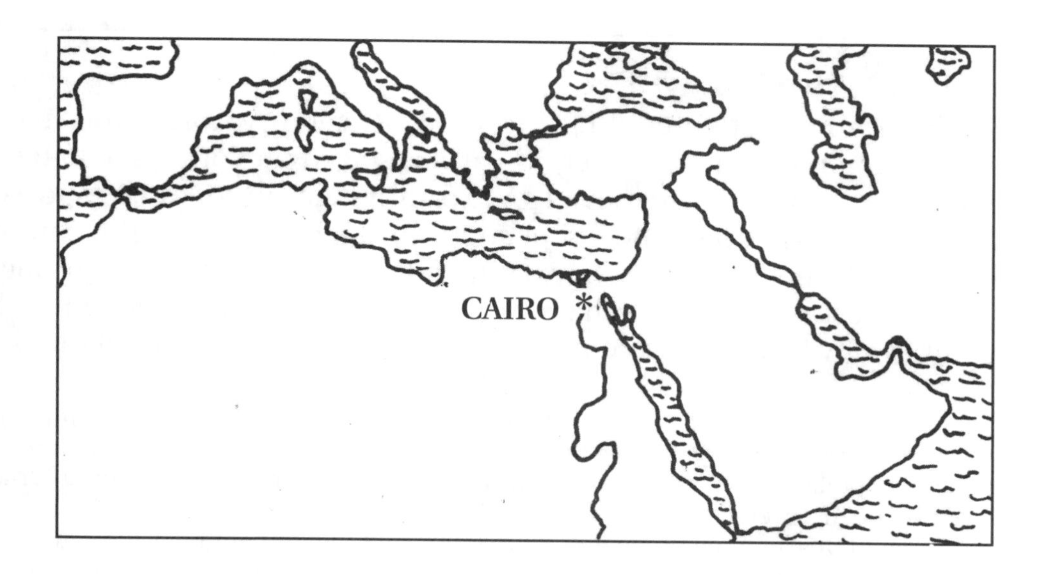

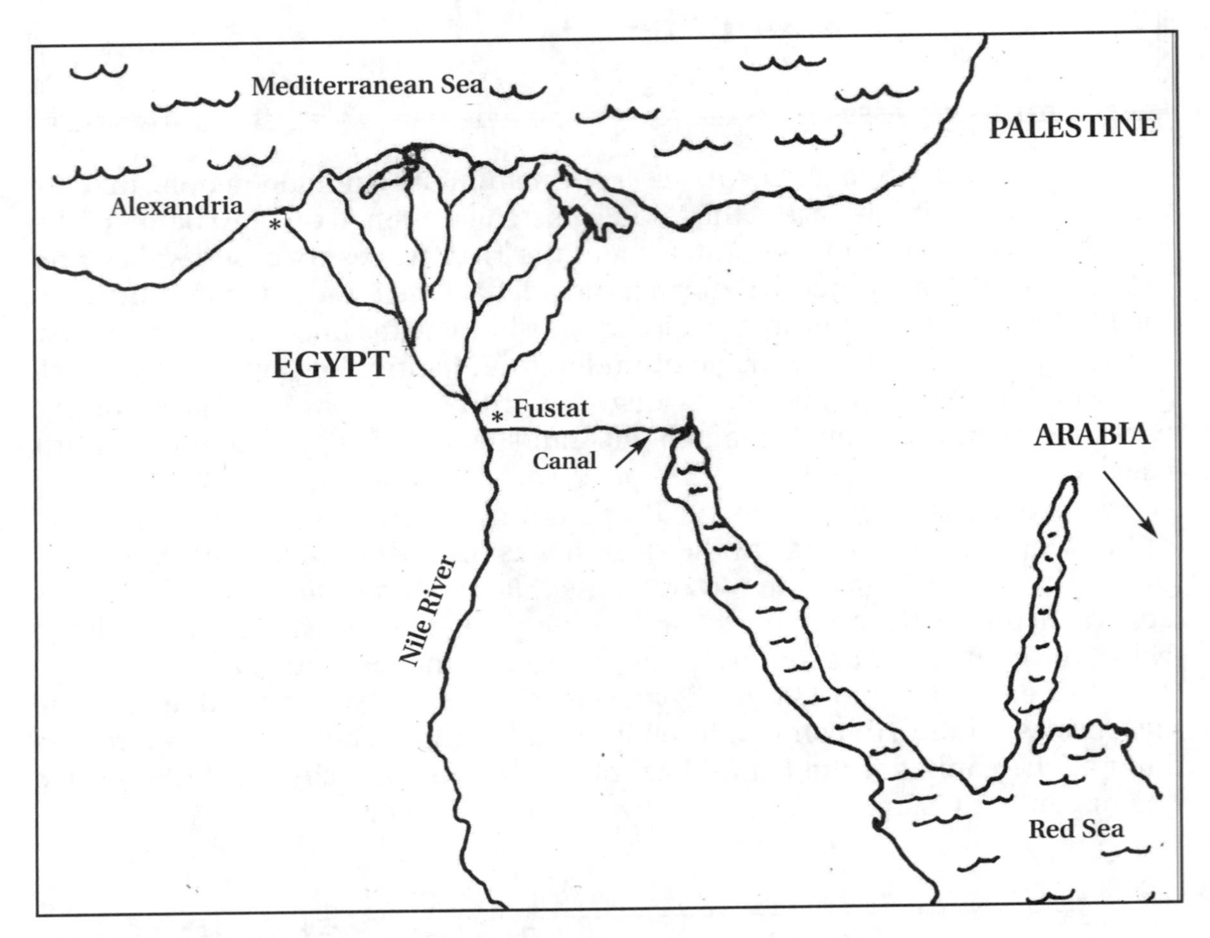


## The Muslims Arrive in Egypt

Muslim armies first entered Egypt in the 7th century during the rule of Umar. Arab commander Amr (AH mer) ibn al-Aas seized the fortress of Babylon from the Byzantines in 640, then moved on to capture Alexandria, a busy port on the Mediterranean. From there he swept south through the rest of the country and made it a Muslim province. Egypt's lucrative trading activities brought wealth to the treasury of the caliphate, while its rich farmlands provided the great quantities of wheat that were needed for the growing city populations in Arabia.

Amr intended to make Alexandria the capital of the new province, but

According to popular legend, Amr left his tent standing when he moved on to Alexandria. Upon his return, he discovered that a dove had built a nest among the tent's goat-hair hangings. He considered this a sacred omen and gave orders that the tent not be disturbed until the dove had raised her brood and departed. The tent was then taken down, and the first shovel of dirt for the new city was dug where it had stood.

Umar preferred a location more accessible to Medina. So the commander chose a site on the east bank of the river just north of Babylon. The new capital was called *Fustat* ("the Settlement of the Tent"), since it was built where Amr had set up his campsite before laying siege to Babylon. Following the Arab tradition of those early years, Fustat was divided into sections for each of the tribal units in the army. The top officers were housed in the center, and it was here that Amr built Africa's first mosque. Like Muhammad's mosque in Medina, its roof was supported by the trunks of palm trees. Amr excavated the old Roman canal, which had silted up since Roman times, and Fustat became an important commercial hub.

The Amr Mosque was rebuilt several times over the centuries, most recently in 1797. Little of the original remains.

Most Egyptians were Coptic Christians, a sect that differed with the Orthodox Church over the doctrine of the dual (human and divine) nature of Christ. (The Copts believed Christ was purely divine.) The Byzantines were staunch supporters of the Orthodox Church, which was based in Constantinople, and persecuted those who did not accept its views. This religious intolerance as well as an oppressive Byzantine tax burden made life so difficult for the Egyptian population that they welcomed the Arabs as liberators. Amr quickly set up a working government in Fustat, recruiting a staff of civil servants among the local people who had previously served the Byzantines. As in other Muslim provinces, Christians and Jews were free to practice their own religions but were expected to pay a poll tax (which was lower than the Byzantine taxes).

After the Umayyads came to power in 661, Egypt was governed by prefects sent from Damascus. Arabic became the official language and Islam was gradually adopted by many city dwellers. (Many converted to avoid the taxes.) When the Abbasids overthrew the Umayyads in 750, they built a new capital, al-Askar, in a suburb of Fustat. In time, the two cities would merge into one. The Abbasids increased taxes throughout their empire to fund their building projects. The burden became so great that the Egyptians rebelled, and al-Mamun himself had to travel to Fustat to restore the peace. By the middle of the 9th century, the Abbasid caliphs were having their own troubles at home (this is when they moved their capital to Samarra) and the oversight of Egypt grew rather lax.

## The Tulunids

In 868 Ahmad ibn Tulun was sent as deputy governor to Egypt. He was the ambitious son of a Turkish slave, who had been educated in Baghdad and risen to the role of commander of the household troops of the caliph. Once in Egypt, he organized an independent army and used the local treasury to pay its salaries. Then he declared Egypt an independent state, which he successfully defended against the Abbasid armies sent to unseat him. He established the Tulunid dynasty, which would rule Egypt for 37 years.

Tulun reduced the revenue Egypt sent the Abbasids to a limited tribute. But he was careful to maintain economic ties with Baghdad to protect his trading interests. He took advantage of the political unrest in Samarra by gradually extending his borders into Palestine and then Syria. Back in Egypt, he built a complex to house his family, ministers, and soldiers on a knoll of high ground east of Fustat. It was known as *Al-Qatai* ("the wards") because it was divided into districts, each housing a separate segment of the population. The palace ("Dome of the Air") stood on the highest part of the knoll, overlooking a large field where Tulun and his officers played polo. A new mosque featured a minaret inspired by the one in Samarra. It was three stories tall, each story having a different shape (from bottom to top, square, round, and octagonal), with a spiral staircase leading up to the balcony of the *muezzin*. (It is pictured to the left.)

Tulun's son and successor, Khumarawayh (koo mar uh WAY), spent most of his time and money embellishing his palace complex. He had a large hall decorated with sheets of gold bearing images of himself and his wives, a pond filled with glistening mercury, and the tropical trees and shrubs of an exotic garden lined with water pipes, which turned them into fountains. He also built a zoo with running water in every cage and a huge horse track, where races were held almost every day and night. After spending a huge amount of the treasury on his "home improvements," Khumarawayh dipped into it again for a lavish dowry for his daughter, who married Abbasid caliph al-Mu'tadid in 895. The year after the wedding, Egypt's spendthrift ruler was found strangled in his bed. Since few funds were left for his successor to pay his soldiers, the government foundered and lost control of the country. Syria was reclaimed by the Abassids in 905. The following year an Abbasid general reclaimed Egypt and put an end to Tulunid rule. He destroyed Tulun's palace and moved the capital back to Fustat. Egypt was again a province ruled, although not very effectively, by governors sent from Baghdad.

> Polo is probably the world's oldest equestrian sport. It is played by two teams of mounted players, who use mallets with long handles to drive a ball down a grass field between two goal posts. Polo originated in Central Asia over 2,000 years ago, probably among teams of Turkic tribesmen battling for possession of an inflated goat bladder. Polo spread gradually throughout Asia, into China, Japan, Tibet, India, Persia, and Egypt. In the early centuries of Islam the sport was frequently played with large numbers of horsemen and was considered training for cavalry officers.

## The Fatimids

The Fatimids were a political dynasty that would bring a distinctive new flavor to Egypt. They belonged to the Ismaili sect of Shi'ism. As we've learned, the Shi'ites believed that Ali was the rightful successor to Muhammad. They considered him the first *Imam*, the divinely inspired leader of the *umma*. Upon his death, the *Imamate* (position of *Imam*) had been passed on to his sons, Hasan and then Husayn, and afterwards to Husayn's direct descendants. Although they had no political power, the *Imams* were considered infallible intermediaries between God and mankind. The death of the sixth *Imam* (Ja'far) in 765 brought about a division among the Shi'ites. Ja'far had two sons — Ismail, the elder, and Musa, the younger. Although Ismail appeared to be next in line, his father disinherited him (allegedly for drinking wine) and appointed Musa as his heir. The majority of Shi'ites recognized Musa, but a minority believed that Ismail was the legitimate seventh *Imam*. When Ismail died before his father, his

The various sects within Shi'ism differ over the path of succession of the *Imamate*. They include the Fivers (who considered Zayd, son of the 4th *Imam* who died fighting the Umayyads in 740, the fifth and last *Imam*), the Seveners (Ismailis, tracing the line from Ali to Ismail, the seventh *Imam*), and the Twelvers (the largest sect). The Twelvers believed that ten *Imams* succeeded Ali, passing the *Imamate* down to their sons in hereditary succession. However, when the eleventh *Imam*, Hasan al-Askari, died, his son, Muhammed al-Mahdi, the twelfth *Imam*, hid himself and remained in hiding. This "hidden *Imam*" would continue to guide the religious men (*mujtahids*), who were chosen to preside over the Shi'ite community until Judgment Day, when he would return. (Today, the most learned of the *mujtahids* are called *ayatollahs*.) The Twelvers acknowledged the following listing of the rightful sucessors of Muhammad:

(1) Ali ibn Abu Talib
(2) Hasan bin Ali
(3) Husayn bin Ali
(4) Ali Zayn al-Abidin
(5) Muhammad al-Baqir
(6) Jafar as Sadiq
(7) Musa al-Kazim
(8) Ali ar Rida
(9) Muhammad at Taqi
(10) Ali al-Hadi
(11) Hasan al-Askari
(12) Muhammad al-Mahdi

followers, known as Ismailis, believed that his (Ismail's) son should be the next *Imam*. But the son mysteriously disappeared. The Ismailis then resolved to wait for *al-Mahdi* ("the Divinely Guided One") to reappear and guide the people.

The Ismaili community was divided into two levels — the lower level (the majority), who lived according to the revealed message of Muhammad, and the intellectual elite, an esoteric group whose religious beliefs combined elements of astrology and abstract philosophy. This sect had its roots in Khurasan and later spread to Yemen and then to North Africa. In the first decade of the 10th century, Ubaydallah, an Ismaili descendant of Muhammad, founded the Fatimid Dynasty in present-day Tunisia. (The dynasty was named after his ancestor Fatima, daughter of Muhammad and wife of Ali.) His dream was to overthrow the Abbasids and replace them with his own dynasty, correcting what he considered the grave error made when Ali was ousted from power. The Fatimids extended their territory by military means and through a vast missionary network of secret agents and clandestine cells. The armies of the fourth ruler, al-Muizz, extended Fatimid borders to Algeria and then continued westward. When a commander named Jawhar reached the Atlantic coast of Morocco, he sent al-Muizz a gift of ocean fish kept alive in salt water. Al-Andalus at that point was ruled by the Cordoba Caliphate, so the Fatimids turned east.

In 969 Jawhar led an army of 100,000 Berbers to Egypt and took over the city of Fustat. He immediately began construction of a new city, *al-Qahira*, on the site of his army camp. According to legend, he marked the perimeter of his city wall with wooden stakes. Ropes were strung between the stakes, and on to these were attached a number of bells. The plan was that when the astrologers determined the time was just right, the ropes would be tugged, ringing the bells as the signal to begin digging the trench for the wall. Hundreds of workmen were assembled and stood ready. Suddenly, a crow landed on the ropes and jangled the bells. The workmen took this as the signal and started digging. The astrologers, startled at first, quickly came up with an explanation. Noting that the planet Mars (in Arabic *al-Qahir*, "The Triumphant") was currently ascendent, they announced that this was a favorable omen and that the city should be named after the planet. The English version of *Al-Qahira* is Cairo, which is how we'll refer to it.

The city was square, each side measuring nearly a mile and facing one of the four cardinal directions. The top of the city wall was wide enough for two patrolling horsemen to ride side by side. Cairo was an exclusive royal complex of palaces for the Fatimid ruler and his court, his government officials, and his guard. No ordinary citizen could set foot inside the walls unless ordered to do so. Even ambassadors would be met outside and led through the proper gate. Jawhar laid the foundation for the al-Azhar mosque (named after *Fatima az-*

*Zahra,* "Fatima the Splendid") while the city walls were still being built. It was constructed of huge blocks of stone dating from the times of the pharaohs.

In November 972 al-Muizz set out for Egypt. His huge caravan of heavily laden donkeys and camels took six months to get there. He arrived in the month of Ramadan. When the period of fasting ended, he conducted prayers at al-Azhar and formally established Cairo as his new capital. The relocated Fatimid government was divided into three branches: bureaucratic, military, and religious. While the bureaucratic branch organized an efficient taxation system, the military branch focused upon ways to absorb Abbasid territories. As a first step, armies were sent into Palestine and southern Syria. The religious branch oversaw the large network of missionaries. Al-Aziz, successor to al-Muizz, created a formal school of theology within the mosque of al-Azhar to train future missionaries. He provided living expenses and housing for 35 scholars, who taught the doctrines of the Ismaili faith.

The oldest street in Cairo bears the name of al-Muizz .

Al-Hakim was one of the more enlightened Fatimid rulers. He invited astronomers, astrologers, mathematicians, and scholars to his court, and he expanded the royal library so that by 1000 CE it filled up 40 rooms. He established a center to teach astronomy and philosophy, which he called the Hall of Wisdom (after Baghdad's House of Wisdom). Astronomer Ali ibn Yunus worked in the observatory there for 17 years. He produced a book on astronomy which included detailed tables of the cycles of the moon and planets. He also provided data for determining Muslim, Coptic, Syrian, and Persian calendars, with tables to convert the dates between these calendars.

In the later years of his rule, al-Hakim grew mentally unstable. He abandoned the religious toleration of his predecessors and passed a series of laws against the Christians and Jews. He confiscated the possessions of the churches and monasteries. He banned wine among non-Muslims (a hardship for Christians, who used it during communion rites) and had all the grapevines cut down. He persecuted Christians in Palestine and destroyed the Church of the Holy Sepulcher in Jerusalem. (The church was later rebuilt by his successor.) His attacks extended beyond religion. He ordered all of the dogs in Cairo be killed because their barking annoyed him, he outlawed the playing of chess (a favorite game among the educated people), and he had all the honey (an Egyptian specialty) poured into the Nile. He forbad women to wear jewelry, to go to the public baths, or even to walk in the streets. In an effort to keep them indoors, he even banned the sale of women's shoes. Being a night owl himself, al-Hakim ordered all shops to close during the day and to stay open from dusk to dawn. He also oversaw a large number of executions for seemingly unimportant crimes, many involving his own aides. Perhaps his most offensive act was to proclaim himself the earthly incarnation of God. One night in February 1021, this eccentric man

The Druze are a small religious sect who still believe in the divinity of al-Hakim. They are still waiting for him to return to earth and usher in a great new age of Islam.

rode his gray donkey through the Muqattam hills east of Cairo and was never seen again. His clothes were found several days later stuffed in a well. Most Egyptians were relieved to hear of his demise.

Al-Haytham was a scholar from Basra, who was once summoned by al-Hakim to study ways to deal with the annual flooding of the Nile. Believing the flow of water could be regulated, he led an engineering team upstream to find a place to build a dam. But, as the story goes, when he saw all the marvelous temples built by the ancient Egyptians, he decided if the floods could be prevented, they would have known how to do it. So he abandoned his project. Fearing the wrath of al-Hakim, who was known to behead people who displeased him, he pretended to be mad. He was confined to his house, where he spent his time on scientific experiments. After al-Hakim's death in 1021, he reemerged in society and lived for the rest of his life in Cairo, teaching and writing books.

Al-Haytham's great work, *The Book of Optics,* proposed revolutionary views about vision. The early Greeks had believed that human sight resulted from the eyes sending out a ray of vision, encompassing an object, and bringing it back to the soul. Galen thought sight had something to do with a lens of the eye, and even theorized that a nerve connected the eye with the brain to make vision possible. Al-Haytham took Galen's concept as his starting point and began a series of experiments to test the way light travels through translucent substances (such as glass, water, and ice). He concluded that light is emitted by radiant sources, such as the sun, that it travels in straight lines, and that when it falls on objects it is reflected back to the eye, making sight possible. His book included a detailed anatomy of the eye and descriptions of the role played by the brain in interpreting images that are seen. (It also contained descriptions of simple experiments with pinhole cameras.) The book remained unknown until the 13th century, when a commentary was made upon it. Latin editions then became available, and his ideas laid the foundations for the revival of optics as

When a Muslim boy reached marriageable age (about 18), his mother chose a wife for him (a girl of about 12 or 13). The girl's father checked into the boy's financial position and decided whether the two families were compatible. Weddings were held on Friday. The bride arrived at the home of the groom and retired to the bridal chamber, but she sat there alone. The groom had already gone to the mosque, where the marriage ceremony took place without her being present!

When the groom returned home, he entered the bridal chamber. The bride removed her veil, and the couple saw each other for the first time. The groom gave his new wife a gift and then rejoined the men for a wedding feast. The bride had her own wedding feast in a separate room. Finally, her husband rejoined her.

a modern science by Roger Bacon.

The warriors of the Fatimid armies proved to be a nearly invincible force. By the 11th century the dynasty controlled two thirds of the Muslim world — a vast territory extending from Morocco to Syria and including Sicily, the Red Sea coast of Africa, the Hijaz, and Yemen. In 1056 a Fatimid general even succeeded in seizing Baghdad, although he was driven out the following year by the Seljuk Turks. The Fatimids enticed merchant vessels from the Indian Ocean to ports on the Red Sea, bypassing the Persian Gulf and further weakening the Abbasid economy. As their treasury filled with revenues from import taxes and tribute, several Fatimid rulers built lavish palaces and imposing mosques and mausoleums. The wealth of the court spurred the development of luxury items, such as ceramic and glass objects, carved wood and ivory, exquisite jewelry, and elaborately decorated manuscripts. An inventory of the treasures of a palace storehouse included 36,000 pieces of crystal, 22,000 amber figurines, a gold peacock studded with jewels, a model garden made entirely of silver, and a lifesize silver sailboat. But despite Cairo's prosperity, the propaganda campaign on behalf of Ismaili beliefs met with little success. The vision of the sect was too narrow and elitist to appeal to more than a small number of intellectuals. While the majority of the Egyptians became Muslims, they embraced Sunni rather than Shi'ite Islam.

The later Fatimid rulers were not particularly gifted, and, lacking a strong central authority, the empire gradually fell apart. The process began with the breaking away of Algeria and Tunisia, and in 1070 Syria and Palestine fell to the Seljuk Turks. The state was further weakened by in-fighting within the army between the Berbers and Turkish mercenary soldiers. Matters became desperate when the country was hit with a seven-year drought and a widespread plague. Ruler al-Mustansir had to send his family to Baghdad to ride out the storm. The drought ended in 1073, and in an attempt to restore order, al-Mustansir appealed to Badr al-Jamali, the governor of Damascus, to come to Cairo. Badr agreed to come, but he insisted upon bringing along his Syrian soldiers. Once in Egypt, the soldiers took over the local army and Badr confined al-Mustansir to the royal palace, where, like the Abbasid caliph, he became a powerless figurehead. Badr assumed the roles of commander of the army, director of missionaries, and vizier, turning Egypt into a tight military regime.

Badr and al-Mustansir died in the same year, 1094. The usurper had profited greatly, leaving his family a huge legacy including six million gold *dinars*, thousands of satin robes, 250 bags of silver *dirhams*, 30 camel loads of golden boxes, and 100 jeweled turbans. He was succeeded by his sons, and then by a series of Syrian generals who had no interest whatsoever in Ismaili beliefs. The Fatimid regime was on its last legs.

## Saladin

In the late 12th century, the Crusaders were planning to wrest Egypt from the hands of the faltering Fatimids. Seljuk emir Nur al-Din (ruling from Damascus) sent an army to Egypt to prevent them from doing so. The army was led by general Shirkuh and his nephew, Salah al-Din, better known in the West as Saladin (Sah lah DEEN). In 1168 Shirkuh took over as governor of Egypt. When he died the following year, power passed to his nephew.

Saladin abolished the Fatimid caliphate and returned Egypt to the fold of Sunni Islam. He ordered the reading of the name of al-Mustadi, the puppet Abbasid caliph in Baghdad, in the Friday prayers and had his face depicted on the local coinage. He reclaimed Egypt's lost territories in North Africa. When Nur al-Din died in 1174, Saladin took advantage of the disruption in Damascus and named himself sultan of the independent state of Egypt, founding the Ayyubid dynasty.

When Saladin first assumed power, the Fatimid royal household remained isolated in its palaces in Cairo. But after the young caliph died a few days later (of natural causes), Saladin sent his family and their retinue into exile. Then he opened the gates of Cairo and allowed Egyptian citizens to enter and eventually settle within the city walls. After two hundred years, the city was no longer an exclusive royal enclosure. Saladin fortified a large domed pavilion standing on high ground to guard the city (his citadel still stands today) and extended the city walls to encompass both Cairo and Fustat. He introduced the *madrasa* into Egypt, founding five schools in Cairo alone, and he transformed the Ismaili seminary at Al-Azhar into a major center of Sunni theology.

In 1174 Saladin extended his authority to Syria. Eight years later, he turned over the reins of government to his brother, al-Adil, and led an army north to consolidate his power. He would never return to Egypt. In 1187 he defeated a Crusader army at the Battle of Hattin and proceeded to recapture Jerusalem. Muslim pilgrims could once again visit the Dome of the Rock and pray at al-Aqsa. Unlike the violent Christian conquest of the city the previous century, the Muslim occupation was relatively peaceful. Saladin spared the civilians and ordered churches and shrines untouched. He took over Saint John's Hospital, built earlier by the Crusaders, renamed it Al-Salahani Hospital, and

> The Crusaders were greatly impressed by many aspects of Muslim culture they encountered in the Holy Land. They returned home with spices that would make European cuisine much more palatable as well as carpets and rugs to decorate the walls and floors of wealthy estates. Their fascination with the *hammams* led to the introduction of soap and weekly bathing, a great hygienic improvement in the medieval towns and castles of Europe.

had it expanded. Saladin's capture of Jerusalem launched the Third Crusade. For the next ten years, Muslims fought against Christian warriors until the Crusaders occupied only a narrow coastal strip. When Saladin died in Damascus in 1193, his empire stretched from Syria to the central coast of North Africa. Much of this territory was soon divided into several small sultanates controlled by members of his family. Egypt, however, remained a strongly united state, the chief Muslim power in eastern Mediterranean basin.

For Muslim historians, the Crusades were a minor series of skirmishes. They did, however, write at length about Saladin, who was revered for bringing Egypt back into the Sunni fold and returning Jerusalem to *Dar al-Islam*. Saladin even won the respect of the Crusaders, not only for his courage and military prowess, but also for his magnanimous spirit. According to legend, when English King Richard the Lion-hearted was wounded, Saladin offered the services of his own physician and ordered some of his soldiers to carry ice down from the mountains to comfort him. And when Richard lost his horse, Saladin sent him two replacements. Saladin's name became a byword in medieval Europe for chivalry — a concept that can be traced back to the Bedouin virtue of *muru'ah* ("manliness"), which embraced courage, loyalty, and generosity.

## The Mamluks

When Saladin first set out for Palestine and Syria, he had filled the ranks of his army with Mamluks, slaves of Turkish origin (from Central Asia) who had converted to Islam and been trained to fight. (*Mamluk* means "possessed by one's master.") The new soldiers were highly disciplined and proved to be formidable warriors. Those who rose through the ranks could win their freedom, although they still owed allegiance to their former masters. After their return to Cairo after the death of Saladin, the Mamluks comprised two major groups — the *Bahri* and the *Burji* — named for the location of their garrisons. The *Bahri* ("River") Mamluks were stationed on Roda Island in the Nile River, while the *Burji* ("Tower") Mamluks resided in the Citadel.

Shajaret-al-Durr was a Turkish slave who became the wife of al-Saleh, the last Ayyubid ruler. When he died in 1249 with no strong successor, she took his place. This was the first time in Islamic history that a woman became a nation-

> Mamluk officers served as emirs of the various provinces of the empire. They were given endowments of land consisting of villages or fractions of villages, whose revenues paid for their upkeep and that of their men. Many an ambitious emir sought to become sultan, usually through intrigue and violence. Once in power, a sultan had to worry about being overthrown, or worse. Of the 53 sultans who ruled, only 10 died in office of natural causes — 19 were assassinated, murdered or executed, and many died in battle.

al leader. She ruled single-handedly for 80 days but was then pressured into marrying a Mamluk chief officer, Aybek. Even then, she continued to run the country from behind the throne. By 1257 Aybek had tired of taking orders from Shajaret and took a second wife. When Shajaret found out about this, she arranged to have her husband killed. Shortly afterwards, she, too, was murdered — by Mamluks. This episode was a forerunner of the violence that would characterize the next 267 years in Egypt.

Several Mamluk officers vied for power after the death of Shajaret, but the internal disorder didn't prevent the government officials from keeping an eye on the international scene. In 1260, two years after he had sacked Baghdad, Mongol leader Hulagu and his warriors charged into Syria and Palestine. The Mamluks were alerted to the imminent danger by a chain of signal fires stretching all the way from Mesopotamia to Egypt. Baybars, commanding officer of the Mamluk army, met the Mongols at Ayn Jalut ("The Well of Goliath") in northern Palestine, dealing them their very first defeat and stopping them in their tracks. (The Mongols would eventually settle down and convert to Islam. In later years, Mongol rulers actually became among the greatest of art patrons.)

> Baybars is one of the few Muslim rulers to be the subject of an epic poem (*Sirat Baybars*).

Soon after his victory, Baybars became Sultan of Egypt, establishing a dynasty of *Bahri* Mamluks. He brought the son of the last Abbasid caliph to Cairo, an act intended to add legitimacy and prestige to his position as a Muslim ruler. The prince and his successors would serve the Mamluks as "shadow caliphs," their only real duty being to supervise religious endowments. Baybars' government was divided into civil and military administrations, both controlled by Mamluk officers. Local Egyptians continued to staff the civil offices.

> Mamluks also ruled the Sultanate of Delhi in India in the 13th century.

Like Saladin, Baybars united Syria and Egypt into a single state, this time more permanently. He rebuilt all the Syrian fortresses that had been destroyed by the Mongols and commissioned new arsenals and warships, with a fleet based in Alexandria. When he died in 1277, he was buried in a mausoleum in Damascus. (Like many Mamluk rulers, he died an unnatural death — in his case, from poison.) Baybar's successors drove the last Crusaders from Syria and extended the Mamluk empire to Anatolia.

> Muslim women of Cairo's middle class often became professional weavers. Since they could not trade in the marketplace, they hired middlemen to sell their cloth. Others became midwives. Many upper class women bought and sold property, invested in trade, endowed the arts, commissioned the building of new mosques, and even studied with renowned scholars.

Al-Azhar

Under the Mamluks, Cairo became the political, economic, and cultural center of Islam. It was one of the largest and most cosmopolitan cities of the medieval world. As the population soared, space became so tight that new buildings were as tall as six stories, many with rooftop gardens. New mosque complexes sprang up throughout the various quarters of the city. Water was brought in by aqueducts and the paved streets were covered to protect the citizens from the hot desert sun. The Nile was lined with kiosks and cafes, where patrons sipped cool water flavored with rose petals and nibbled on figs, dates, and pistachios. (A favorite dish was *harisa,* a kind of hamburger made of ground lamb and wheat fried in fat.) Ibn Battuta, a 14th century Moroccan explorer who traveled widely (logging 73,000 miles in 30 years), was impressed by Cairo's "peerless in beauty and splendor," calling it "the crossroads of travelers."

Al-Azhar grew as a major seat of learning, drawing scholars from many distant parts of the Islamic world for lectures, debates, and research. (Scholars fleeing from the Reconquest in Spain found an intellectual haven there.) Apart from religious studies, courses were taught on philosophy, literature, chemistry, astronomy, medicine, mathematics, geography, and history. Al-Damiri was a zoologist who gave lectures at al-Azhar. His encyclopedic work, *A Zoological Lexicon,* described in alphabetical order the 931 animals mentioned in the *Quran* and *sunna* as well as in Arabic poetry and proverbs. It proposed a theory of survival of those animal species best adapted to their environment, predating by over 400 years English naturalist Charles Darwin, who independently worked out a similar theory. (So had al-Jahiz. See page 64.)

The Mamluk sultans loved books and oversaw the writing of huge chronicles, bibliographical dictionaries, and encyclopedias. Cairo competed with Damascus in the production of the most beautiful copies of the *Quran* and the most lavishly illustrated secular works. There were also more modest examples of the written word among the common people. The Banu Sasan were a group of ingenious street people who mass-produced strips of paper printed with verses of the *Quran* and sold them as amulets. This involved inscribing the verses on small clay tablets, baking the tablets to harden them, and then pouring molten tin across the parts inscribed with the words. When the tin hardened, it formed a plate with raised letters in reverse. By inking a plate and pressing it against a strip of paper, they could print a copy of the words. The printed strips were rolled up and placed in clay holders that were worn around the neck on a cord. They were believed to bring the wearer good luck. This is the only known example of printing in the Islamic world before the 18th century.

Like every major Muslim city, Cairo had excellent hospitals. Some specialized in particular diseases, including psychological ones. (One dealt only with insomnia.) The largest hospital was the Mansuri, built by Sultan Qala'un. It treated over 4,000 patients every day. Before becoming sultan, Qala'un had fought the Crusaders. He was wounded and taken to the renowned An-Nuri Hospital in Damascus. After he recovered, he vowed that one day, if he became sultan, he would build a hospital even greater than An-Nuri in Cairo. Once he came to power, the hospital was his highest priority. The Mansuri was built in less than a year.

Ibn al-Nafis was chief of physicians at the Mansuri. He wrote detailed commentaries on the medical knowledge available up to his time, but his greatest contribution to medicine was the discovery of the blood's circulatory system. Galen had written that blood was manufactured in the liver as needed by the body and that it flowed back and forth between the left and right sides (ventricles) of the heart through a hole between them. Al-Nafis contradicted this theory, explaining that the right side of the heart pumped blood to the lungs where it was purified and then returned to the left side of the heart, which pumped it out through the arteries to the rest of the body. It then passed through the veins and returned to the right side of the heart, and the process started over. A book about his discovery was translated into Latin in the 16th century, and a century later English physician William Harvey would actually demonstrate the circulation of blood in animals in a laboratory.

The Mamluks are known for many the huge mausoleums they built in Cairo. These were shaped as squares or polygons covered with domes that were richly decorated with carved masonry. The magnificent Mosque of al-Nasir

> Al-Nafis did not figure out how the blood got from the arteries to the veins. That was left to his contemporary, Ibn al-Quff, a surgeon in Damascus. He described how tiny capillaries allowed the blood to flow from the arteries to the veins. He also discovered that cardial valves in the veins and heart chambers open in only one direction, keeping the blood flowing the same way throughout the entire circulatory system.

Mamluk craftsmen produced beautiful gilded mosque lamps like the one above. These lamps were suspended on chains from the roof beams of prayer halls. Massed arrays of the lamps created spectacular effects in the mosques as the lights of their flames were reflected from one another. An association is made between God and just such a lamp in this verse from the *Quran*:

*God is the Light of the heavens and the earth;*
*The likeness of His light is as a niche*
*Wherein is a lamp*
*the flame within a glass,*
*the glass as it were a glittering star*
*lit with the oil of the Blessed Tree,*
*neither of the East nor of the West,*
*whose oil appears to light up even though fire touches it not --*
*Light upon Light!*

*Quran* 24: 35

Hasan cost 20 million *dirhams*, making it the most expensive monument ever built in the city. At the time, there was public opposition to the construction of such a grandiose monument, and when one of its minarets collapsed in 1361 killing 300 people, the tragedy was taken by some as God's judgment on the sultan's extravagance.

In the 14th century Sultan al-Malik was visited by Mansa Musa, the Muslim ruler of the West African kingdom of Mali that had become rich from the salt trade and the mining of gold. Mansa Musa set out on a pilgrimage to Mecca in 1324, stopping in Cairo on the way. His huge caravan included a personal retinue of 12,000 slaves, all clad in beautiful silk brocade. Each of his 80 camels carried 300 pounds of gold. Once in Cairo, the king impressed the local people with his own splendid attire and his noble bearing. He spent his gold so lavishly (that which he didn't give away outright) that he flooded the market, causing a decline in the value of gold in Egypt for a dozen years. When he returned to Mali, Mansa Musa was accompanied by a number of Egyptian architects and scholars. In time, the West African city of Timbuktu would become an important center of Islamic scholarship.

The Black Death, a plague that originated in the steppes of Central Asia, reached Egypt in the autumn of 1347. Nearly half the population of Cairo died of the disease.

The *Bahri* Mamluks ruled for a little over a century. Most of the sultans had short reigns that ended in violence. Making matters worse, the officers were constantly divided into quarreling factions, and the *Bahris* and *Burjis* were continually at odds. In 1382, the rule of the *Bahris* ended with the election of a *Burji* sultan, Barquq. The *Burjis* ruled Egypt for the next 135 years. Their reign proved even bloodier and more unstable than that of the *Bahris*.

Ibn Khaldun, the Tunisian historian (see page 98), traveled to Cairo in 1382. He was invited to deliver a series of lectures to an audience of scholars and court officials at al-Azhar. Much impressed by Ibn Khaldun's learning and elo-

Despite devastating most of the cities he conquered, Tamerlane built a capital, Samarkand, that was one of the most beautiful cities in the world. After each campaign, he rounded up the local architects and artisans and marched them, with their native materials and treasures, to his capital. In a remarkably short space of time, he had a city of ornate palaces, graceful formal gardens, bustling bazaars, madrasas, mausoleums, and imposing blue-tiled mosques. The Bibi Khanum mosque, completed in 1404, was the largest and most beautiful mosque in central Asia. Its turquoise dome rested on an earth-toned drum faced with glazed mosaics that spelled out verses from the *Quran*. Just outside the city lay a ring of workers villages, which Tamerlane named after great cities had had conquered, including Baghdad, Damascus, Shiraz, and Delhi.

quence, Sultan Barquq appointed him to teach jurisprudence at a major *madrasa*. Years later, the aging historian had an encounter with an infamous conqueror that might have changed the destiny of Cairo. The conqueror was Tamerlane, a Turkish warlord from Mongolia. He was a Muslim, but his approach to religion had little in common with the piety of the *Sufis* and the *ulama*. Claiming hereditary ties to his hero, Genghis Khan, he had formed a coalition of Mongol and Turkish nomads and set out to conquer the world. His forces swept through Central Asia and by 1387 had subjugated the Iranian highlands and the plains of Mesopotamia, slaughtering countless thousands and then building pyramids with their skulls. In 1398 Tamerlane descended upon India, where he massacred thousands of Hindus and devastated Delhi. He then moved on to Syria, where he destroyed the city of Aleppo and stood poised to take Damascus. It seemed like Egypt would be next.

This is when Ibn Khaldun, now 70, accompanied Sultan Faraj on a campaign to defend Damascus. After setting off, Faraj learned of a threatened coup and returned to Cairo. The historian continued on. When he reached the outskirts of Damascus, he was led to Tamerlane's camp and into his presence. With the help of interpreters, the two got on amazingly well. The aged scholar remained in the camp for more than a month, during which time he and Tamerlane discussed many issues. They might even have played chess, at which the warlord was a known master. After playing a role in the surrender of Damascus, Ibn Khaldun departed for Cairo. Once he was out of sight, Tamerlane allowed his troops to sack Damascus, burning the Great Mosque of the Umayyads. Then he led his army north into Anatolia rather than continuing south. We'll never know whether or not Ibn Khaldun had saved Cairo, but it's likely that he did.

Egypt continued to flourish for another century as a center of trade, despite the constant fighting among the Mamluk ruling class. In 1498 Portuguese navigator Vasco da Gama landed in India by sailing around the Cape of Good Hope of Africa and then returned to Lisbon with a cargo of spices. By opening a new sea route from Europe to the East, bypassing Egypt, he greatly weakened the Egyptian economy. The Mamluks would continue their rule of the country, however, until they encountered a force much stronger than themselves — the mighty Ottomans. The next and final chapter is devoted to them.

## Review Questions:

1. What were the advantages of Fustat's location?
2. What is a Coptic Christian?
3. What were some of Tulun's accomplishments?
4. Who were the Ismailis?
5. What was the goal of the Fatimids?
6. What was the original function of Cairo?
7. Describe the "two sides" of al-Hakim.
8. What were some of the weaknesses of the Fatimid regime?
9. What contributions did Saladin make to Egypt?
10. Compare the Christian conquest of Jerusalem with that of Saladin.
11. Who were the Mamluks?
12. What was the importance of al-Azhar?
13. What was al-Nafis' main contribution to medicine?
14. Why did Ibn Khaldun travel to Syria?
15. What effect did Vasco da Gama's voyage have on Cairo?

## Questions for Discussion:

1. Despite its political fragmentation, Islam maintained a great degree of cultural unity throughout the medieval era. A Muslim from Spain visiting Cairo, Baghdad, or Damascus — or even more distant cities such as Bukhara — would have felt quite at home. What aspects of daily living did not vary from one place to another within Dar al-Islam?
2. Why were the Europeans so taken with Saladin? What explains his becoming a legend in their eyes? In what major ways did Muslim conquerors differ from Europeans?
3. In what ways did Islam contribute to Western culture during the Crusades?
4. What are some of the major weaknesses of a government run by a military aristocracy? What are some of the advantages?
5. Compare and contrast the regime of the Umayyads (a military aristocracy) with that of the Mamluks.

# Chapter 7 — ISTANBUL

Istanbul, the capital of Turkey, lies on both sides of the Bosporus Strait, a narrow channel of water separating Europe and Asia. In ancient times, the Greek settlement of Byzantium stood here on the European shore. It grew rich through its control of the shipping lanes linking the Mediterranean and the Black Sea. Byzantium became the capital of the eastern half of the Roman Empire in the 4th century. Emperor Constantine I renamed it Constantinople ("city of Constantine") and expanded it until it covered seven hills, like Rome. Under Constantine, Christianity replaced paganism throughout the empire. (It was Constantine who built the Church of the Holy Sepulcher in Jerusalem.)

When the western part of the Roman Empire fell in the 5th century, the eastern half, known as the Byzantine Empire, continued to prosper. Latin, the language of ancient Rome, was gradually replaced by Greek. Constantinople became one of the most beautiful and sophisticated cities in the world. In the 6th century Emperor Justinian built a magnificent church — the Hagia Sophia (HIGH yuh so FEE yuh, Greek for "Holy Wisdom."). At that time, the Byzantine Empire nearly encircled the Mediterranean, but over the centuries its territory was gradually whittled away through warfare.

The long conflict between Muslims and Byzantines finally ended when Constantinople fell into the hands of the Ottomans in the 15th century. Renamed Istanbul, it would enter the modern age as the glittering center of a new Islamic empire, one that extended well into Europe as well as Asia and Africa.

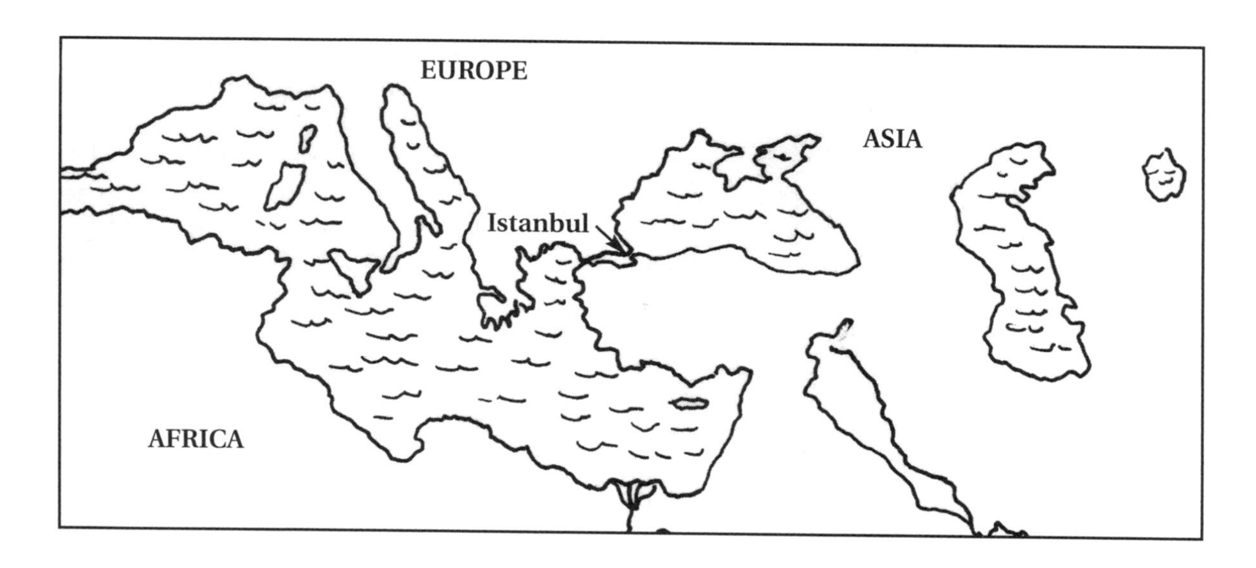

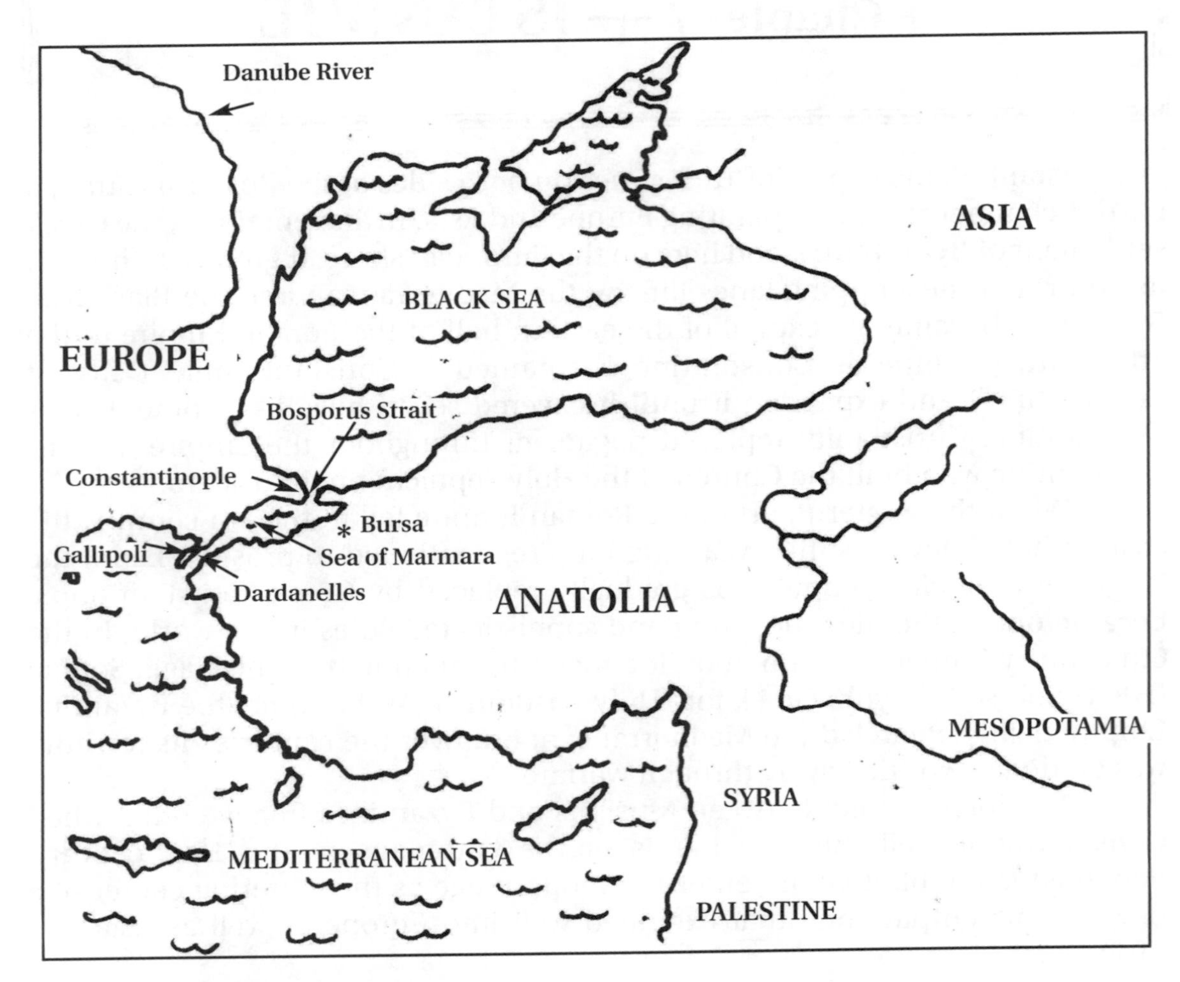


## The Rise of the Ottomans

Around the 13th century, some of the nomadic Turkic tribes that had settled in Anatolia began to form small principalities. In 1281 a tribesman named Osman (Turkish for Uthman) defeated several of the local princes and created a kingdom, founding a dynasty known as the Osmanli (Ottoman in English). Osman's son and successor, Orkhan, took the title of sultan. He conquered the Byzantine city of Bursa (in western Anatolia) and made it his capital. Orkhan established diplomatic relations with the Byzantine emperor and even married one of his daughters. But this did not prevent him from crossing into Europe and occupying a long strip of land along the coast of the Sea of Marmara from the peninsula of Gallipoli to within a few miles of Constantinople.

Orkhan's successor, Murad I, conquered the city of Adrianople, just west of Constantinople, and made it his European base for further expansion into the Balkans (Greece and the region to its north). By 1372 he had seized the greater part of what remained of the Byzantine empire and reduced the emperor to a dependent ally. Constantinople was nearly surrounded. Murad created an elite corps of infantry soldiers known as the Janissaries. ("Janissary" comes from the Turkish *Yeni Ceri* meaning "new soldiers.") The corps was made up of young Christian prisoners of war who converted to Islam and were trained in the military arts. Like the Mamluks, the Janissaries were slaves of the sultan, but unlike the Mamluks, they could not win their freedom. At first, the corps numbered only about a thousand men, but in time their numbers would increase dramatically.

Murad's son and successor, Bayezid, was so determined that his rule not be challenged by any family member that he initiated a grisly new tradition — imperial fratricide — by ordering the strangulation of his younger brother, Yakub. From then on, the first act of a newly crowned sultan would be to execute all his brothers and nephews. Bayezid became known as "the Thunderbolt" because of his speedy campaigns. After seizing any remaining principalities in Anatolia, he marched into Europe and crossed the Danube River into Hungary. In less than ten years he doubled the size of the Ottoman Empire, which now occupied about equal parts of Europe and Asia. Bayezid besieged Constantinople, intending to make the city his capital. But his plans for the future were foiled and the Ottoman Empire was nearly snuffed out by one man — Tamerlane. We met him in the last chapter. After sacking Damascus, the infamous warlord had moved into Anatolia. In 1402 his army defeated the Ottoman forces, capturing Bayezid himself. (The sultan died in captivity.) Tamerlane restored the Anatolian principalities and then left for Samarkand, never to return.

The next two sultans, Mehmed I (MEM et, Turkish for Muhammad) and Murad II, pieced the empire back together again and set the government back on course. Murad had an appreciation for Western and Eastern scholarship, and he saw to it that his son, the future Mehmed II, was well educated in European and Islamic history, classical philosophy, science, and literature.

## The Conquest of Constantinople

When Mehmed II came to the throne in 1451 at the age of 19, his eyes were fixed upon Constantinople, the prize that had eluded his forebears for so long. The city sat high on a promontory above the Bosporus, where the waters of the Black Sea mingled with those of the Sea of Marmara and of a small inlet known as the Golden Horn. This lofty location as well as 14 miles of heavily fortified walls (100 feet high and 30 feet thick) had enabled the city to withstand centuries of attack. But the challenge of breaking into such an impregnable stronghold only whetted the appetite of the ambitious young sultan. He assembled an army of over 100,000 men, including 10,000 Janissaries and a large artillery corps equipped with catapults, battering rams, and other siege equipment. In March of 1451 he set out from his naval base at Gallipoli with a fleet of 125 warships. He sailed up the Dardanelles and across the Sea of Marmara, landing on the outskirts of Constantinople. There he constructed a fortress, which gave him command of the Bosporus strait and served as a base for an assault upon the city.

Mehmed hired a Hungarian engineer named Urban to build a cannon for the fortress tower. (Gunpowder had recently been introduced into western Asia and Europe by the Mongols.) The cannon was made in record time, and Mehmed was so impressed by its performance that he ordered another twice its size, one that might breach the walls of Constantinople. This second cannon, named "Urban" after its designer, required 15 pairs of oxen to haul it from the foundry where it was cast. Its barrel was nearly 27 feet long, and it shot a 1200-pound cannonball that traveled a mile before burying itself in six feet of earth. The explosion could be heard for ten miles. Mehmed also ordered a number of smaller cannons to back up his new superweapon.

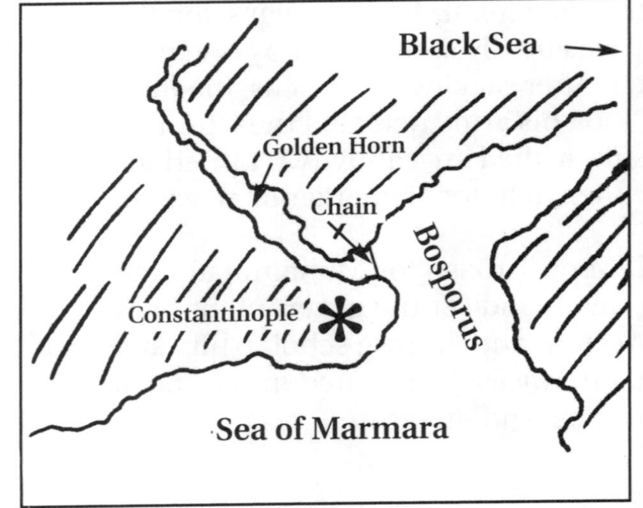


The population of Constantinople had shrunk since the days of Byzantine glory, numbering less than 50,000, and the city was defended by only about 7,000 troops. The emperor, Constantine XI, was the 80th Byzantine ruler since his namesake, the city's founder Constantine I. He now prepared for the onslaught, ordering the city gates closed and the bridges across the outer moat demolished. A chain of wooden floats was placed across the entrance to the Golden Horn to protect the northern seawall.

Mehmet arrived at the western wall of the city on April 2,1453. Before laying a siege, he sent messengers to Constantine with a flag of truce offering freedom of life and property to all inhabitants in return for his voluntary surrender. When the emperor refused the offer, the bombardment of cannons and catapults began. It would continue without a break for six weeks. Urban proved a disappointment. It could not penetrate the thick walls, and it required so much time to reload that the Byzantines were able to repair most of the damage after each shot, using planks of wood, piles of rocks, and barrels of earth. Eventually, the massive cannon collapsed under its own recoil.

The Ottoman engineers were more successful in dealing with the chain blocking the Golden Horn. They laid a track of greased timbers along the northern shore of the inlet. Seventy-two warships were hoisted by pulleys out of the water, placed on metal-wheeled cradles, and drawn along the track by teams of oxen. The sails were hoisted, flags were flown, and from the city it appeared that the fleet was actually sailing across the distant landscape. When they reached a point behind the chain, the ships were slid off the cradles and into the water. They were then lined up side by side to form a bridge, allowing infantry to cross the Golden Horn from the north. Constantinople was now completely surrounded.

Mehmed sent the emperor a message demanding unconditional surrender. When this was refused, he prepared for a major offensive. On May 27 his soldiers worked all through the night by the light of torches filling in the moat surrounding the city walls. The next day they rested, and an eerie silence engulfed the enemy campsite. That evening, the emperor ordered all defenders who were not on duty along the walls to congregate in the Hagia Sophia to pray for the city's salvation. He appeared shortly before midnight, prostrated himself before the high altar and took Communion. Then he returned to his palace, said goodbye to the members of his household, and rode to his command post.

At two o'clock in the morning watchmen on the towers heard a loud commotion and ordered the ringing of all the church bells of the city to alert the populace. Defenders ran to their posts, women hurrying after them to help mend any gaps made in the walls, while old people and children crowded into the churches. Mehmed launched his attack on the northwestern walls, which were more recently built than the other sections and were not as thick. The first wave of the Ottoman infantry soon made its way up the scaling ladders. These were the weaker soldiers, sent out simply to weary the defenders, and they were easily forced back. After two hours, a second wave of better fighters took over. The cannons blasted away and finally made a breach in the wall, but any soldiers entering through it were driven back by showers of stones and arrows. Then the Janissaries charged, spurred on by the sounds of trumpets and cymbals. Nothing could keep them back, and they were soon engaged in hand-to-hand combat with the Byzantine soldiers in the streets of the city. Someone discovered a gate that had been left unlocked, and the rest of the Ottoman army rushed

Historians consider the capture of Constantinople an important turning point in western civilization. Greek scholars fleeing the Ottoman advance took their ancient texts to Europe, rekindling the flame of classical learning that had started in al-Andalus and led to the Renaissance. It marked the beginning of the modern era.

in. When Constantine realized the battle was lost, he dismounted his horse, tore off his royal insignia, and plunged headlong into the melee of the oncoming Janissaries. He was never seen alive again.

## The New Ottoman Capital

Late that afternoon, Mehmed rode into Constantinople. He proceeded directly to the Hagia Sophia, dismounted at the front steps, and fell to his knees, sprinkling a handful of earth over his turban as a sign of humility. He then entered the church, walked to the altar, and offered prayers to God. He later announced that the church was to be converted into a mosque. Constantinople was soon renamed Istanbul (from the Greek words often heard by the Ottoman troops, *is tin poli*, meaning "to the city"). Fulfilling Bayezid's dream, the city became the Ottoman capital and a major bridge between Europe and Asia. It would remain so for nearly five centuries.

Mehmed considered himself the successor not only of the caliphs and sultans who had preceded him but also of the rulers of the Roman and Byzantine Empires. In fact, he added Caesar to his many titles. It became his mission to restore his new capital and make it better than it had ever been, blending the traditions of Byzantium and Islam with those of his Turkish ancestors. This would be a major undertaking. Constantinople had been in decline for some years, with entire sections uninhabited, and many families had fled just before the siege. To quickly repopulate the city, Mehmed proclaimed a general amnesty to any former residents who returned within a specified time, adding that they could practice their religion freely and be exempted from taxation. He even offered aid for the rebuilding of houses and shops. At the same time, he ordered provincial governors throughout his empire to send families to occupy deserted houses, and he brought in thousands of captured prisoners from earlier campaigns to settle and farm the surrounding countryside.

The conversion of the Hagia Sophia into a mosque involved adding a *mihrab*, a *minbar*, and four tall, slender minarets (one for the *muezzin* to give the call to prayer and the other three simply ornamental). The cross on the church's dome was replaced by a crescent pointing toward Mecca. Mehmed admired the figural mosaics in the church and preserved them, in defiance of the Islamic prohibition of human form in religious places.

The non-Muslim residents of the city lived in communities according to their religion. Each community was granted authority in religious matters and in most legal disputes. Greek Christians made up the largest and most literate non-Muslim community. Mehmed appointed a new patriarch of the Orthodox Church and offered him a new church, since the Hagia Sophia was now a mosque.

A Greek architect was hired to build the city's Great Mosque, the Mosque of *Fatih* ("the Conqueror"), on a 25-acre site on the fourth of Istanbul's seven hills. This site was presently occupied by the Church of the Holy Apostles, the second largest church in the city and the burial place of the Byzantine emperors. It was demolished to make room for the new structure, which was modeled on the Hagia Sophia. Mehmed converted and enlarged a former monastery to create a residence for himself and his royal retinue. A new government complex was begun in 1465 on a point of land where the Bosporus, the Sea of Marmara and the Golden Horn meet. It came to be known as *Topkapi* ("Cannon Gate"), because it was situated near the cannon gate of the ancient city walls.

The conquest of Constantinople led to the creation of a new Ottoman flag — a star and crescent on a field of red. This logo had its origins in ancient times. The Roman city of Byzantium had been dedicated to Diana, goddess of the moon, and the crescent was her symbol. When Constantine renamed the city, he rededicated it to the Virgin Mary, and her star symbol was added to the crescent. The star and crescent appeared for centuries on the Byzantine flag. When Mehmed's troops took the city, they found many of the flags and adopted them as their own battle standards. Mehmed then usurped the star and crescent for his own flag. Today it is a symbol of Islam, the crescent moon symbolizing Islam's use of the lunar calendar and the five points of the star indicating the Five Pillars of Islam.

Mehmed invited renowned scholars from Europe and the Islamic world to his court. He collected a number of classical Greek and Latin manuscripts, together with writings on the Christian religion, and had them translated into Turkish. He personally visited the site of Troy in 1462 and commissioned a copy of *The Iliad* soon after he returned. Inspired by the great epics of Persian poet Firdawsi (see page 75), he had lavish verses written about his own accomplish-

Mehmed's curved battle sword, complete with the scratches and nicks incurred during his many military campaigns, is on exhibition at Topkapi Palace. So is his talismanic shirt, which he wore under his armor. Inscribed with prayers and verses from the *Quran*, it was intended to protect the wearer from evil.

ments, and he commissioned Greek scholar Kritovulos to write his biography. Mehmed himself wrote 80 poems in Turkish, earning himself the epithet of "the Rhyming Sultan." He also patronized European painters and sculptors. Venetian painter Gentile Bellini came to Istanbul in 1479 and painted several portraits of the sultan. One of these (shone left) is now in the British Museum in London.

## The Ottoman State

Each of the two halves of the Ottoman Empire (Anatolia and the European part, called Rumelia) was divided into provinces that were controlled by military governors. Mehmed's central government had four branches. The top branch was headed by the grand vizier, the sultan's right-hand man. He held the seal of state and supervised the appointment and work of all other high-level officials. The second branch was that of the judges (the *qadis*), who enforced the law. The third branch handled financial matters, while the fourth consisted of the chancellors who drew up the sultan's edicts. The *Diwan* (DEE wan) was a council of the top men in the four government branches. It met four days a week. Earlier sultans had presided in person over the council meetings, but Mehmed let his vizier take over this position. However, he often looked down upon the proceedings, unseen, from a latticed window known as "the Eye of the Sultan." The *Diwan* also acted as a law court to try high government officials suspected of abusing their power. Those found guilty were subjected to very harsh punishments, even execution.

By this time, all top government and military positions were held by non-

The Turkish word *diwan* is derived from the Persian term for a bundle of papers on which government accounts were written. It came to refer to the assembly of government officials. The Ottoman ministers sat on low cushioned sofas with no arms or backs. Westerners visiting Istanbul mistakenly referred to these sofas as "diwans," associating them with the men who sat on them, and before long, the divan (Anglicized as DIGH van) became a popular piece of furniture in European homes. The term "Ottoman" is still used to describe a cushioned footstool.

Turks selected through the *devsirme* (def SHUR mee), the recruitment system derived from Murad I's scheme for filling the ranks of his elite army corps. Every few years, an imperial recruiting commission went around the Christian provinces to interview boys and unmarried young men in their teens. They selected those who were healthy, intelligent and moral, who did not have a trade, and who were not only sons. These recruits were sent to Istanbul and soon converted to Islam.

Those of the highest ability were trained in the Palace School at Topkapi. Apart from instruction in the *Quran* and the principles of Islamic theology and law, they studied languages — Turkish for everyday activities, Arabic for reading the *Quran*, and Persian for poetry and court activities. They also studied mathematics, science, and history, with an emphasis on statecraft and military strategy. Physical training involved gymnastic exercises, archery, wrestling, swordsmanship, javelin throwing, and polo. Every recruit also learned a trade or craft. (Even sultans mastered a special skill. Mehmed II was an enthusiastic gardener and his great grandson, Suleiman, would be a talented goldsmith.) The recruits studied religious subjects with the *ulama* and the other disciplines with the scientists and literary figures of the court. At the age of 21, the more intellectual young men were assigned to administrative posts in the palace or sent to provinces to act as minor officials. According to their record, they could rise to the highest levels — even grand vizier. Those with a love of fighting were sent to train at military camps to become Janissaries.

The Ottoman Turkish language was a unique blend of Turkish grammar with a heavy dose of Arabic and Persian vocabulary. It was written in the Arabic script.

Al-Jazari was a mechanical engineer living in Anatolia whose *Book of Knowledge of Ingenious Mechanical Devices* appeared in 1206. In the book he described in great technical detail how to construct mechanical devices that told the time, poured water on demand, or played music. His design for a clock run by water operated with a complex system of reservoirs, floats, and pulleys. Every hour of the day, a figure emerged from one of the twelve doorways in the arcade below the signs of the zodiac, and the two falcons on the sides came out and dropped balls from their beaks. Every hour during the night, one of the twelve circles in the lower arch lit up. At the sixth, ninth, and twelfth hours, the musicians played their instruments. Centuries later, astronomer Taqi al-Din published a book in Istanbul that included data on weight-driven clocks. These indicated hours and minutes and could determine the time of prayer "without having to observe the heavenly bodies."

Using the works of al-Jazari and Taqi al-Din, the Ottomans were the first among Muslims to construct an elaborate mechanical timepiece. The first Turkish clocks were made in the monasteries of the Mevlevi (Whirling) Dervishes. The Mevlevis had an interest in making mechanical clocks to help initiates of their order observe fixed prayer times during long periods of meditation.

## The Growing Empire

Mehmed hoped his dynasty would eventually rule over all the lands once held by the Romans. He created a large navy with shipyards at Gallipoli and gradually extended his power around the shores of the Black and Aegean Seas and into the Adriatic. Upon his death, his empire stretched from the Danube River to the Euphrates. Mehmed's successor, Bayezid II, was a peace-loving, contemplative man. He had no interest in further conquests. (He was the first Ottoman ruler not to lead armies into battle.) After a long reign of 30 years, Bayezid was deposed by his son, Selim.The new sultan had the warlike spirit of his grandfather. He spent the first two years eliminating all family members who might advance a claim to the throne. Because of his ruthlessness, he is remembered as "Selim the Grim." His victims also included seven viziers who apparently disagreed with him — he executed almost one a year!

The Ottomans' major rival in the east was the Safavid Empire of Persia, which had been established in the 14th century. Although its founder was a Sunni, his successors were Shi'ites. In the early 16th century Ismail I took the pre-Islamic title of *Shah,* an act intended to recall the glories of ancient Persia. After extending his borders to include Mesopotamia, he gazed menacingly at the eastern edge of the Ottoman Empire. Selim hastened eastward with his army, and in 1514 he defeated Ismail in the valley of Chaldiran on the eastern bank of the Euphrates River. The Safavids, having no gunpowder, were no match for the Ottoman artillery. Selim's troops then sacked the Safavid capital of Tabriz. Ismail withdrew to the east and adopted a "scorched earth" policy, burning all fields of crops that might be used to feed invading enemy troops. For two centuries, his successors would continue this policy, effectively keeping the Ottomans out of Persia.

The Safavids created the greatest Shi'ite empire since the fall of the Fatimids. In later years, their capital, Isfahan, would become one of great cities of Islam, promoting a revival of ancient Persian literature and art.

In 1516 Selim marched into Syria and defeated Mamluk Sultan Al-Ghawri at Aleppo. He took as prisoner Abbasid puppet caliph al-Mutawakkil, who had accompanied the Mamluk sultan. Selim then captured the cities of Damascus, Beirut, and Gaza. When Mamluk Tuman Bey proclaimed himself the new sultan

The commemoration of the death of Husayn had become the emotional core of Persian Shiism, and a pilgrimage to Karbala was as important as one to Mecca. The tombs of other *Imams*, especially that of Ali at Najaf, were also important pilgrimage sites. Around the 10th century Shi'ite *ulama* compiled their own accounts of Muhammad's life and words. They also drew a slightly different interpretation of the *Quran*. In modern Iran, religious scholars, the *mujtahids*, interpret the Islamic texts in light of current events. The most notable of these are recognized as *ayatollahs*.

back in Cairo, Selim crossed the Sinai Desert into Egypt. He sent al-Mutawakkil and a large military escort ahead to Cairo with the message that he intended to deal kindly with the people of Egypt — but not their ruler. The Egyptians responded by reading Selim's name in the Friday prayers, officially acknowledging him as leader of the *umma*. Selim soon arrived in Cairo, defeated Tuman Bey, and added Egypt to his empire. Cairo retained an eminent position as the center of the richest, most populous, and (with al-Azhar) the most culturally prestigious province under Ottoman rule. With the conquest of Egypt came control of the Hijaz. Selim had the standard and cloak of Muhammad transferred from Medina to Istanbul to symbolize his own status as leader of the Muslim world. He further strengthened his image by bringing the Abbasid caliph to the capital. The Ottoman Empire now stretched from the Danube all the way to the Nile and from the Adriatic Sea to the Persian Gulf. An Ottoman poet compared it to the setting sun, which cast a long shadow over the earth.

Selim the Grim also had a gentler side. He enjoyed literature and had a talent for poetry, writing a book of odes in Persian. On his campaigns he took along bards and historians to record the events and to celebrate his exploits. During his stay in Damascus after the Egyptian campaign, he ordered the rebuilding of the tomb over the grave of the great Sufi ibn Arabi, whose writings were taught in Ottoman *madrasas*.

## Suleiman Takes Charge

Suleiman (SOO luh mahn), the son of Selim, became sultan at the age of 25 in 1520. Astrologists proclaimed he would be great because he was closely associated with the Number 10 — he had been born in the 10th century after the founding of Islam and was the 10th sultan of the Ottoman dynasty. As it turned out, his 46-year reign marked the high point of Ottoman political, economic, and cultural development. He is known in the West as "Suleiman the Magnificent" because of the splendor of his court and his remarkable military achievements.

Suleiman is Turkish for Solomon, and this sultan proved to be a worthy successor to his namesake, the biblical King Solomon, who was praised in the *Quran* for his great wisdom.

Suleiman was well-prepared for his role. At the age of seven, he had been sent to live with his intellectual grandfather Bayezid II, where he studied history, science, literature, and theology with a famous scholar. During his teens he received practical training under governors in several provinces, and he was later appointed to a governorship in Anatolia.

When Suleiman came to power, two elites directed the lives of the Ottoman people — one religious (the *ulama*) and the other secular (the sultan, his ministers, and the provincial governors). Each of these elites was associated with a set of laws. The *ulama* oversaw the enforcement of Islamic law, the *sharia*. However, some issues, such as land tenure and the amount of interest allowed on loans, fell outside its guidelines. The decisions made on these issues formed the *kanun*, which fell under the authority of the government. In 1520 the *kanun* was a confused jumble of custom and practice. Suleiman immediately set out to organize and reform it, collecting all the judgments that had been issued by the nine Ottoman sultans who preceded him and reviewing them in light of present-day circumstances. After eliminating duplications and choosing between contradictory statements, he issued a single legal code, being careful not to violate any aspect of the *sharia*. His new code, known as the Ottoman Laws, would last for more than 300 years. Today, Suleiman is revered by Muslims as *Kanuni* (Turkish for "Lawmaker").

## Military Matters

The Janissary corps now numbered nearly 20,000 men. The soldiers were assigned to regiments called *ortas*. *Orta* means "hearth," which reflects the fact that life in the barracks centered around the great copper cauldrons in the cooking hearth. This is where the men gathered to eat and socialize. Every Friday the *ortas* stationed in Istanbul marched with their cauldrons to the great palace kitchen and received the next week's rations of rice and mutton. Beyond its practical use, a regiment's cauldron had a symbolic function, much like a flag or standard. It was carried in front of an *orta* on the march and even paraded in public ceremonies. The greatest disgrace to a regiment was to lose its cauldron. Should this happen, all officers in the unit would be expelled from the corps. In later years, if the Janissaries disapproved of something the sultan did, they would turn their cauldron upside-down. Janissaries could increase in rank only within their own *orta* and only through seniority. Rank was distinguished in the uniform by the cut of the coat, the shape of the headdress or turban, and the color of the boots. Janissaries could not wear beards (a beard was a sign of freedom), only a moustache.

Even the titles of the officers were drawn from the camp kitchen and included First Maker of Soup, Chief Cook, First Pancake Maker, First Cake Maker, and First Carrier of Water.

In the mid-15th century the printing press was invented in Germany. However, it was difficult to make type for the Arabic script. Compared to the 250 individual pieces of type needed for a complete Latin font, an Arabic font needs at least 600. Besides, Muslims greatly revered the calligrapher's art, considering it the only acceptable means of transcribing the *Quran* and other important books. Printing, therefore, was not introduced to Istanbul until the 18th century, when it was used for reproducing secular works.

While the Janissaries (who were always infantry soldiers) formed the backbone of the army, they received support from other divisions. The artillery corps which was responsible for maintaining the large weapons and conducting sieges, usually marched separate from the rest of the army, slowed down by the heavy weaponry. The other major division was the cavalry. Army supplies — food, fodder, tents, and ammunition for firearms — were transported on military campaigns by donkeys and camels. A contingent of tailors, shoemakers, and doctors accompanied the troops.

Suleiman's first military task was to strengthen Ottoman power in Europe. He aimed to achieve by imperial conquest in the West what his father, Selim, had in the East. In 1521 he led an army up the Danube valley into central Europe, where he attacked Belgrade, the anchor of Hungary's southern defense line. His victory there sent shock waves throughout Europe. The following year, he turned his attention to the island of Rhodes in the Mediterranean, where a Christian military order known as the Knights Hospitallers of Saint John was headquartered. These were skilled seamen who preyed upon Ottoman ships, particularly those carrying Egyptian grain to Istanbul. Suleiman attacked the island fortress with his heavy artillery. After a siege of 145 days, the Knights surrendered.

In 1525 Suleiman mobilized an army of 100,000 men for a second invasion of Hungary. That August they faced and defeated a greatly outnumbered Hungarian army on a marshy plain near the little town of Mohacs. From there, they proceeded to capture the cities of Buda and Pest (modern Budapest). Suleiman took up residence in the palace and ordered the royal collection of books, paintings, and Roman statues transported to Istanbul. The greatest prize of this campaign was two huge cannons that Mehmed II had abandoned after an unsuccessful siege of Belgrade. They had been proudly displayed by the Hungarians. Teams of oxen hauled them back to the Ottoman capital.

To avoid wintry conditions, military campaigns were carried out only between the months of April and September.

Musicians were prominent at Suleiman's court. The principal instruments were the *kemence* (a kind of violin), the *kanun* (a sort of dulcimer), the seven-stringed lute, and the *ney* (a flute). Drums ranged in size from huge copper kettledrum to the *darbuka* (a small earthenware pot with sheepskin stretched across the top). Extra rhythm was provided by castanets and wooden spoons. Military bands performed on ceremonial occasions, using woodwind *shawms* (an early oboe), trumpets, drums, cymbals, fifes, and tambourines. Many government officials had *mehters* (army bands) assigned to them. Suleiman's *mehter* woke the inhabitants of the palace half an hour before dawn for morning prayers, performed after the noon prayer on Fridays, and played when pilgrims left for Mecca and at the start of military campaigns. The Janissaries always paraded to the beat of a *mehter*.

In 1529 Suleiman set out on another European campaign with a larger army than before. They marched through torrential rains, and the roads became so waterlogged that the heavy artillery had to be abandoned. In September they laid siege to Vienna. The defenders were able to hold off the Ottomans by constantly repairing the damage done by their light cannons. After a month, Suleiman withdrew. Winter was coming and supplies were running short. As the Ottomans trudged back along the waterlogged roads, the bells of the churches of Vienna, silent through the siege, pealed in triumph. The Ottoman borders would never extend beyond Hungary.

From 1534 until 1553 Suleiman waged three campaigns against the Safavids. Since Selim's victory at Chaldiran, relations between the two countries had been relatively quiet. But when the Shah had the governor of Baghdad (an Ottoman ally) murdered and replaced by one of his supporters, Suleiman led an army east. He took Baghdad (now a small provincial center) as well as the Shi'ite shrines of Karbala and Najaf. His two later campaigns in 1548 and 1553 were less successful, as he had difficulties supplying an army so far from his home base. In 1555 he agreed to the Peace of Amaysa by which he retained present-day Iraq (allowing Shi'ite pilgrims to visit their holy shrines) but renounced all claims to Safavid territories further east. The Ottomans were never able to extend their sway over the eastern part of the Muslim world. As a result, a distinctive western and eastern flavor of Islam would evolve.

Despite his setbacks in the east, Suleiman ruled one of the most powerful empires in the world. It surrounded the eastern half of the Mediterranean Sea and stretched from Budapest to Baghdad. He controlled all the major land and sea routes linking Europe and Asia. The taxes and duties his officials collected made his dynasty fabulously rich. His great-grandfather, Mehmed, would have been pleased.

After being driven from Rhodes, the Knights Hospitallers reestablished themselves on the island of Malta and resumed their acts of piracy. In 1533 Suleiman summoned Khayr ad-Din, a Turkish sea captain who had built up his own pirate fleet in the western Mediterranean, and placed him in charge of the Ottoman navy. Ad-Din is known as Barbarossa or "Red Beard." He turned Suleiman's navy into a first-class fighting force and carried out a series of attacks against the coastal towns of Italy, the Greek islands, and cities of northern Africa. In 1538, 200 Italian and Spanish ships bore down on Barbarossa's fleet off the western coast of Greece. With help from hurricane force winds, he turned them back, securing the eastern Mediterranean for the Ottomans.

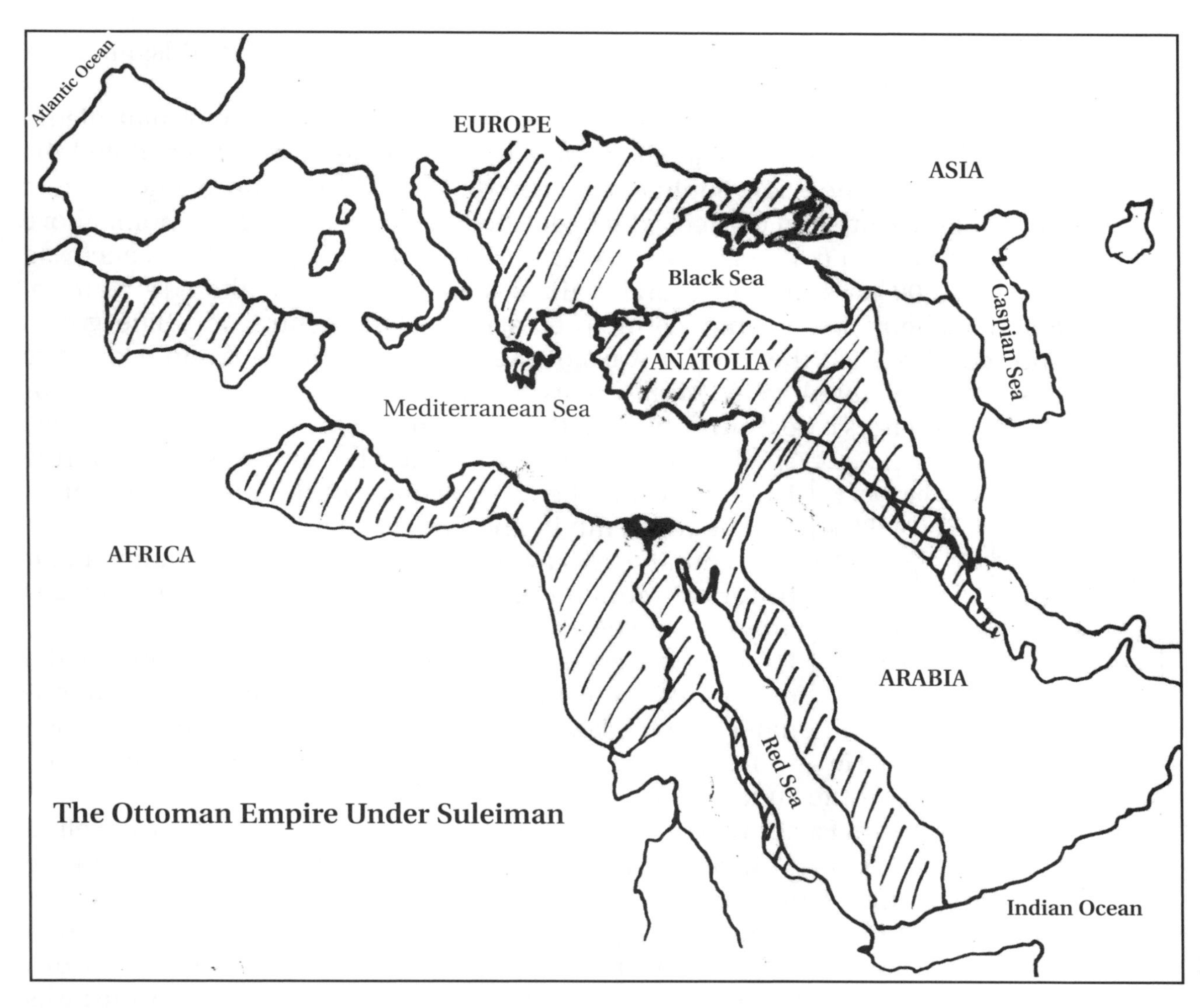


The Ottoman Empire Under Suleiman

## The Ottoman Golden Age

Suleiman's court included a dazzling collection of artists, poets, and philosophers drawn from many parts of his empire. Mimar Sinan (see NAN) became the most celebrated Islamic architect of all time. He was born of Greek parents in Anatolia and was recruited through the *devsirme*. He trained as a Janissary and started a career as a military engineer. His skill in designing siege equipment, fortifications, and bridges brought him to Suleiman's attention, and he was made the sultan's chief of artillery. As he traveled on campaigns, Sinan took great interest in the local building styles. In 1539 he left his army duties to become chief court architect, and he began adapting his technical skills to the design of civil and religious buildings. He combined Byzantine and Islamic elements to form a unique Ottoman style.

Sinan's greatest work was Suleiman's imperial mosque and mausoleum (the *Suleimaniye*), built on a hill overlooking the Golden Horn. He adapted the ground plan of the Hagia Sophia to the needs of Islamic worship, using the great dome of the Christian church, which glorified the altar, as the focal point above the large Muslim congregation. The dome rose 174 feet high and was enclosed by nearly 200 glass windows, some stained, some clear, which filtered streams of incoming light. Small domes counterbalanced the large central one. Blue, green, and red tiles lined the interior walls of the mosque, with floral and geometric designs highlighted by *Quranic* verses written in elaborate calligraphy. Four slender minarets rose from corners of the courtyard. Some say the four minarets symbolized Suleiman's being the fourth sultan to rule Istanbul, while the ten balconies of the minarets signified that he was tenth in line from Osman.

Sinan designed buildings across the empire for three successive sultans — a total of 70 mosques, 34 palaces, 33 *hammams*, 19 tombs, 55 schools, 7 *madrasas*, and 12 *caravanserais*. He lived to be 99 years old.

Sinan oversaw repairs and additions to many major historical monuments. In Jerusalem he constructed walls around the central sanctuaries, which remain to this day. He had the crumbling Umayyad-period mosaics on the exterior of the Dome of the Rock replaced with predominately blue glazed tiles, with *Quranic* verses inscribed across the top. He also refurbished an enormous water reservoir that has come to be known as "the Sultan's Pool."

Topkapi Palace had become the imperial residence in the time of Selim. After a great fire in 1574, Sinan made extensive renovations that resulted in the sprawling complex of buildings, courtyards, and gardens seen today. (Topkapi and the Alhambra are the only pre-modern Muslim palaces that are still fairly intact.) The palace had three distinct areas — the Outer Court, the Inner Court, and the *Harem* — surrounded by three miles of high walls. The Outer Court was open to the public. Every day thousands of people entered to attend official meetings and submit petitions to the sultan. Included in this area were an arsenal, hospital, bakery, arsenal, and mint. The Inner Court held the chamber where the *Diwan* met, the treasury, and the palace kitchens. (The kitchens employed a thousand cooks who fed up to 10,000 people a day. Every three

The Imperial Corps of Architects was in charge of practically everything related to the empire's civil engineering, architecture, and urban development activities: water supply, sewerage systems, roads, building regulations, permits and their control, fire prevention, wages of architects and workers, the standardization of building materials and their quality and price control, and the building of bridges, forts and other military works in wartime.

months, the Janissaries assembled there to be paid. Their giant shop cauldrons can be seen there today.) The *Harem* was a closely guarded area containing the private apartments of the sultan and the quarters of his mother, wives, children, and concubines — plus their servants and guardians. Virtually none of its inhabitants, apart from the sultan, had the freedom to leave at will, and almost no one from the outside world was ever admitted. A pavilion in one of the gardens had a glass dome, over which water cascaded in hot weather. Sitting there must have seemed like being under a waterfall. The servants, gardeners, and other workers of Topkapi lived within the walls of the complex in dorms. They wore color-coded attire for ease of identification.

*Harem* comes from the Arabic word harim means "forbidden" or "sacred." The words was first used to connote a holy place; later, it came to designate the private area in a Muslim household where the women lived.

A palace studio was set up in the Outer Court for artists and artisans to train and work. They included painters, bookbinders, calligraphers, carpenters, jewelers, architects, masons, and goldsmiths. This group was known as "the Society of the Talented." They entered as apprentices and advanced to the rank of master, the most outstanding rising to head their group. They were assigned daily wages according to their level of accomplishment. These wages were generally higher than those of civil servants working at the palace, reflecting the sultan's high opinion of art. Suleiman personally inspected the work produced in the palace studio and rewarded the artists with silver coins for outstanding achievements.

This elegant example of stylized calligraphy expresses the Muslim doctrine of faith: *There is no god but God.*

The works of art were usually made to order for the sultan and his court. Among the most cherished items were the manuscripts. There was a popular saying that "The *Quran* was revealed in Mecca, recited in Egypt, and written in Istanbul." Calligraphers were trained to write flawlessly and elegantly in the Arabic, Persian, and Turkish languages, copying texts onto sheets of paper and leaving appropriate spaces for the illustrations and decorations. The studio artists also created two-dimensional miniature paintings to illustrate secular books. Many of these depicted major political and social events of the times as well as scenes from ordinary life, providing a colorful record of this period in history.

The studio became famous for its designs, which represented a unique blend of European, Islamic, and Turkish traditions. Those used in manuscript decoration were also applied to textiles (cloth), rugs, metalwork, jewelry, and ceramic tiles (an Ottoman specialty). One decorative style was called *saz*, an ancient Turkish word meaning "enchanted forest." It depicted an imaginary world of intertwined branches and vines with long feathery leaves and huge composite flowers inhabited by lions, dragons, *senmurvs* (phoenix-like birds), *chilins* (strange four-legged creatures), and *peris* (fairies). Another style featured spring flowers, such as tulips, carnations, roses and hyacinths, which grew from clusters of leaves amid blossoming fruit trees.

Under the Ottomans carpet-weaving was transformed into a state industry. The carpets were used as wall hangings and table covers as well as floor coverings. Some of the finest pieces were made for the Ottoman court or sold to be displayed in the great castles of Europe. Cardinal Wolsey of England purchased 60 carpets to furnish his palace at Hampton Court.

As we've seen, poetry played an important role in Islamic society since earliest times. Suleiman created within his court the post of Imperial Rhyming Chronicler, a kind of Ottoman poet laureate, whose duty was to versify current events in the manner of Firdawsi. The sultan himself composed odes in Turkish and Persian, many of which he sent to his favorite wives under the pseudonym *Muhibbi* ("Affectionate Friend"). He took great pride in attending competitions

Public festivals were held on special occasions. The people enjoyed free food, drink, and entertainment — acrobatics, juggling, fireworks, concerts, dances, and shadow plays. One of the most lavish festivals was held in 1530 in honor of Suleiman's sons. In the center of a great field outside the city walls, the sultan presided over the activities from a lofty pavilion.

After three weeks the festivities came to a close. Suleiman then asked his vizier, Ibrahim, who had recently married the Sultan's sister, "Whose celebration was finer? Mine, which has just been completed, or your own wedding feast?" Ibrahim considered thoughtfully, then replied, "There never was an occasion equal to my wedding." This might seem like an unwise thing to say, since the Sultan had the power of life or death over his subjects. When Suleiman inquired how that could be, the vizier replied, "Because my wedding was honored by the presence of Suleiman, the Sultan of Sultans, the Caliph of Islam, the Protector of Mecca and Medina, the Lord of Syria and Egypt, the Caliph of the Lofty Threshold, and the Lord of the Residence of the Pleiades. Your festival had no guest of such majesty."

where the most respected poets received prizes. A new genre, known as *diwan* (in this case, the word meant "a collection of poems"), stressed form over content, using rhyme, a careful choice of words, and the skillful use of onomatopoeia (employing words that sound like what they describe, such as "boom" or "cuckoo") to achieve a musical effect. The poets were content to express the very same ideas, but in different, inventive ways. The most famous was Baki, whose *diwan* reflected the pleasures of courtly life in Istanbul. Many of his poems lamented the elusive nature of happiness and prosperity, urging the reader to enjoy the pleasures of love and wine while he could. The Ottomans also produced a long line of official historians. Mustafa Ali, the most notable, felt free to criticize the bad decisions of the great and powerful, even the sultan. (This says quite a lot about the open-mindedness of Suleiman.)

A typical "book" consisted of several folded bundles of ten pages each, placed inside a leather case. Today, more than 10,000 illuminated manuscripts are preserved in the Topkapi Museum.

## Daily Life in Suleiman's Istanbul

By the mid-16th century Istanbul had a population of about 500,000, of whom over half were Muslim. The Muslim section of the city was divided into thirteen districts, each named after the mosque complex that formed its center and focus. The districts were subdivided into neighborhoods in which people of similar professions lived. (The butchers and tanners lived in a district noted for strong odors!) Each district was surrounded by a wall with gates that closed at night.

The wealthy families lived in houses two or three stories high built of stone and brick. Each floor projected beyond the floor underneath, a design that protected the house's entrance from sun and rain and made the upper levels more spacious. Lead or tiles covered the sloping roof. The inner walls and ceilings were often carved or painted. Carpets lay on top of rush matting, and people took off their shoes at the door so the carpets would last a long time. The families sat on low sofas covered with silk and satin cushions. Beds usually consisted of two or three cotton-stuffed mattresses piled one on top of the other, with a silk sheet spread on top. The rooms were heated by charcoal-burning braziers (small metal grills). People of lesser means lived in simple, one-floor dwellings made of brick or wood with dirt floors. They sat on wool cushions on the floor and slept on rugs that were unrolled at night. Every house maintained separate quarters for women, the *harem.* In a rich household, women often had their own building, while in a humbler abode the women's section was shut off by a thick felt cloth suspended from the ceiling.

Istanbul was famous for its spring flowers, particularly the red and yellow tulips. They filled the gardens of Topkapi Palace, lined walkways and courtyards, encircled fountains, and added splashes of color to window boxes throughout the city. Gardening was a favorite pastime among all classes of society. Suleiman's supreme judge, Ebussuud Efendi, spent hours tending his flowers. And, as we've seen, the tulip was a favorite motif of Ottoman art.

Thousands of artists and craftsmen not associated with the palace studio had workshops scattered throughout the city. Every craft was controlled by a guild, which set the product standards and determined how many men could practice the craft, a measure that set the level of competition. The guilds made loans to members, helped those who fell ill, and even paid for funerals. They also distributed food to the poor and sponsored readings of the *Quran* at the local mosques. There were about 150 major guilds, and each one had a representative who met with government officials to decide upon prices and the margins of profit. The typical craft workshop was made up of apprentices (beginners), jour-

Although it is today associated with Holland, the tulip is actually native to eastern Anatolia and the Iranian plateau, where it grew wild for centuries, along with other bulbous plants such as the narcissus, the hyacinth, and the daffodil. For centuries the Persians admired the wild tulips, but the Turks were the first to cultivate them in flowerbeds and window boxes.

In 1554, Baron Ogier Ghiselin de Busbecq, the Flemish-born Austrian ambassador to the court, upon arriving in Istanbul, was amazed to see the great abundance of flowers blooming when there were still patches of snow on the ground. He wrote home about them, remarking that the Turks were so fond of the flowers that the marching soldiers were under strict orders not to trample on them. He took some bulbs back with him to Vienna and cultivated them in his garden. Before long, tulips were growing in many Viennese parks. In 1587 Charles de L'Ecluse, professor of botany at the University of Leiden in Holland, obtained a number of bulbs from Vienna. He used them to develop new varieties. And so the Dutch tulip was born.

neymen (experienced craftsmen), and masters. A journeyman studied with a master for several years, and when he felt ready, he exhibited examples of his work to the guild council. If they were approved, he became a member of the guild, and the objects he had made were auctioned off at prices high enough to enable him to set up his own shop.

The *madrasas* of Istanbul were known as the "eight paradises of knowledge." Students received free room and board and a monthly allowance. The most promising graduates went on to study law or medicine.

Covered markets throughout the city were made up of small shops that handled one particular kind of product (books, carpets, fabrics, saddles, and so forth). A section of the market served as a bank. Uncovered markets, known as bazaars, sold local grain, meat, and vegetables, as well as rare and exotic spices and delicacies from other parts of the world. Markets were open from sunrise to sunset (except Friday, the Muslim Sabbath, when many closed at noon). They were patrolled by inspectors, who checked to make certain that goods were weighed and measured properly. Anyone caught trying to cheat a customer was beaten on the soles of his feet with thick wooden rods.

A typical man living in Istanbul wore a shirt and trousers, with a wide sash tied around his waist. If he was wealthy, he also wore a caftan of luxurious cloth, such as silk brocade. He wore soft-soled leather slippers indoors and put on heavy leather shoes over the slippers to go outside. Students and religious scholars dressed in long flowing gowns. A wealthy woman wore full trousers and an embroidered smock with a high neck and elbow-length sleeves, and over this a long-sleeved waistcoat and a close-fitting caftan tied with a sash. She wore leather slippers indoors. Poorer women wore trousers and a smock and usually went barefoot in the house but put on shoes when going outdoors.

The turban did not become common among the Ottomans until after the capture of Constantinople. Mehmed began the fashion, winding a long narrow piece of cloth around his felt cap. As in other Islamic states, this headdress was worn only by Muslims. With the Ottomans, the higher one's social status, the larger the turban. The cloth could be as long as 12 feet — even longer. Turbans worn by the sultan were huge, and were often decorated with gems and gold

Every morning Suleiman put on a new caftan, with twenty gold coins in one pocket and a thousand pieces of silver in the other. At the end of the day, the caftan, together with the gold and silver, became the property of his chief attendant. Every night he slept on a couch made of three crimson velvet mattresses, with his head resting on green-tasseled pillows. Above his couch was a golden canopy and around it stood four tall candles on silver stands. By each candle stood an armed guard.

embroidery. The *ulama* wore gold-embroidered skullcaps wound round with white muslin, forming flat turbans. Both rich and poor women wore felt caps with kerchiefs draped across the tops.

Most city dwellers had a simple breakfast of bread with cheese or fruit jam after reciting the first prayer of the day. Lunch was often a dish of yogurt. Dinner was the main meal of the day and always included rice. Lamb and mutton were the main meats. A popular dish was the *kebab* — chunks of meat grilled over a flame on a skewer. The Turks loved pastries sweetened with *pekmez* (a thick molasses made from grape sugar) and candies like *halvah (*sesame seeds mixed with honey). Rather than eat at a table, diners sat on cushions on the floor and served themselves from a tray that was placed on a low stool. The only utensils were spoons, which were used for soup. The rest of the food was cut into small pieces and eaten with three fingers. The rice was taken by the handful and pressed into a ball, then popped into the mouth. Coffee, a favorite beverage, was often enjoyed in special coffeehouses.

The English word "tulip" derives from *tulband,* the Turkish term for turban, which the flower's shape seems to resemble. Above is a portrait of Suleiman wearing his huge imperial turban. Below is a tulip.

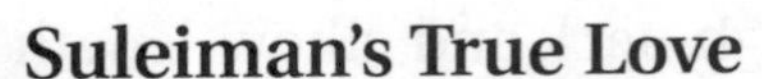

## Suleiman's True Love

Like other Muslim rulers, the sultan had a large *harem.* Women were carefully selected from prisoners of war and from slave markets. (A few were gifts from a foreign ruler to seal a political alliance.) Many of the women never saw the sultan and were merely servants in the *harem.* They usually ended up marrying one of the government officials. Those of extraordinary beauty and talent were trained in calligraphy, poetry, dance, singing, the playing of musical instruments, sewing, and embroidery. They became the concubines of the sultan.

Before Suleiman was crowned, the imperial *harem* was ruled by his mother, Hafise. (Being parent of the heir to the throne gave her the highest status.) She introduced her son to a young slave from the region of the Black Sea. She was called *Hurrem* ("The Smiling One") because of her pleasant disposition. Suleiman fell in love with her and wrote her poems, which were copied and illuminated by the court artists. She bore him many sons.

When Suleiman came to the throne, his heir was Mustafa, the eldest son born to the second highest ranking concubine, Gulbehar ("the Rose of Spring"). Mustafa was intelligent and shrewd, promising material for a sultan. To guarantee her son's right of inheritance, Gulbehar persuaded Suleiman to make her his legal wife. This was the first time in six generations that a sultan had formally married a concubine. (It had been feared that royal wives might place their own family interests ahead of those of the state.) After Suleiman's mother died, Gulbehar became the top woman in the *harem*.

Hurrem worried that her eldest son, Selim, second in line to the throne behind Mustafa, might be killed to avoid disputes about the succession of power. (This had become the Ottoman tradition.) Selim had few qualities and was known for his excessive drinking. (He was often referred to as *Sarhos* ["the Sot."]) He was opposite in nearly every way to the talented Mustafa, but his mother was determined that he should one day rule the empire. In 1553, while Suleiman was on campaign in Persia, his vizier, in league with Hurrem, convinced him that Mustafa was conspiring to usurp the throne. The sultan had the poor fellow strangled with a bowstring. The way was now clear for the disreputable Selim.

The first coffee plants grew wild in Ethiopia, perhaps as early as the 6th century BCE. There is a popular legend about a goat herder who noticed his animals were friskier after eating the red berries of a nearby shrub with dark shiny leaves (they were coffee beans). He tried the berries himself and felt stimulated (from the caffeine). He later took some berries to a local monk, and before long chewing coffee beans had become popular at monasteries because it helped the monks keep awake during long hours of prayer. The beans were at first eaten alone, but travelers learned to grind them up, mix them with animal fat, and press them into small lumps for snacks on the road. Coffee beans later spread from Ethiopia to Yemen through trade.

The Arabs were the first to cultivate the coffee plant. After harvesting the beans, they removed the skins, crushed the beans, then added water and boiled the brew, creating a drink they called *qahwa* ("that which prevents sleep"). Over the centuries, the new beverage became popular in places far from Yemen. But it was not until the 14th century that the beans were roasted and ground. And even then, the grounds were consumed along with the liquid. Coffee as we know it (roasted and brewed, without the grounds) was introduced to Istanbul in the time of Mehmed II. The world's first coffee house opened there in 1475. The Turks often flavored their coffee with spices, such as clove, cinnamon, cardamom, and anise. The English word "coffee" comes from the Turkish word *kahveh*, derived from the Arabic *qahwa*.

## The Final Years

When Hurrem died in 1558, Suleiman had her laid to rest beside his own tomb at the *Suleymaniye*. As he grew older, the sultan became increasingly inward, still mourning the death of his beloved concubine. His health grew poor, and his face became so pale that he took to wearing rouge to have a more healthy appearance. Perhaps to break away from his gloom, he turned to what had once been a great source of pleasure, a military campaign. Although his fleet controlled most of the Mediterranean Sea, many of the Knights of Saint John had relocated to the island of Malta and were once again preying upon Ottoman ships. In 1565 Suleiman set out to capture the island and secure his domination of the Mediterranean once and for all. The struggle over Malta proved bloody, with casualties running into the thousands on both sides. Ultimately, the Ottomans were stricken with illness (probably malaria) and Suleiman was forced to withdraw.

The next year, the aging sultan set out at the head of his army to fight his old enemies in Austria and Hungary. He was now nearly 70 and so weak that he could no longer ride his horse. (He had to be carried in a litter.) After his forces laid a siege of Hungarian fortress of Szigetvar, they dug under the walls, placed explosives there, and fired them. The blast shattered the fortress walls, ensuring an Ottoman victory. But Suleiman died in his tent a few hours before the city fell.

His death was kept a secret for more than three weeks, as the army returned to Istanbul. His body was secretly embalmed, then dressed in the imperial robes and set up in his tent as if he were still alive. His vizier forged his signature on the documents that continued to be issued in his name. This gave Selim time to get to Belgrade and assume command. Only then was it announced that the sultan was dead. His remains were taken to Istanbul for burial beside Hurrem at the *Suleymaniye*.

Suleiman had ruled for nearly half a century and made the Ottoman empire a world power. Although almost constantly at war, he brought to the diverse peoples of his empire the benefits of peace, promoting the art and culture that would strongly influence European as well as Muslim civilizations. His successors would rule until 1922, making them the longest-surviving dynastic state in Islamic history.

## Review Questions:

1.Describe the founding of the Ottoman dynasty.
2. Who were the original Janissaries?
3. What was Mehmet II's first major act as sultan?
4. Why had Constantinople survived attacks for such a long time?
5. What was Urban?
6. What was the Hagia Sophia, and how was it transformed by Mehmed II?
7. What actions did Mehmed take to restore the former city of Constantinople?
8. What was the *Diwan*?
9. How were candidates for government office and the Janissary corps recruited and trained?
10. Why did Selim attack the Safavids?
11. Why is Suleiman known as *Kanuni*?
12. What was the extent of Suleiman's empire?
13. In what ways were Sinan's mosques a blending of Byzantine and Islamic styles?
14. What were the three parts of Topkapi Palace?
15. What was the Society of the Talented?
16. How would you describe the poetry of Suleiman's court?
17. What do a turban and a tulip have in common?
18. Why did Suleiman's heir, Mustafa, never become sultan?
19. What was Suleiman's last battle?

## Questions for Discussion:

1. In what major way was the Ottoman state, under the rule of Suleiman, a more genuine Islamic institution than the regime of the Abbasid caliphs?
2. In what ways did the Ottomans seem to ignore the egalitarian traditions of Islam?
3. By the end of the 12th century the minaret, in the form of a slender freestanding shaft, had become the universal symbol of Islam from the Atlantic to the Indian Oceans. Discuss the origins of the minaret, and describe the various styles you have encountered in your study of early Islam.
4. For many European observers the 16th century Ottoman empire seemed to be the model modern state. What might they have admired about Suleiman's imperial regime? What were its strengths? Its weaknesses?
5. We have learned how an overly strong military force can lead to the downfall of a dynasty. What predictions might you make about the Janissaries in the years following the death of Suleiman?
6. During Suleiman's reign, the major European powers were ruled by young men of outstanding ability — Charles V of the Habsburg empire, Francis I of France, and Henry VIII of England. These rulers all considered Suleiman one of the great rulers of all time. What do you know about these three Europeans? How might their approach to government have differed with that of a Muslim sultan? What similarities might they have shared with Suleiman?

Sinan's Selimiye Mosque

# EPILOGUE

We've reached the end of the story of early Islam. After Suleiman, the Ottoman Empire began a long period of decline. The sultan lost much of his authority to his viziers and the Janissaries, while territory was lost in a series of military defeats. The end came at the close of World War I, when the Ottoman provinces were divided up among European powers. The heartland — Anatolia and the region around Istanbul —became the nation of Turkey in 1923, and the sultanate and the caliphate were formally abolished. Meanwhile, other Muslim regions in the Middle East, India, Arabia, Malaya, and Africa had been colonized by various European powers. In many cases the Muslims were forced into a process of modernization which led to great resentment on their part towards the West. After World II all the Arabic-speaking countries of the Middle East and northern Africa gained their independence, and others followed. Today, *Dar al-Islam* is made up of a great number of independent nations, many with non-religious governments.

Although Islam is the second largest religion in the world and the fastest growing, its basic doctrines have not changed since its origin over a millennium ago. The words of the *Quran* are still as central to the lives of Muslims as they were at the very beginning. The Five Pillars remain at the core of Islam, as do Muhammad's teachings about responsibility toward others and the equality of all members of the community. But divisions that occurred in earlier times have also remained. We have seen how the issue of who should succeed the Prophet and the very nature of the leadership of the *umma* led to the schism between Sunnis and Shi'ites. Differences in the religious and political views of these two groups continue to divide Muslims of the world. (Today, the majority are Sunnis, with Shi'ites making up about 15%. Shi'ites outnumber Sunnis in Iraq and Iran, however.)

The interpretation of the *Quran* and the *sunna* caused another long-standing debate. While the early traditionalists took the words literally and tried to duplicate the life of Muhammad in every way possible, the rationalists sought to relate these values to contemporary circumstances. The pendulum swung back and forth until the 12th century, when the works of al-Ghazali put a freeze on empirical inquiry. In the 18th century, Muhammad ibn Abd al-Wahhab led a puritanical movement in Arabia that eliminated all practices not specifically sanctioned by the *Quran* and the *sunna*. A hundred years later, reform movements in Egypt, Turkey, Syria, and Iran attempted to modernize traditional Islamic societies and institutions along Western lines, and the pendulum swung back to the left. In the 20th century Wahhabism reemerged. It was closely linked with the founding of Saudi Arabia, whose government was based on a literal reading of the *Quran*. But despite its intent to return to the simplicity of the original *umma*, the country's conservative values were not the same as Muhammad's. Women, for example, were shrouded from view and secluded, a discriminatory treatment at great variance from the Prophet's respect for women's rights. And like the Abbasid caliphs, who used state revenues for the enrichment of their exclusive and lavish courts, Saudi Arabia's ruling elite flaunted their wealth while fellow countrymen lived in relative poverty.

The 20th century also bore witness to an increase in tensions between Islamic and Western cultures. The creation of the Jewish state of Israel in 1948 led to the displacement of nearly a million Palestinians (Muslim and Christian Arabs). Western support of Israel (particularly that of the United States) has been viewed by many Muslims as a sign of indifference to the plight of the Palestinian refugees. Warfare has occurred frequently in modern times even among Muslim states, although this is forbidden by the *Quran*. Much of the fighting has been over the control of the rich oil fields of the Middle East. In the 1980's Iraq battled Iran over this issue, and in 1990 Iraq invaded Kuwait for the same reason. The involvement of the United States and European nations in these wars further fanned the conflicts between Islam and the West.

Fundamentalism in its truest sense refers to a reverence for the basic values of a religion. This is inherent in Islam. But extremism in any context leads to a distortion of beliefs and an intolerance of other points of view. In the middle of the 20th century an Egyptian revivalist named Sayyid Qutb preached a form of Islam that distorted the message of the *Quran* and the life of Muhammad. He proposed that Muslims separate themselves from mainstream society, just as Muhammad had migrated from Mecca to Medina, and engage in violent *jihad* in order to establish a new Muslim state. But, as we have seen, Muhammad's battles against the Meccans were largely for self-defense, and he ultimately won over his adversaries through peaceful means. Furthermore, the *Quran* condemns aggressive warfare and opposes the use of force in religious matters. It also denounces intolerance and exclusiveness. Osama bin Laden and his followers, those responsible for the attack upon the United States on September 11, 2001, were fundamentalist extremists inspired by Qutb. Their violent acts in the name of Islam were an unconscionable abuse of a religion founded upon peace, brotherhood, and compassion.

In these violent times, experts in the field of international relations believe that Islam must look within and reform itself if there is to be world peace. Ways must be found to accommodate the fundamental doctrines of the faith in the modern setting and to foster a meeting of minds among traditionalists and rationalists, Sunnis and Shi'ites. The stakes are too great to do otherwise.

# DATELINE

| | |
|---|---|
| 570 | Birth of Muhammad |
| 610 | First Revelation |
| 619 | The Night Journey |
| 622 | Migration to Medina |
| 624 | Battle of Badr |
| 625 | Battle of Uhud |
| 627 | Battle of the Trench |
| 628 | Treaty of Hudaybiyya |
| 629 | Muhammad's first *hajj* to Mecca |
| 630 | Muhammad occupies Mecca |
| 632 | Death of Muhammad |
| | |
| 632-61 | Rightly Guided Caliphs |
| 634 | Battle of Aynadyn |
| 640 | Founding of Fustat |
| 636 | Battle of Yarmuk, Battle of Qadisiyya |
| 638 | Muslim occupation of Jerusalem |
| c 650 | Standard version of the *Quran* appears |
| 656 | Ali becomes caliph, Battle of the Camel |
| 657 | Battle of Siffin |
| 661 | Death of Ali |
| | |
| 661 | Founding of Umayyad dynasty |
| 680 | Husayn is killed at Karbala |
| 685 | Building of the Dome of the Rock begins |
| 705 | Muslim armies reach Atlantic coast of Morocco |
| 706 | Building of the Great Mosque of Damascus begins |
| 711 | Muslims enter Spain |
| 732 | Battle of Poitiers, Charles Martel defeats raiding party of Muslims from Spain |
| 750 | Battle of the Great Zab |
| | |
| 750 | Founding of Abbasid dynasty |
| 756 | Cordoba Emirate is established |
| 762 | Building of the Round City of Baghdad begins |
| 786-809 | Rule of Harun al-Rashid, peak of Abbasid caliphate |
| 813 | Al-Mamun begins caliphate |
| 830 | House of Wisdom established |
| 836 | Samarra becomes Abbasid capital |
| 868 | Founding of Tulunid dynasty |
| 874 | Samanids begin rule in Khurasan and Transoxiana |
| | |
| 929 | Cordoba Caliphate Established |
| 945 | Buyids seize power in Baghdad |
| 969 | Founding of Cairo |

| | |
|---|---|
| 972 | Fatimids move capital to Cairo |
| 998 | Mahmud of Ghazni comes to power |
| 1031 | Taifas begin rule in al-Andalus |
| 1055 | Seljuk Turks enter Baghdad |
| 1071 | Battle of Manzikert |
| 1085 | Toledo falls to Christian armies |
| 1086 | Almoravids begin rule in Spain |
| 1095 | Pope Urban calls for the First Crusade |
| 1099 | Crusaders conquer Jerusalem |
| 1147 | Almohads begin rule in Spain |
| 1174 | Ayyubid dynasty founded |
| 1187 | Saladin defeats Crusaders at Battle of Hattan, recovers Jerusalem for Islam |
| 1238 | Nasirids dynasty founded in Granada |
| 1250 | Mamluks establish dynasty in Egypt |
| 1236 | Fall of Cordoba |
| 1258 | Mongols sack Baghdad |
| 1260 | Battle of Ayn Jalut |
| 1288 | Founding of Ottoman dynasty |
| 1325 | Visit of Mansa Musa to Cairo |
| 1370 | Tamerlane begins conquests |
| 1453 | Mehmed II, Ottoman sultan, conquers Constantinople |
| 1492 | Granada is conquered by Christian armies |
| 1502 | Safavid dynasty founded by Ismail |
| 1513 | Portuguese traders reach China |
| 1514 | Battle of Chaldiran |
| 1517 | Ottomans take Egypt and Syria from the Mamluks |
| 1520 | Suleiman becomes sultan of Ottoman Empire |
| 1522 | Ottomans conquer Rhodes |
| 1525 | Battle of Mohac |
| 1529 | Failed siege of Vienna |
| 1534 | Ottomans occupy Baghdad |
| 1543 | Ottomans conquer Hungary |
| 1566 | Death of Suleiman |

# MAJOR CHARACTERS IN THE STORY OF ISLAM

**Abu al-Abbas** — first Abbasid caliph (ruled 750-54)
**Abu Bakr** — Companion, first of the Rightly Guided Caliphs (632-34)
**Abu Sufyan** — leader of opposition in Mecca against Muhammad, later joined up against Ali
**Adud al-Dawlah** — Buyid ruler, built al-Adudi Hospital in Baghdad, 982
**Ahmad ibn Tulun** — founder of Tulunid dynasty in Egypt, 868
**Aisha** — favorite wife of Muhammad, daughter of Abu Bakr, battle of the camel, opposition
**Al-Arabi** — (1165-1240) Andalusian mystic and philosopher; writer
**Al-Bakri** — Andalusian geographer, wrote *The Book of Highways and of Kingdoms*
**Al-Battani** (868-923 ) — mathematician, pioneer in trigonometry
**Al-Biruni** (963-1048) — scientist and geographer, wrote *The Book of India*
**Al-Farabi** (c 878-950) — rationalist philosopher, wrote *The Perfect City*
**Al-Ghazali** — (1058-1111) theologian, brought Sufism into the mainstream of Sunni Islam, wrote *The Incoherence of Philosophers* and *Revival of the Religious Sciences*
**Al-Hakam II** — Cordoba caliph (961-976), promoted *Convivencia*
**Al-Hakim** — Fatimid ruler (996-1021), established Hall of Wisdom, later became mentally unstable
**Al-Haytham** (965-1039) — scientist, wrote *The Book of Optics*
**Al-Idrisi** (1099-1166) — Andalusian geographer, wrote *The Book of Roger*
**Al-Jahiz** ( 776 -868) — zoologist, wrote *Book on Animals*
**Al-Khwarizmi** (780-847) — mathematician and astronomer, introduced Indian numerals, wrote first book on algebra
**Al Kindi** (c. 800-867) — first major Muslim philosopher
**Al-Malik** — Umayyad caliph (685-705), builder of Dome of the Rock
**Al-Mamun** — Abbasid caliph (813-33), creator of the House of Wisdom
**Al-Mansur** — Abbasid caliph (754 -75), builder of Baghdad
**Al-Muizz** — Fatimid ruler, established Cairo as Fatimid capital, 972
**Al-Mu'tasim** — Abbasid caliph (833-42), moved capital from Baghdad to Samarra
**Al-Rahman I** — Umayyad prince, set up Emirate of Cordoba in 756, built *La Mezquita*
**Al-Rahman III** — established Cordoba Caliphate in 921, built *Madinat al-Zahra*
**Al-Rashid** — Abbasid caliph (786-809), character in *One Thousand and One Nights*
**Al-Razi** (864-930) — physician, wrote *The Comprehensive Book on Medicine*
**Al-Tabari (Abu Jafar)** (d 923) — historian, wrote *History of the Prophets and Kings*
**Al-Walid** — Umayyad caliph (705-715), builder of Great Mosque of Damascus
**Ali ibn Abi Talib** — cousin and son-in-law of Muhammad, fourth Rightly Guided Caliph, First Imam, murdered in 661, revered at his shrine at Najaf.
**Amr ibn al-Aas** — military commander, conquered Egypt in 640, built settlement of Fustat
**Baybars** (d 1277) — the first and greatest Mamluk sultan
**Banu Musa** — three brothers, scholars of the House of Wisdom
**Firdawsi** (c 940-1020) — poet, wrote great epic, *The Book of Kings (Shahnama)*
**Hulago** — Mongol khan, captured and destroyed Baghdad in 1258
**Hurrem** — favorite concubine of Suleiman I, mother of Selim II
**Husayn ibn Ali** — (d 669) second son of Ali, third Shiite Imam, killed at Karbala and mourned annually during rites of Ashura

**Ibn al-Nafis** (1210-1288) — physician in Cairo, discovered the blood circulatory system
**Ibn Arabi** — Andalusian philosopher and mystic, wrote *The Meccan Revelations* and *Bezels of Wisdom*
**Ibn Baytar** (1188-1248) — Andalusian botanist and physician, wrote *The Practical Manual of Treatments and Diet*
**Ibn Hayyam** (721-815) — developed chemistry as a distinct science
**Ibn Ishaq (Muhammad)** (d 773) — biographer, wrote *Life of the Messenger of God*
**Ibn Ishaq (Hunayn)** (808-873) — physician, translated the works of Hippocrates and Galen into Arabic, wrote *The Introduction to the Healing Arts*
**Ibn Khaldun** (c1332-1406 )— historian, founder of social science, author of *An Introduction to History*
**Ibn Rushd** (1126-98) — Andalusian scholar and philosopher, wrote commentaries on the works of Aristotle
**Ibn Sina** (980-1037) — physician and philosopher, wrote *The Canon of Medicine* and *The Book of Healing*
**Ibn Zaydun** (1003-1071)— Andalusian poet, forerunner of French troubadours
**Ibn Zuhr** (1091 - 1161) — Andalusian physician, wrote *The Practical Manual of Treatments and Diet*
**Khadija** — first wife of Muhammad and mother of his surviving children, first to convert to Islam
**Mahmud of Ghazna** — sultan of Ghaznavids (998-1030), patron of Persian art and culture
**Maimonides** (1135-1204) — Andalusian Jewish physician and philosopher, wrote *Guide of the Perplexed*
**Mansa Musa** — Muslim ruler of Mali, visited Cairo in 1324 en route to Mecca
**Mehmed II** — Ottoman sultan (1451-61), conquered Constantinople (renamed Istanbul), established Ottoman state
**Muawiyya** — first Umayyad caliph (661-80 )
**Murad I** — Ottoman sultan (1360-89), created the Janissary corps
**Nizalmulmulk**— Persian vizier of Seljuks (1063-92), built first *madrasas*
**Omar Khayyam** (1048-1131) — mathematician, astronomer, and poet, author of *The Rubaiyat*
**Osman I** (1281-1326) — founded the Ottoman dynasty
**Rumi** (1207-1273) — Sufi leader (founder of the Mevlana) and poet-author of *The Rhymed Discourses*
**Saladin** (Salah ad-Din) (1137- 1193) — Sultan of Egypt and Syria, founded Ayyubid dynasty
**Selim I** — Ottoman sultan (1512-20), extended empire to include Mesopotamia, Syria, and Egypt
**Shajaret-al-Durr** — Turkish slave who became ruler of Egypt for 80 days in 1249
**Sinan** (1490-1588) — Ottoman architect, builder of the Suleymanye mosque, established Ottoman style of architecture
**Suleiman I** — Ottoman sultan (1520-1566), oversaw Ottoman civilization at its peak
**Tariq ibn Zijyad** — army lieutenant, led Berber army across Strait of Gibraltar to Spain, 711
**Tughril Beg** — Seljuk warlord, captured Baghdad in 1055, founded Seljuk Sultanate
**Umar ibn al-Khattab** — Companion, second of the Rightly Guided Caliphs (634-644)
**Uthman ibn Affan** — Companion, third of the Rightly Guided Caliphs (644-656)
**Yazid I** — Umayyad caliph (680-683), responsible for the death of Husayn at Karbala

These names are listed according to the forms by which the individuals are best known.

# GLOSSARY

**adhan** — the call to prayer

**Allah** — the God of Islam

**amir** — a governor of a Muslim province

**Ashura** — the tenth day of the Islamic month of Muharram and the time of mourning among Shi'ites for the death of Husayn at Karbala

**ayah** — a verse of the Quran

**basmalla** — phrase written at the beginning of nearly every chapter of the *Quran* and at the beginning of all important documents ("In the name of God, the Most Gracious, the Most Merciful")

**caliph** — "successor" to Muhammad, leader of the Islamic community

**Companions** — the closest associates of Muhamad

**Dar al-Islam** — lands under Islamic rule

**dinar** — gold coin

**dirham** — silver coin

**dhimmis** — "protected people" of monotheistic religions, such as Christians, Jews, and Zoroastrians

**fatwa** — a non-binding legal opinion or authoritative opinion on a point of Islamic law given by a learned legal expert (mufti)

**fiqh** — the study and application of Islamic law

**hadith** — tradition relating to what Muhammad said or did

**hajj** — annual pilgrimage to Mecca, which each Muslim should undertake at least once in his or her lifetime, if possible

**harem** — private quarters in a home reserved for the women

**hijab** — screen or veil that shields a Muslim woman from public view

**Hijra** — the emigration of Muhammad to Medina in 622; the date when the Islamic calendar begins

| | |
|---|---|
| **imam** | for Sunnis, the prayer leader in a mosque; for Shi'ites, the divinely guided leader of the community (Imam) |
| **Islam** | willing obedience to God's authority and guidance |
| **jihad** | literally "struggle"; a personal struggle against inner weakness or a community struggle against unjust treatment to Muslims |
| **jinns** | supernatural beings or spirits who inspire poets and sometimes meddle mischievously in the lives of humans; known in the West as genies |
| **Kaaba** | cube-shaped shrine in Mecca, Islam's most venerated place of worship |
| **madrasa** | a college primarily for teaching Islamic law; means "place of study" |
| **mawali** | non-Arabic Muslims during Umayyad caliphate |
| **Mamluk** | slave-soldier of Asian origin; militaristic dynasty that ruled Egypt, Syria and Arabia from 1250 to 1517 |
| **mihrab** | niche in the wall of a mosque indicating the qibla or direction of Mecca |
| **minbar** | pulpit in a mosque |
| **mosque** | place of Muslim worship |
| **mozarab** | "Arabized" non-Muslim (Christian or Jew) in al-Andalus |
| **muezzin** | "crier" who calls the Muslim faithful to prayer five times daily |
| **Muslim** | one who submits himself to the will of God |
| **Pillars of Islam** | the five requirements of Islam: confession of faith of God, daily worship, almsgiving, fasting during Ramadan, and hajj to Mecca |
| **pir** | a Sufi master (Persian term) |
| **qadi** | Muslim judge who rules on points of religious law |
| **qibla** | direction of prayer, at first toward Jerusalem and since 623 toward Mecca |
| **Quran** | the holy scripture of Islam |
| **Quraysh** | the rulers of Mecca in pre-Islamic Arabia; the tribe of Muhammad |
| **Ramadan** | ninth month of the Muslim calendar when fasting is required from dawn to sunset |

**Rashidun** the first four "Rightly Guided" caliphs: Abu Bakr, Umar, Uthman, and Ali

**salat** formal prayer, undertaken five times daily, during which Muslims turn toward Mecca, prostrate themselves, and worship God

**shahada** profession of faith: "There is no god but God, and Muhammad is His messenger"

**sharia** rules and regulations that govern the daily lives of Muslims, based on the Quran and hadith

**shaykh** literally "old man," the tribal chief, religious leader, or head of a Sufi community

**Shi'ite** sect of Islam that rejected the historical succession of caliphs and insisted that Ali and his descendants should have rightfully succeeded Muhammad

**shura** council or committee to chose a new leader

**sira** biography of Muhammad

**Sufi** a mystic seeking union with God through meditation and ritual

**sultan** Muslim ruler, a title first used in the 11th century

**sunna** customary procedures to Muslim living based upon the hadith and sira

**Sunni** mainstream Islam (as opposed to Shi'ite) based on the Quran and sunna; orthodox sect that accepted the historical succession of caliphs

**suq** marketplace in an Islamic town or city

**sura** chapter in the Quran

**tajwid** the science of Quranic recitation

**tawaf** the seven ritual circumambulations of the Kaba

**ulama** community of learned religious men, "the ones possessing knowledge"

**umma** the Muslim community

**waqf** endowment used for the support of mosques, hospitals, *madrasas*, etc.

**zakat** giving to the poor

# REFERENCES AND RESOURCES


Armstrong, Karen, *Islam: A Short History*. New York: Random House, 2002
Armstrong, Karen, *Muhammad*. New York: Harper Collins, 1992
Aslan, Reza, *No god but God: The Origins, Evolution, and Future of Islam*. New York: Random House, 2005
Bloom, Jonathan and Sheila Blair: *Islam: A Thousand Years of Faith and Power.* New Haven, Connecticut: Yale University Press, 2002
Cook Michael, *The Koran: A Very Short Introduction*. New York: Oxford University Press, 2000
Esposito, John, *Islam: The Straight Path*. New York: Oxford University Press, 1992
Esposito, John, *The Oxford History of Islam*. New York: Oxford University Press, 1999
Esposito, John, *What Everyone Needs To Know About Islam*. New York: Oxford University Press, 2002
Fletcher, Richard, *The Cross and the Crescent*. London: Penguin Books, 2003.
Freely, John, *Istanbul: The Imperial City*. London: Penguin Books, 1998.
Holt, PM, Ann Lambton and Bernard Lewis, editors, *The Cambridge History of Islam*. Cambridge, England: Cambridge University Press, 1980
Hourani, Albert, *A History of the Arab Peoples*. New York: Warner Books, 1992
Irwin, Robert, *Islamic Art*. New York: Harry N. Abrams, 1997
Kennedy, Hugh, *When Baghdad Ruled the Muslim World*. Da Capo Press, Cambridge, Massachusetts, 2004.
Kinross, Lord, *The Ottoman Centuries*. New York: William Morrow and Company, 1977
Lewis, Bernard, *The Arabs in History*. New York: Oxford University Press, 2002
Lunde, Paul, *Islam*. London: DK Publishing, Inc., 2002
Mandel Khan, Gabriel, *Muhammad The Prophet*. San Diego, CA: Thunder Bay Press, 2004.
Macaulay, David, *Mosque*. New York: Houghton Mifflin, 2003
Newby, Gordon, *A Concise Encyclopedia of Islam*. Oxford, England, Oneworld Publications, 2002
Nicolle, David, *Historical Atlas of the Islamic World*. London: Mercury Books, 2003
Raymond, Andre, *Cairo*. Cambridge, Massachusetts: Harvard University Press, 2000
Schimmel, Annemarie, *Islam: An Introduction*. Albany, New York: State University of New York Press, 1992
Watt, W. Montgomery, *Early Islam*. Edinburgh: Edinburgh University Press, 1990.

DVDs:
*Islam: Empire of Faith* (PBS)
*Inside Islam* (The History Channel)
*Inside Mecca* (National Geographic)

Websites:
Council on Islamic Education www.cie.org
Institute of Islamic Information and Education www.iiie.net
International Institute of Islamic Thought www.iiit.org
Islamic Art and Architecture Organization www.islamicart.com

# INDEX